B109

LUCAS

FROM THE STREETS OF SOWETO
TO SOCCER SUPERSTAR

The authorised
biography by
**RICHARD
COOMBER**

796. 334092

GREAT-N-ORTHERN

Dedicated to Alan Berry and Andrew Smith,
who gave a 40-year-old novice the chance to write

Great Northern Books
PO Box 213, Ilkley, LS29 9WS
www.greatnorthernbooks.co.uk

ISBN: 978-1905080-73-1

Design and layout: David Burrill

Printed in Great Britain

CIP Data
A catalogue for this book is available from the British Library

CONTENTS

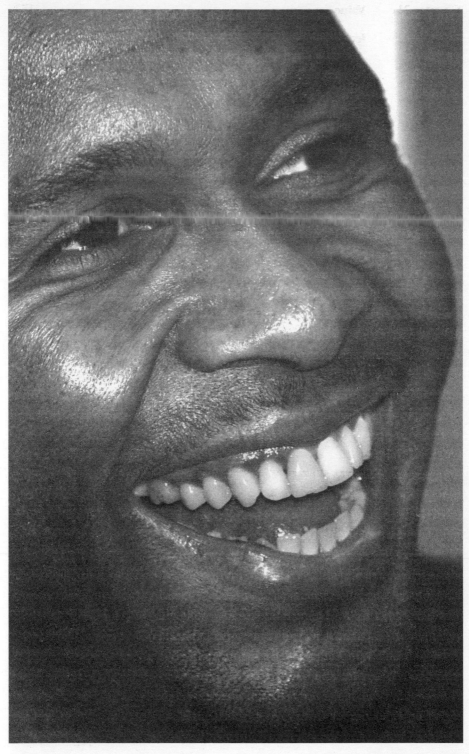

The first thing you notice.

Foreword 1

by Eddie Gray MBE

Howard Wilkinson made many astute signings during his time managing Leeds United but I have no doubt that none turned out better than Lucas Radebe. At just £250,000 Lucas was arguably one of the best value for money purchases in Premiership history, but his contribution went far beyond just a return for a transfer fee.

I was at the club in a number of positions throughout Lucas's time there and I know he found it hard to settle at first but he never complained. He got his head down, worked hard, listened to advice and went on to become one of the best central defenders in the country. His ready smile and friendliness sometimes mean people underestimate the fact that he was a hard defender. He wasn't afraid to put his foot in and let opponents know he was there, but it was not done maliciously or with the intention to hurt anyone. I remember vividly how Lucas and Jimmy Hasselbaink used to battle with each other in training. Lucas would give him a dig and as Jimmy went down protesting, he'd say with a big grin: 'The ju-ju man got you.'

In many ways I think Lucas was like Norman Hunter, a man who loved to defend and to dominate the person he was marking but who was always willing to help them up with a smile and shake their hand at the end of the match.

Some people were surprised when Lucas was made captain of South Africa and then Leeds; they feared he wasn't demonstrative enough. But Lucas was one of those rare people – Bobby Moore was another – who didn't have to shout a lot or shake their fist to make an impact. He led by example and the other players had so much respect for him that they were willing to follow. Players saw how he pushed his body to the limits so that he could fulfil his obligation to club and country, and they learned a lot about loyalty.

Part of that respect was built up when the players were first starting to emerge through the youth team. Paul Hart and I were coaching a particularly special bunch of youngsters, who won their league as well as the FA Youth Cup, and the lads all loved Lucas because he would spend time talking to them, advising and encouraging them. There was already a bond between them and their captain when they stepped up into the first team.

It was as true off the pitch as on it. It's not always easy to persuade players to make personal appearances at charity or community events – most footballers are happier performing in front of 40,000 in a stadium than going where they might have to talk to half a dozen strangers one on one. But Lucas was always the first to put his hand up. He believed he had a duty to give something back and because he led the way, others followed.

It's not too difficult to captain a side when things are going well, but Lucas was also a leader in the bad times. When I took over as caretaker manager, trying to halt the slide as Leeds spiralled downwards after living the dream, I always knew I could rely on Lucas to give me 100 per cent even on the occasions when he shouldn't have been on the pitch because of injury.

The thing that stands out most for me about him is how much he appreciated the opportunities football had given him. I suspect that is partly because of the way he was brought up and partly from his experiences as a young man in South Africa. But the key thing was that he never lost it. Some players start to take the privilege of being a footballer for granted but Lucas never did and even when injuries took their toll later in his career, he always remained positive and wanted to be back playing, even if that meant waking up the next day hardly able to get out of bed.

Lucas Radebe is one of the nicest men you would ever want to meet. His story is an inspiration for everyone, whatever his or her field of endeavour. I'm delighted to have been asked to write these few words.

Eddie Gray
July 2010

Foreword 2

by Kaizer Motaung
Executive Chairman, Kaizer Chiefs

I could speak volumes about Lucas Radebe the football player but I choose instead to look deeper into that which distinguished him from his colleagues. I could also speculate on his private life, but as a man who reveres my own privacy, I choose never to attempt it because a man's privacy is his stronghold and refuge.

When mentioning Lucas Radebe, I am immediately attracted to the leadership qualities that he naturally possesses as his anointing, a rare quality often found in athletes whose career is christened by personal awards and pitfalls that scale beyond their athleticism.

For many that harvest the glamour of a successful career in sports, our ultra-ego often takes measure to catapult our reputation as heroes and role-models; the ultimate identity that we carry as a chip around our shoulders. On many occasions, it is this ego that often makes us lose ourselves and plunges us into depths of self-destruction. Used and managed correctly, the same ego sustains our livelihood and places us as a cut-above-the-rest and opens doors for opportunities of responsibility when our bodies have resigned from carrying our careers beyond our achievements.

In Lucas Radebe, it has been difficult to associate his rise to prominence to an ultra-ego purely because of his grounded demeanour that exhumed nothing else but pure personal leadership. This quality makes him stand against his past and present colleagues as a true Chief and an icon of stature who has graced our sports and social scene.

Football thus provided the platform to live his anointing as records of his achievements both on and off the field could testify. When he joined Kaizer Chiefs from Lehurutshe ICL Birds United, the lanky and exceptionally talented defender caught our eyes as a hard-working yet humble person. He immediately and naturally blended with our brand of football whilst carrying his smile to warm the hearts of the many supporters he led.

Consolidating his talents was a natural inclination to command, initiate, and organise his colleagues in a manner that had leadership written all over. This at a time when Kaizer Chiefs dominated the late eighties and early nineties by sweeping everything that was on offer, the challenge to find a true leader proved to be major in our undertakings. Our successes were frequent to overwhelm the youngsters that had swelled our ranks and we could only rely on the anointing of a true leader to regulate professional behaviour both on and off the field.

In the words of Dr. Myles Munroe "the purest form of leadership is influence through inspiration"; Lucas Radebe qualified to wear the captain's armband after displaying these characteristics. He naturally drew the best out of others whilst maintaining a steady but combative athletic behaviour that settled for nothing but a winning mentality. In executing his duties, Lucas was never intimidated by our previous record of achievement but embraced the challenges to carry the Kaizer Chiefs' baton forward just like a seasoned combatant.

It therefore came as no surprise when he attracted the attention of Leeds United who signed him together with Philemon 'Chippa' Masinga in 1994 after serving the Kaizer Chiefs family with dedication and commitment. Taking his leadership qualities along, Leeds discovered exactly what we at Kaizer Chiefs had and appointed him captain. This achievement placed him in football record books as the first Black South African to captain a European team that campaigned in the Premier League. He was a great export. Lucas guided Leeds United to greater heights and earned respect from the often hard-to-please supporters that later affectionately bestowed the title of "The Chief" to their South African import.

The Chief went on to campaign for his team whilst subtly gaining a positive ambassadorial role for South Africa, a country that had just embarked on a road to transformation following the democratic elections of 1994. At this time, our national team obviously carried a much more intense socio-political role of unifying the nation than merely lifting the Africa Cup of Nations trophy that was staged for the first time on South African soil.

The period 1996 heralded yet another achievement in his illustrious career as a member of a South African national team that lifted the Africa Cup of Nations trophy in a match that crowned our readmission into world football. Again Lucas proved his worth by overcoming niggling injuries when he outwitted the lethal Ghanian Tony Yeboah, his colleague from Leeds United. His efforts helped South Africa secure a berth in the final against Tunisia whom they dismissed in front of a partisan crowd to lift the coveted trophy.

Wearing the Bafana Bafana captain's armband in the FIFA 1998 World Cup in France further endorsed his leadership qualities and lifted his stature as a true South African sportsman. Whilst the team returned after the first round, Lucas had demonstrated a tenacious spirit of leadership that also saw him captaining the national team in the 2002 FIFA World Cup in South Korea/Japan. This was to be his final appearance for the national team and perhaps his exit from competitive football following a stream of injuries.

Today Lucas Radebe remains in our books as the most successful leader and ambassador of the Kaizer Chiefs brand. His time with us and the life he dedicated to serve the millions of our supporters and those of the country as a whole is by far the humblest gift he shared. His role as ambassador of FIFA for the SOS Children in South Africa qualified his persona as a free-spirited and free-giving model to society. Ranked 54th amongst the Top 100 Great South Africans in 2004 surely adds to the many awards he amassed beyond his playing days.

As you read this book, may I invite you to spread your thoughts beyond his successes on the field of play but afford yourself an opportunity to scan his model life that has risen to iconic status. He is the most sought after role model with a serene lifestyle that he leads by his humble and good natured personality. The unpretentious smile that grace our billboards remains the same he shared when he was first introduced as a lad from the controversial former homeland of Bophutatswana, his refuge during the tumultuous riots of the eighties.

I am thus proud to have shared the challenges and achievements of Kaizer Chiefs with Lucas Radebe. I just hope this book is widely read by all South African youth and beyond particularly those that have yet to master the art of personal leadership before stardom and fame beckons. In it I hope they gather lessons in commitment, dedication, focus and humility, as character traits and weapons of personal success and glory.

I also pray that you discover the role that soccer has played in unifying a nation that had previously belonged to the doldrums of sporting isolation. As the dust settles to bury the historical achievements of our successful hosting of the FIFA 2010 World Cup, may we know that the likes of Lucas Radebe and many others had paved the way for us. Regrettably though, is the fact that they could not be actively seen fighting it out on the field of play; but they surely carved their names as warriors that withstood the pressures of the erstwhile reintroduction of South Africa into the world arena of sports.

May I therefore on behalf of the Kaizer Chiefs family congratulate Lucas Radebe and present him through prayer into the hands of the Almighty whose glory shone through his private and professional life. We are truly blessed to be associated with his name as he continues to scale the ladder of success through the many pursuits of his interest.

Kaizer Motaung
August 2010

Introduction

On 25 April 2010, the Professional Footballers' Association held their annual dinner at the Grosvenor House Hotel in London's Mayfair. Alongside the Player of the Year award to Wayne Rooney, the PFA presented their Special Merit Award for 'outstanding contribution to professional football for both club and country.' The list of former winners includes some of the greatest names in the game, starting with Sir Bobby Charlton and also including Denis Law, Bill Shankly, Sir Tom Finney, Sir Matt Busby, Bob Paisley, Bill Nicholson, Ron Greenwood, Sir Stanley Matthews, Brian Clough, Eusebio, Pele, Sir Bobby Robson, George Best and Sir Alex Ferguson. Now the name of the former Leeds and South Africa captain, Lucas Radebe, was added to that stellar list.

Before handing Lucas the glass crystal vase, PFA chairman Chris Powell read a letter he had received from the Nelson Mandela Foundation. It read:

'This is to express the pride and gratitude of the Nelson Mandela Foundation on you conferring this prestigious award on our countryman, Lucas Radebe.

'Football in South Africa has provided enjoyment and entertainment for the whole nation for many years and we are very proud that as hosts of the first World Cup to be staged in Africa, the world will be invited to see the beauty of our homeland.

'As captain of Bafana Bafana and throughout his distinguished career, playing for Leeds United in England, Lucas has always upheld the highest values of sportsmanship and fair play combined with sporting excellence.

'His celebrity has always been used to great effect supporting charitable initiatives both at home and in the UK, therefore it is fitting that his achievements are to be recognised in England.

'South Africa is very proud of the achievements of Lucas Radebe and congratulates him on receiving this award from the PFA in London.'

As a journalist covering Leeds United, I've known Lucas since he arrived at Elland Road in 1994 and during the years I co-wrote the club's match-day programme, I probably interviewed him more than most. I admired the footballer, I liked the man and I was impressed by his willingness to give back to the community, especially his work for SOS Children's Villages. I was intrigued by his childhood and the glimpses I saw of his iconic status in South Africa.

The main downside I found in all those years was that he tended to forget that he'd arranged to meet at the training ground for an interview and by the time I arrived at Thorp Arch, he'd gone home. But it wasn't personal – he did it to everyone – and you always forgave him. Other people reacted to him in exactly the same way. Mention Lucas's name and words like 'legend', 'gentleman', 'great bloke', 'ambassador', 'icon', 'hero' and 'role model' are commonplace. The first things everyone talks about are the dazzling smile and his ability to be positive in adversity.

So when I started on this project, I realised it would be easier to write a 'kiss and tell' book about Mother Theresa than a 'warts and all' biography of Lucas. I'm not claiming he's perfect – who of us is? And I have included stories that don't reflect well on Lucas. But they don't form the dominant theme of the book even though the bestseller lists tell us digging the dirt sells. Why? Because whatever his shortcomings, Lucas's life has been mainly a positive one and any biography that didn't reflect that would not ring true with almost everyone who has had contact with him.

I did ask a few people what was the worst thing they could say of about him. The results were hardly the stuff to excite a tabloid editor. Gary Blumberg, long-time friend, adviser and chairman of Lucas's company, told me that one of his most endearing qualities, the inability to say 'no', can be as much a problem as a strength. Former Leeds United physio Dave Hancock said, 'I heard stories that he would go missing sometimes on his way back from South Africa.' Ex United press officer Dick Wright, who was as close to Lucas as anyone at the club, complained the South African would come into his office and sweep all the carefully arranged papers on to the floor before dashing off laughing. And he would go away in the summer, forgetting to cancel the milk and papers or to arrange for the lawn to be cut at home, leaving Dick to sort things out. 'He'd even left the key in the door, but that's Lucas,' Wright said.

Perhaps the most interesting 'criticism' came from another friend, Emma Joussemet, who worked closely with Lucas in his charity and community work. She said: 'At times I've thought that he didn't realise quite how much power he had to influence people's lives. If that could have been harnessed even more and used in something like education, the results might have been incredible.' But she then thought for a moment and added: 'But it was his modesty that helped make him so appealing…so who knows?'

Along with that modesty, another strong trait that comes across when you look into Lucas's life is his unswerving loyalty. He had one club in South Africa and one in England, and anyone who witnessed the crazy schedules he suffered in order to play for both Leeds and South Africa in the space of a few days, can have no doubts about his loyalty to his country. And interestingly, at a time when commercial relationships often seem as short-lived as Hollywood marriages, Lucas has trusted his affairs to Gary Blumberg since his early days at Elland Road, and several other members of 'Team Lucas' would be coming up for testimonials if they had been footballers.

In many ways writing this book has been my dream job because along with Lucas's life, it has allowed me to explore a unique moment in South Africa's history, to follow the re-emergence of that country's football team from the international wilderness, with all that meant to its people, and to revisit the rise and fall of Leeds United, a story I covered day by day but which is much clearer in retrospect. Lucas played a part in all these narratives and his life cannot be separated from them.

At that same PFA dinner where Lucas picked up his Merit Award, former Leeds United manager Howard Wilkinson, who brought Lucas to England, said of him: 'The fact that he is South Africa's World Cup face and he stands there alongside Nelson Mandela is in many ways appropriate because they both came from very humble backgrounds. But both of them are able to engage with people at any level.' When someone with the rare combination of intelligence and bluntness as Howard Wilkinson puts Lucas in the same company as Nelson Mandela, I'm not going to argue. And speaking for myself, I haven't seen the same mixture of world-class footballer and likeable man, revered by fans of all clubs, since I was fortunate enough to spend a year working with England World Cup captain Bobby Moore on his promotional work and soccer schools. Like Bobby, Lucas is simply 'a bit special'.

So, for anyone who has bought this book hoping for another scandal-packed saga of an overpaid soccer star, I apologise up front, but I make no apology for writing it. Lucas's story is worth telling. It reminds us that it remains possible for kids born in tough circumstances to make the most of their talent if they are willing to put in the effort. It shows that not all highly paid sportsmen and women are in it for what they can take out. It restores your faith in people.

Richard Coomber, August 2010

Chapter One
Hail to the Chief

Leeds United fans were disillusioned. They had swallowed the shame and the pain of relegation to the Championship - a fancy title for football's old second division in England - because they were confident their side would bounce straight back 'where they belong', not just *in* the Premiership but near the top, battling for the title and a place in the UEFA Champions League.

But a year on, the season had been a massive anti-climax. Instead of chasing promotion, Leeds floundered in mid table. Instead of taking on and beating AS Roma, AC Milan and Lazio, Leeds had been second best to Crewe Alexandra, Rotherham United and Gillingham. The ever-loyal fans, thousands of whom watched them home and away, hadn't seen their side win more than two games in a row all season. And even the good news - the takeover of the club in January to protect it from administration and a ten-point penalty that would almost certainly have led to a second successive relegation - was received with trepidation. After all, the saviour was former Chelsea owner Ken Bates, a man Leeds fans loved to hate and of whom they were deeply suspicious. They were grateful to the irascible 73 year old with the Father Christmas beard and tight-lipped smile but they couldn't help being concerned. The first time Bates took his seat in the directors' box, the Kop let him know how they felt, greeting him with a favourite chant, but with the volume cranked up even higher than usual: 'We hate Chelsea! We hate Chelsea!'

Yet on 2 May 2005, Bank Holiday Monday, and with the final, meaningless league game a few days away, there was a carnival atmosphere as Leeds fans flocked to the stadium at Elland Road. For the first time in ages, they smiled as they took their seats. Early arrivals made their way to the statue of Billy Bremner on the concourse outside the towering East Stand and discussed the approaching game animated with anticipation. They weren't expecting great football but they were confident they would see some star names. More importantly, this was their chance to say thank you to a man they had come to love over the previous 11 years, a man who epitomised the Leeds United they cared about. He had not only performed brilliantly match after match, but had overcome massive injuries in his determination to play for Leeds; he had made great personal sacrifices to pull on the white shirt; he'd turned down lucrative offers to go to Spurs, Roma and the hated Manchester United; he had thrown himself whole heartedly into working for the community and to improving United's too-often tarnished image; this was a man who had taken a pay cut to stay at Elland Road when others scurried as far from the beleaguered club as they could get.

Kick-off was still some way off when the chant first arose from the Kop and was taken up around the ground:

Radebe!

Radebe!

Radebe, Radebe, Radebe!

Radebe-e, Radebe-e, Radebe-ee-ee-ee-ee!

LUCAS!

It was because they believed that Lucas shared their passion for Leeds United that so many people turned up to watch a testimonial match. He recalled: 'We had talked about it before the game and some of the organising committee thought we might get 25,000. I thought 20,000 would be nearer the mark. When I went out to warm up, I looked around and I thought it looked about half full and that pleased me. But when I came out again just before the match, I couldn't believe what I saw. The place was packed. It was very emotional. I had to tell myself not to cry but it was hard.'

In fact 37,889 paid their way into Elland Road that day, the biggest crowd of the season and that with no visiting supporters. It has rarely been passed since. To put it into perspective, the previous testimonial, three years before, had been for popular Irishman Gary Kelly when just over 26,000 turned up, including a good contingent from Celtic who provided the opposition. And even back in the club's golden years, United's most famous captain Billy Bremner attracted 37,708 and World Cup winner Jack Charlton 34,963, each boosted by opposition fans, while the joint match held for international giants John Charles and Bobby Collins was attended by 13,671.

Supporters and players travelled from across the UK and beyond to be at Elland Road. Lucas's parents, Emily and Johannes came over from South Africa, together with several members of his family and were proudly sitting alongside his wife Feziwe and other close friends. Also in the crowd was playwright, author and Yale University lecturer Caryl Phillips, who flew in from New York especially for the match. In recent years he had interviewed Lucas and written about him and this match was one he simply could not miss. 'I wouldn't have made the trip from New York for any other post-Revie player,' he said.

Phillips first arrived in Leeds, aged four months, when his family emigrated from the Caribbean island of St Kitts. He became a United fan at the age of five and followed the side through the many triumphs under manager Don Revie in the 1960s and 70s, and even though the racism in the crowd eventually drove him away from the ground for a number of years, he never lost his passion for the club. He summed up what Lucas's testimonial meant to him: 'I had a profound sense of pride in Leeds during the Revie era, but I also felt that I was the only black person in the crowd and so felt waves of isolation and loneliness sweep over me. For me, therefore, it was so important to see a black footballer who was not only respected enough that Elland Road was full, but that his peers turned out to pay tribute to him. Lucas had won the respect of those people who understood what he represented, not just as a cultural ambassador but also his importance as a footballer. Jack Charlton was a terrific centre half but I think Lucas Radebe is the best defender Leeds have ever had. When he was injury-free at the peak of his career he was an astonishing defender.'

But Phillips believes Lucas's significance extends beyond his talent as a footballer: 'As a black South African he did a lot to heal the wounds of guilt that many Leeds fans felt about Albert Johanneson, who played in the Revie team and died alone, a victim of depression and alcoholism. We had the opportunity to have another black South African occupy a central role at the club and this time we got it right, we didn't allow him to be marginalised. And, for Leeds to sign Lucas and Philemon Masinga back in 1994 was significant, not only in terms of Leeds' history but also in the way African players started to become an integral part of British soccer. Leeds' signing of those two guys opened the flood gates to African players generally.'

The news of Lucas's testimonial was greeted with pride in South Africa where he had also written his name in the history books and earned his place in the hearts of the fans. After abandoning plans to train as a teacher for the riskier career of a footballer, he quickly made an impact at his country's biggest club, Kaizer Chiefs. He played in South Africa's first international after sanctions were lifted and they were allowed back into world football; he shrugged off a career-threatening injury to be part of the side that won the African Cup of Nations on home soil to spark a massive party, not just among the soccer-mad black majority but the white minority as well; he proudly captained South Africa to their first World Cup finals; and he was a friend of Nelson Mandela, who had his own name for him, Mthimkhulu which means 'big tree'.

As the familiar figures drifted out of the changing rooms to warm up for the testimonial match, the fans greeted them enthusiastically. There was a special cheer when Gordon Strachan, David Batty, Gary McAllister and Gary Speed appeared - the irresistible midfield behind Leeds' 1992 title winning side reunited. Only a handful recognised Philemon 'Chippa' Masinga, the South African striker who had joined Leeds at the same time as Lucas. Fewer still knew who South African superstar Doctor Khumalo was when he trotted out but it meant a lot to Lucas that his countrymen had made the trip especially to play on his big day. Nigel Martyn, David Wetherall, Jimmy Floyd Hasselbaink, Olivier Dacourt, and Tony Yeboah were welcomed back, symbols of a time when Leeds 'lived the dream'.

There was an especially warm reception for Vinnie Jones, the hod carrier turned footballer, turned film star, whose stay at Elland Road had been brief, but long enough for United fans to recognise him as one of their own. The Leeds faithful - and few clubs have more steadfast fans - love to see talented ball players and over the years have drooled over midfield maestros like Bobby Collins, Johnny Giles and John Sheridan. But they will forgive those, like Jones, who may not be blessed with silky skills but who always give 100 per cent to the cause and wear their Leeds heart on their sleeve - or in Jones's case on his leg, in the form of a white rose tattoo to mark winning promotion from the old Division Two in 1990.

But the biggest cheer was reserved for Lucas. As he beamed his unmistakable smile and waved to the crowd, it was hard not to reflect on the enormity of the odds against him being there at all. Many of the Comrades with whom he had grown up in Diepkloof 4, a township neighbouring Soweto on the outskirts of Johannesburg, had been killed or ended up in jail during the anti-apartheid struggle in which he too had played a part in the 1970s and 80s. Having survived the running battles, police oppression and gang warfare that marked the fight against the apartheid regime in South Africa, Lucas had started to make his mark as a footballer for the Chiefs only to come close to death once more when a bullet tore through the side of his car, into his back and out through his thigh, somehow miraculously missing the bones and vital organs.

Even his cut-priced move to Leeds United looked doomed to failure in the early days. On his debut, as a sub against Mansfield in the League Cup, the TV commentator introduced him as 'Leeds United's other South African' and as he turned to face the play, his back revealed the number 27 and his mis-spelled name REDEBE. Struggling to make an impact, he, like Masinga, had no chance of playing in the 75 per cent of first team matches necessary to have his work permit renewed but unlike 'Chippa', he picked up the first of many serious injuries and was therefore reprieved while his team-mate had to move on. Despite all those potential pitfalls, here he was, the man they called the Chief, idolised and respected for his contribution to Leeds United.

Many of the United side who dominated English football in the golden era of the 1960s and 70s are held in high esteem by the supporters. Whenever Eddie Gray, who served the club as player, coach and manager, is introduced it is as though the first two names given him by his parents were Leeds Legend. Legend is also regularly attached to the names of the club's first big star, John Charles, and to Don Revie, Billy Bremner, Johnny Giles, Peter Lorimer and Norman Hunter. As the club's fortunes fluctuated over the years, the word has been used less and less. Of the 1992 championship-winning side, only David Batty has earned the right. Since then, in an era of high drama, near misses, but no trophies, followed by a rapid and catastrophic decline, only one man is accepted as a Leeds legend - Lucas Radebe.

Chapter 2
Ntuba

In 1948, Johannes Radebe and Emily Tlhong were still school children, living in the Magaliesberg region of South Africa, when their status as second-class citizens was enshrined into law. They were soon to feel the full force of the apartheid rules, which in later years would continue to dominate the lives of their children, especially their fourth child, Lucas Valeriu, known to them as Ntuba.

Magaliesberg, a region about an hour's drive north-west from Johannesburg, is known as the birthplace of humankind. The mountains, it is claimed, are older than Everest and the valleys have been home to people for hundreds of thousands of years – archaeologists found the skull of 'Mrs Ples' in the region and dated it as 2.15 million years old. Throughout history native tribes raised families, worked and fought in the area, the Tswana, the Zulu, the Matabele. In the 19th century white explorers arrived from England and from Holland, delighted to discover gold and diamonds, and fertile farmland. They killed each other and they killed the native people to secure for themselves the wealth of a country overflowing with valuable resources. Life for the black population would never be the same. They were patronised, colonised and turned into mere labourers in their own land. Harshest of all, they were segregated, forced to live apart from the ruling whites and often from their own families.

When the English won the decisive Boer Wars at the end of the 19th century, they embraced the defeated Afrikaaners in the new Union government and with a higher population of vanquished than conquerors, it was the Dutch who dominated the political landscape from which the majority black population was excluded. A desperate situation grew worse for the native peoples when, fearing a growing restlessness in the black community, the whites went to the polls in 1948 and voted into power the extreme National Party. In his book *South Africa 1948-1994*, author Martin Roberts explained: 'The 1948 election was a turning point in that it brought to power a new government with particularly racist policies. This government was to stay in power, increasingly out of step with world opinion, for more than forty years. Also new was the confidence the government had in its policies and its ruthlessness in carrying them out.' An Afrikaaner was heard to say after the election, 'At last, a kaffir is a kaffir again.' To black South Africans, being called a kaffir was the equivalent of an American being called a nigger.

A fever of legislation followed, which among other things prohibited marriage between the races; forced registration of every citizen into a racial group; declared certain areas and facilities were for use by whites only; tightened pass laws, ordering every black person, known as Bantu, to carry an identity card as a way of limiting their movement; and set up government controlled schools that ensured blacks received only a basic education. Each loss of freedom was justified to the world by the National Party leadership in ways that take the breath away today. On education, South African prime minister Dr Hendrik Verwoerd said: 'The natives will be taught from childhood to realise that equality with Europeans is not for them…What is the use of teaching the Bantu mathematics when he cannot use it in practice…There is no place for the Bantu child above the level of a certain form of labour.'

The small farm school in the village of Hekpoort attended by Johannes and Emily was already very basic with children sharing books and desks and being taught by teachers who themselves had not enjoyed much of an education. Their prospects looked bleak. Emily, living with her grandmother after being orphaned at the age of 15, had little to look forward to. Johannes would either have to leave to find work in the city or scrape a living as a farm labourer. He gambled on finding a job in Johannesburg with all the restrictions that entailed, and even when he came back to marry his childhood sweetheart, the pass laws forced him to return to the city without her.

It is sometimes hard for those brought up outside South Africa to understand just how extreme the racism was in a country where a newspaper like the Johannesburg Star could carry a headline that read, 'Farmer makes native run 22 miles in front of his horse at a trot, thrashing him when tired' or 'Piccanin dies as result of a thrashing.' For years black political leaders tried to shake off the yoke peacefully by demonstration, defiance and negotiation, seeking to introduce a 10-point charter they had drawn up, which concluded 'These freedoms we shall fight for side by side throughout our lives until we have won our liberty.' But the government responded with banning orders and arrests.

Young blacks grew impatient with their leaders whose approach was proving ineffective. A new man, Dr James Moroka, became President of the black's leading political organisation, the African National Congress, and he was joined on the executive by passionate young campaigners including Walter Sisulu, Oliver Tambo and a young lawyer named Nelson Mandela, also known by his tribal name of Madiba.

Any hope they had of a non-violent end to oppression disappeared on Monday

21 March 1960. A young policeman lost his nerve during a noisy demonstration around the police station in Sharpeville. He fired his gun and that spooked his colleagues, who also opened fire. By the time they stopped shooting, 69 demonstrators were dead and 180 wounded. In a separate incident on the same day at Langa township in the Cape, police baton-charged a demonstration and then opened fire on the crowd, killing two people and wounding 49. Enough was enough. Mandela invoked an African saying: 'the attacks of the wild beast cannot be fought off with only bare hands'. He and others went underground, forming Umkhonto we Sizwe, the Spear of the Nation, otherwise known as MK. Force would be met with force.

Emily had finally managed to secure the correct papers to move to Johannesburg and be with Johannes and in the year of the Sharpeville massacre, their first child, Abram, was born. Having lived with relatives in the early years, they were finally allocated a house of their own. It was in Zone 4 of Diepkloof, a township to the south west of Johannesburg, neighbouring Soweto. It was a modest building, similar to the hundreds of others that filled street after street in the area. It consisted of just four small rooms with no running water indoors, no electricity and with an outside toilet. Situated towards one end of dusty Modisa Street, the single-storey 'matchbox' house was under the shadow of a bare, mine-filled hill. But it was theirs and Emily immediately set about turning it into a home.

With only three of them, the size of the house wasn't a problem at first. It was slightly more crowded five years later when Elizabeth was born, followed within a year by Billy Abednego. Money was tight. Johannes wasn't earning much at a tyre factory, so he started a taxi service in the evenings. Soon he was working weekends as well, driving workers to and from their families in Magaliesberg.

The political situation in South Africa was becoming more and more tense. In 1961 the politicians declared South Africa a republic. In response, it was thrown out of the Commonwealth. Keen to avoid loss of life, MK embarked on a programme of sabotage, blowing up power lines and government offices. Eventually their leaders were arrested and tried and in June 1964, Nelson Mandela, Walter Sisulu and six other men were found guilty of 'recruiting people for training in sabotage and guerrilla warfare for the purpose of violent revolution' and they were sentenced to life imprisonment.

Opposition to apartheid was growing around the world, especially in other African nations, and in 1969 a conference in the Zambain capital, Lusaka, issued a manifesto which warned: 'while peaceful progress is blocked by the actions of those at present in power in the states of Southern Africa, we have no choice but to give to the people of those territories all the support of which we are capable in their struggle against their oppressors.' It had no effect on South Africa's rulers. Prime Minister John Vorster replied: 'Let them spit as much fire as they want to about the so called immorality of apartheid…we in South Africa know that it is the only feasible policy.'

This was the uneasy, divided world into which Emily gave birth to her fourth child on 12 April 1969. Another boy, his English name was Lucas but to the family he was, and remains, Ntuba, which means a small hole, like the eye of a needle.

With more mouths to feed, Johannes needed to expand his taxi business. He took on other drivers and worked every hour he could. He and Emily were determined their children would have a better start than they had enjoyed and perhaps become doctors or lawyers or teachers. In order to earn the money to fulfil this dream, Johannes had to work away from home for long periods and it became a family joke that each time he returned a new baby was conceived. Catherine Mphole was born two years after Lucas, Lydia Benge followed in 1973, Lazarus Mpho in 1975, Johannes Shimane in 1977, Thabo Edward in 1979 and two years after that the tenth and final baby, Dikeledi. Life in the four-roomed house was getting crowded.

As one of the older children, Lucas was introduced early to the principle of helping out around the place. Elizabeth spent many hours assisting her mother with cleaning and cooking, while Abram, Billy and Lucas helped their father with his cars. One of Lucas's earliest memories was cleaning the cars every Sunday or, bleary-eyed, going out in the early hours and helping push start a reluctant engine. 'Often there were ten of them parked around our little home,' he recalled in the anthology *My Dad By South African Sons*. 'Dodge saloons, an old Dodge van, a Plymouth, even an old Bedford truck – all big cars and all gas guzzlers.' The family and the neighbours loved to hear the growl of the Bedford truck when it returned home because Johannes often brought back boxes of fruit and vegetables and there was usually enough to go round the family and those living in the immediate area.

Until they were able to extend the house, conditions were cramped and Lucas and some of his siblings slept on foam mattresses on the kitchen floor, with others camped down in the lounge. It meant they had to wake around 4am on the days Johannes was setting off and after helping him get away, they would wearily slip back under the blankets for another couple of hours sleep.

Johannes was a strict father – by modern standards he would be considered harsh. But he was typical of his time and not just in South Africa. He used the sjambok, a leather whip, to punish idleness or misbehaviour. 'He kept them all over the house - in the lounge next to his favourite chair, in the bedroom, even in the kitchen,' Lucas recalled. 'They had to be within easy reach, just in case there was ever any slacking.' Lucas often felt the sting of the sjambok, especially if he arrived home late or Johannes thought he wasn't working hard enough. He has never used corporal punishment on his own children, yet he didn't and doesn't resent the punishments he received. 'That's how things were in our day and we responded well. It never left me or my brothers traumatised and it instilled a sense of discipline in us that has stood me in good stead throughout my life.'

It would be wrong to portray Johannes as an uncaring man. The Radebes didn't live a life of luxury but they didn't go hungry. 'He always provided for his family,' Emily said with pride. And Lucas's siblings see similarities in their father's sense of humour to that which later endeared their brother to so many people. Lydia recalled: 'Dad was funny and when Lucas was playing football in England, one of the first things he would ask us when he got home was to tell him what Dad had been doing or saying.'

If Lucas inherited humour and self discipline from his father, it is easy to see that many of his other characteristics, not least his love of sport, will to win, his work ethic, his resilience, energy and willingness to help others, all had their origins in his mother. With Johannes away so often and so long, she was left to bring up ten noisy, lively children, separated by an age gap of 21 years. Often she was the only one there to feed, discipline, comfort, encourage, nurse and entertain them, all in a four-roomed house. That would have been enough for most people but Emily not only kept an immaculate home and raised well-behaved children, she ran a small crèche to supplement the family income, and organised township kids into a netball team, a football team and a church choir. Even today she has her own football team and her home, bought for her by Lucas in the Richmond area of Johannesburg, is constantly filled with the noise of her children, grandchildren and great grandchildren. She is a woman for whom the word matriarch was coined.

Lucas was a tall lad but quite nervous, especially of the dark. In order to fetch water for the house, he had to go outside to the tap under a large tree where rats lurked. At night he would leave the bucket filling and dash back indoors, afraid to stay amid the movement and sound of wind in the branches. Then, another dash to turn the tap off and rush back indoors, water slopping over the sides of the bucket in his haste. 'It was very dark where we lived,' Lucas recalled. 'There was no electricity, no streetlights. You could hear people but you could not see them. I was scared of the sound of my own footsteps – I would run and the footsteps would run after me. Sometimes when I went to the shops, paper would fly up in the wind and frighten me. My brothers and sisters used to tease me.'

The toilet was also outside, near the tap, and Lucas used to make one of his younger brothers accompany him to keep guard. One day Lazarus was annoyed at being dragged away from his game of football, so he stole Lucas's trousers and hid them. He then went off to continue his game, forgetting all about Lucas who was stuck plaintively calling to his mother to bring him something to cover his nakedness.

Unusually for a boy in the townships, Lucas liked to cook. Lydia remembered: 'He used to slip into our Mum's room and come out wearing a wig, her apron and her shoes and say "Today I'm going to do the cooking." He was quite a good cook.' The family meals were plain but nourishing and Lucas had one strange habit, he loved to dunk pieces of orange in his cups of tea.

Lucas's love of football started early, inspired by Abram who was something of a local star. Most spare daylight hours were spent with the other kids from the neighbourhood chasing a ball made of rolled up socks down the street or on patches of waste ground, returning home hours later his skin and clothes caked in red dust. The ground was rock hard and the bare-foot boys picked up lots of scrapes and knocks but they just got up and played on, allowing the blood to dry on their knees. Sometimes, the injuries were more serious. In his book *Madiba's Boys*, author Graeme Friedman described how Lucas paid dearly for his spectacular style: 'Those scissors kicks! Lucas broke his arm attempting one, and twice woke up in hospital because he had turned so high in the air, only to land on his head, knocking himself out…two days later he would be back at school, turning out for the team at the next match.' It was a resilience that lasted throughout his career.

Lucas looked back on those days with some fondness. He told the Leeds United programme: 'The pitch could be as large as we could make it and it was always far more than 11 a-side. Every day there would be matches between sides from different streets or different zones – we called them challenges. If we weren't involved in a challenge we would pick up teams among ourselves. Sometimes we would play a game with a tennis ball called pole. We would put an old oil drum to one side and you had to hit it to score. You were only allowed two touches. In another game we would all kick into the same goal. Later, when I joined Leeds, these were all things we did in training. I didn't know it at the time but I was being prepared for my future life in England!'

From the age of eight, Lucas started to play in proper teams in Diepkloof and showed obvious talent. Few people took notice because the star player of the family was Abram. He was a winger for one of the township's top teams, United Scientists. 'He was my hero,' Lucas said. 'He was a much better footballer than I ever was. If he'd been born in a different age, he would have been a big star.' But the nine years between Abram and Lucas made an enormous difference. The elder boy was caught in a double bind – the effect of apartheid on black sport and the ban imposed on international sport by the anti-apartheid movement.

South Africa is a sport-mad nation, so all the iniquities that apartheid conceived were apparent in sport. In his book on sport and politics in South Africa, *The Race Game*, academic Douglas Booth tells how South African Indian golfer Sewsunker Sewzolum had to get special permission to play the course in the South African Open championship and still wasn't allowed to use the clubhouse. Black tennis player Mark Mathabane qualified to join the Wanderers tennis club in Johannesburg and he was considered 'a fine tennis player, well mannered and able to speak English' but he was refused membership because of the segregation problems it would create. However, Mathabane was invited to play in a club tournament and the President said, 'I don't think there will be any problems provided you use the servants' bathroom and eat where they eat.'

Just as the white rulers didn't feel it was necessary to provide black children with good schools, sports facilities were also meagre. South African Liberal MP Ken Andrews pointed out: 'The government is spending 2,400 times as much furthering the participation in sport for each white child compared with each black child. Surely there is something seriously wrong with our priorities if we spend more on tug-of-war visitors to South Africa than on 3.6 million black school children when it comes to sports activities?' Football was the black population's favourite sport, yet it was subject to the same international sanctions as the white-supported rugby and cricket. Consequently, from 1964 there was no opportunity to see international players in action and little chance for players to show off their skills and attract attention from overseas clubs. A few like Albert Johanneson made it to England, and more recently Kaizer Motaung and Jomo Sono had become stars in America, but on the whole it was not a way for young men like Abram to make a living. 'We just played football for fun,' Lucas said.

He might also have added for release because the oppression of apartheid hung heavy on the black community. And just as all those years before, when Nelson Mandela and his friends organised the MK and broke with peaceful protest, so in the 1970s it was the young people who decided they had endured enough. And this time they were even younger. It was schoolchildren who rose up, including Lucas.

Chapter 3

Comrades

Faced with someone who doesn't speak their language, most English people sigh, then speak more slowly and much louder - in English, of course. So it comes as a surprise on arriving in South Africa to find that practically everyone speaks at least half a dozen different languages fluently. Although he is a Zulu, Lucas grew up in a house speaking Tswana, the language his parents spoke at home in Magaliesberg, but from an early age he also knew Zulu, English and Afrikaans and he can make himself understood in five other tribal languages.

Lucas was just seven years old, a bright, football-mad pupil at Ikeneng Lower Primary School when language sparked the protest that brought the next major crisis in South Africa's civil conflict. The government ruled that all pupils had to learn Afrikaans, the Dutch-based language of the ruling class, and that exams were to be written in Afrikaans. To the students it was a sign that their education was intended as nothing more than preparation to serve those who oppressed them. In Soweto, children abandoned school and took their protest to the streets, and inevitably the police and army responded with force. On 16 June 1976 around 15,000 chanting and singing youngsters surged through the streets shouting 'Amandla!' 'Inkululeko!' and 'One Azania!' (Power, Freedom in our lifetime and One nation). They were met with warning shots and tear gas. Then bullets raked the protestors as with eyes burning and hearts thumping they scrambled for safety. Hector Pietersen, aged 12, fell to the ground. The picture of a fellow student, his face wet with tears of sorrow and rage, carrying Hector's bloodstained, dying body flashed around the world. There was no way back. The next few years in South Africa were marked by outbreaks of brutality, fear, misery and death.

Of course, it wasn't constant. Lucas carried on going to school, moving up when the time came to Thotlego Higher Primary and then Bopasenatla Secondary School. He continued to shine in local football teams, earning himself the nickname Buick after a Kaizer Chiefs star Buick Makwati. As well as playing for his school he was in a team called Diepkloof Wolf Wanderers and in matches against other township sides he pitted his skills against a number of talented young players like John 'Shoes' Moshoeu and Doctor Khumalo, who would one day be his international team-mates. Lucas seemed to be able to play in any position, including goalkeeper, always performing well, his tongue sticking out in concentration. Not quite as good as Abram, maybe, but a good player. He also managed to run the gauntlet of Soweto gangs to reach the Orlando Pirates' stadium and sneak in to watch his favourite team – the whole family, except Emily, were Pirates fans; she alone supported the Chiefs.

Emily and Johannes's energy was spent on bringing up their family, having to work even harder to afford the fees as each child reached school age. But the fear of violence could never be completely shaken off. Like many parents, they had mixed feelings – they believed in the anti-apartheid cause, they were involved in the struggle, but they also feared for the safety of their children, fretted over how they could protect them. And the children were constantly reminded of the potential dangers. Whispered playground stories of how the police had broken into a neighbour's house in the middle of the night and dragged away the father, or how someone else, thought to have betrayed the cause, had a tyre soaked in petrol, put round his neck and set alight, kept many youngsters awake at night. There was no way they could enjoy a normal life. Lucas's sister Lydia recalled: 'I was nervous. There were soldiers with guns in the yard when you got to school. Sometimes I would run back home by ten o'clock, sometimes I didn't go in at all. If I saw soldiers when I was going home I would just go into the nearest house until they had gone.'

Lucas has seldom revealed much detail of his involvement in the student uprisings of the early 1980s but putting together the clues, it is clear he played his part. In an interview with the BBC he said: 'Many of my Comrades were killed fighting for freedom from apartheid. The riots in the townships were too bad, too many people got involved in some nasty stuff…I was involved at school and that's when my Mum realised this was trouble. I wasn't a ring leader but I think we were very strong at school. I was always on the right side – against the bad guys. We were always going to be troublesome for the authorities because we were trying to do good, but they saw us as the bad guys.' Few listening realised that Comrades was not just another word for friends, but the term used by students for their fellow freedom fighters. In *Young Warriors*, a well-researched and moving description of life among the 'lost generation' in Lucas's home township at the time of the uprising, Monique Marks wrote that to be a Comrade in Diepkloof 'one had to have a concern for the community and to uphold all that is "good" against all that is "evil".'

Her book gives an often-terrifying picture of the unsettled and explosive world in which Lucas and his family lived. 'Diepkloof was renowned for its high levels of violence, both political and criminal,' she wrote. 'In Greater Soweto,

Diepkloof was known as Little Beirut. While the "era of negotiations" brought with it a decline in the activities of the security forces, political violence took on a new and sinister face. Activists in the township continued to be "eliminated". There were constant threats of attack on the Diepkloof community from hostel-based Inkatha supporters. Youths continued to carry out acts of political violence in various forms.'

Later she added: 'In the mid 80s, townships like Diepkloof were buzzing. Meetings, both public and somewhat clandestine, were happening on every corner. Crowds of people marched in protest against poor service delivery, the collapse of schooling and the detention of activists. Barricades set up mainly by the youths were burning on the streets.' Recalling this time, Emily Radebe said: 'They were burning houses, burning cars, burning buses. It was terrible. As a parent you were terrified but what could you do?'

At first glance, some of the actions of the youngsters seem to be turned against their own people. They would meet buses from the city and take away the women's shopping because a boycott had been called against shops in the city. If a neighbour had a company car, they would steal or damage it because it belonged to a company that supported the government. There is no doubt that innocent people suffered. In fact Johannes fell foul of a gang in another township, Orlando West. They forced him off the road and wounded him with a spear before he managed to escape to the safety of a relative's home. The danger was real and most Sundays there would be sombre and simmering processions through the townships as the bodies of more young men and women were carried to their grave.

Lucas admitted to carrying a knife with which to stab tyres in order to sabotage cars and buses, and he and his friends quite often stole cars. Such was the fear of the youth gangs, owners would hand over the keys voluntarily to avoid being hurt. 'I remember we kept one car for some time,' he recalled. 'We drove it around until the gearbox packed up and then we just abandoned it. Sometimes we would sell them to get a bit of money.' Questioned further on his involvement, he added, 'I was always the first to run away. I wasn't as bold as the others. I remember one day we approached a car and the driver put his hand out of the window with the key but as we got closer we could see he had a gun in the other hand. He was probably an undercover cop. I ran as fast as I could, not daring to look back, wondering if I was going to be shot in the back. It was scary. No matter what you were like, if you were part of the gang, you could get dragged into things you wouldn't normally do. Most of my friends got arrested. Some of them died.'

While the overall aim of the campaign was to try to make the country ungovernable and therefore bring about the downfall of the government, it was never easy for leaders to keep control of testosterone-fuelled gangs of teenagers, who realised they held power through fear. As well as fights against the security forces and the government, there were gangland 'turf wars' between townships and if one group attacked or robbed another, retribution had to be self-imposed. No one in Diepkloof trusted the police to solve crime.

It's a sign of his possible seniority that Lucas was a member of a disciplinary committee who were charged with imposing suitable punishment on those who overstepped the mark. 'We never allowed the people from Soweto to just walk into our patch and do whatever they wanted,' he explained. 'They were scared of us. We were a fierce lot and disciplinarians. I remember one of our people was robbed and we went and found some of the gang who did it. Their arms were tied with wire coat hangers so they bled. One of our guys poured water on them and then hit them with sjamboks and spades. They broke one guy's ribs. One tried to run. He was hurt badly and bleeding. He got into the street but he never got far. I had a bottle of Coke and I chased him. I threw the bottle and hit him on the back but I don't think it did much damage. One of our guys picked up an old boiler and he hit him in the face with it. His faced just opened up and the blood poured from the wound.. The guy stood there. He was dizzy and only half conscious. I thought he was dying. I've never been so scared. He tried to run but the messages weren't getting from the braain to the legs and he just blacked out. I ran home. I was so scared. I thought we'd killed him. That was a turning point for me. What was next? Their friends could easily have come back and picked up any of us, looking for revenge. And this time they could have had guns.'

For Emily this was the last straw. Ntuba was getting into too much trouble. He wasn't a naughty boy at heart but it wasn't just the naughty boys who were being hurt or killed. She must get him away from the influence of the gangs. Abram had benefited from going to school in Bophuthatswana and it was time for Lucas to follow the same path.

Bophuthatswana was one of ten so-called homelands, pseudo independent states set up by South Africa for the black population. Each was under the rule of puppet governments, in this case dominated by a dictator by the name of Lucas Mangope, who was later found guilty on 105 counts of theft and two of fraud involving more than R5 million.* He received a suspended two-year sentence. Homelands were also a travesty of justice, giving 70 per cent of the population

* *An explanation of the varying exchange rate for the rand is given in the acknowledgements section at the end of the book*

13 per cent of South Africa's land, much of it unworkable scrub. In addition, a 'state' like Bophuthatswana was in reality seven separate parcels of land stretched over more than 700 kilometres. But from Emily's point of view, its advantage was that it was about three and half hours drive from the troubles at home and she knew that the school run by Mr Hlonga would drum some knowledge into her son who had been neglecting his lessons.

Lucas was reluctant to leave home. Abram had told him the area was very rural and very boring. The only excitement for miles was the local football team, ICL Birds United and he was probably too young to get a game.

Chapter 4

Amakhosi

Lucas moved into one of three houses owned by ICL Birds United in Welwedagt. It was about an hour's walk from Ngotwane school in Lehurutshe that he would be attending. Most of the other boys were older than him, some in their early twenties. Having been used to helping with the cleaning and cooking at home, the domestic aspect of his new life wasn't a problem, but it took him a while to adjust to the extra disciplines of his school. Things had become lax in Diepkloof but here strict rules had to be obeyed or you would be punished by a beating.

Although he was a good student, particularly enjoying the geography classes of the charismatic Mr Joseph, Lucas found his rural surroundings too quiet for a teenager used to the sometimes over-exciting times in the township. He didn't miss the violence and the fear but he did miss his friends and having plenty to do. He was homesick and he was bored and the only release was when the football coach allowed him to join in the team's training sessions. But he wasn't playing in the matches so even that didn't end his frustration. Most of all he looked forward to going home to see his family and friends either travelling by bus or getting a lift with some of the team members who came from Soweto.

Lucas's loneliness gradually eased as he started to make friends and also when his sisters Elizabeth and Lydia joined him at the school. Lydia remembers it as an austere place and recalled: 'many of the local people disliked the South Africans. They said we influenced their children by talking about politics.' Lucas got to know some of the local shopkeepers and found himself a part time job with one of them. A tall, good-looking teenager with a stylish afro hairstyle and some money in his pocket, he also discovered girls and met his first serious girlfriend, fellow student Peggy Makowah. But still the main distraction was football training.

ICL Birds' coach Lumunde Mosia was impressed with the youngster: he had skill, pace and he read the game well. One day, about a year after Lucas arrived in Lehurutshe, Mosia said: 'We need a goalkeeper for the team. Will you play in goal?' Lucas jumped at the chance and in a fairy tale start he saved two penalties on his debut and was carried shoulder high from the field. Soon after, he signed semi-professional forms and started to receive payment for playing – on strict orders from Emily that he wouldn't neglect his studies. He became a regular in the team, growing popular with the home fans and enjoying the camaraderie of his team-mates on the long, often dusty trips to away matches in a battered old 18-seater bus.

As football fans around the world were to discover, Lucas was a brave player – perhaps too brave at times. Only as a last resort would he leave the pitch for an injury as he showed when the Birds played a Castle Cup semi-final against Grinaker Wanderers. Birds had a 2-1 lead when Lucas went out to dive on a through ball. As he went down, the opposing striker's boot caught him in the head and his teeth clamped shut on his protruding tongue. His face was a mess. He had cuts around his nose, several of his teeth were broken and his tongue was pouring blood. But he wouldn't go off. He played the remaining 70 minutes of the game as Birds reached the final and only then went to hospital to be stitched up. For days his face was swollen like a football. Fortunately, Peggy's family took him in and prepared his food so he could drink it through a straw while Peggy brought home books from school so he could keep up with his studies.

Life was pretty good. Lucas was something of a local celebrity, welcome wherever he went. Just as he had gone in goal to fill a gap, his move into central defence came when a player left and the Birds needed a replacement. He quickly showed he was even better on the field than between the posts and people started to talk about him as a possible recruit for one of the big teams in Johannesburg. For Lucas that was dream talk. He enjoyed his football but it would never provide him with a proper living. He knew that a college of education was due to open in Lehurutshe at the time he would matriculate and he planned to be one of the first students. He would become a teacher like Mr Joseph.

He was accepted by the college but what he didn't realise was that he was about to be faced with a major dilemma. One of his boyhood heroes, Ace Ntsoelengoe, had advised Kaizer Chiefs to sign this promising young defender. Ace, who had played in the USA as well as at home for the Chiefs, heard about this kid who had been named Footballer of the Year in his league and even played an 'international' for Bophuthatswana against South Africa. He went to watch him in action and could immediately see what the fuss was about. When he asked Lucas to sign for the Chiefs, the 20 year old had a big decision to make. This was serious stuff.

When Jomo Sono returned a wealthy man from America after playing alongside New York Cosmos superstars like Pele and Franz Beckenbauer, he audaciously bought Highland Park the biggest white club in South Africa and renamed it Jomo Cosmos. While his side enjoyed some success, they couldn't match the achievements of Kaizer Chiefs, another club created with money earned by a player in the States. Former Orlando Pirates star Kaizer Motaung broke away from the Pirates to create a rival outfit but even he couldn't have foreseen how big they would become. Amakhosi, as the Chiefs are known, are the Manchester United of South Africa, the best-supported and most successful team in the country.

Even so, after discussions with his parents, Lucas turned down Ace's offer. Emily didn't want him to come back to Johannesburg, where the violence, although reduced, was still in evidence and where young men were still dying at the hands of the authorities and tsotsi gangs. Anyway, football was too precarious. Better to be a teacher. Lucas accepted her advice.

But Kaizer Motaung wouldn't give up. He visited Emily and Johannes and pleaded with them. He phoned Lucas. 'Just come for a trial,' he suggested. 'Where's the harm in having a trial?' Lucas couldn't argue with that, and when the trial went well and Kaizer said the club would help Lucas continue with his studies, Emily too ran out of arguments. It was Lucas who finally decided that it had to be one or the other, football or studies, and he decided to give Amakhosi his best shot. At the age of 20 he was a fully-fledged professional footballer.

It took him a year to break into the team but in the meanwhile he trained regularly, learning his trade under coach Augusto Palacios, a black, former World Cup player from Peru who had come to South Africa when he retired from playing and quickly learned the strictures of apartheid when he was refused permission to check into a hotel with his white wife. Although not on big wages, Lucas could afford to improve his wardrobe and, against the wishes of his parents, buy his first car, a second-hand, gold BMW. Ironically, having hated his early days in Lehurutshe, Lucas now started to drive up there every couple of weeks to see his old friends at ICL Birds, usually with his pal Monyane along for company. Monyane never bothered to get a passport or ID and as the trip meant passing through check points on the South Africa and the Bophuthatswana sides of the border, Lucas adopted a routine to avoid his friend being stopped. Over the months travelling to and fro, Lucas had got to know the guards quite well. They'd have a brief chat and then wave him through without searching his car, so whenever Monyane was with him, Lucas would stop close to the border, put his friend in the boot and then reverse the process once they were clear on the other side.

What they hadn't reckoned on was the growing anxiety of the South African government. Under pressure from within and without the government had started to make some concessions while still hoping to keep control. While appearing to give way on some things, they tightened up many restrictions. They were particularly concerned about infiltration from neighbouring countries and with tension rising again the government ordered a clamp down on border controls. The searches became more rigorous. Driving home to Johannesburg with Monyane in the boot, Lucas suddenly realised that on the South Africa side he was approaching a roadblock manned by armed soldiers he didn't know. He still shudders at the memory: 'I thought oh shit! What am I going to do? Monyane wanted to get out but I couldn't stop because we were in full view of the border guards from both sides. My mind was racing and all the time the car was still moving forward, getting closer and closer to the soldiers and the guns. They waved down the car in front of me and a guy stepped into the road as though he was going to stop me. By then I didn't have any control of my feelings or actions. My right foot took command. It floored the accelerator and I was gone in a squeal of tyres. I was shaking and sweating. I expected to hear a siren or a bullet but luckily they didn't fire at me or chase after me. I stopped the car down the road and I let Monyane out of the boot. I said, "When we get back home, the first thing you are going to do is get an ID. Man, you are not coming with me again unless you have an ID." I still don't know why the soldiers didn't open fire or chase after us. We were so lucky.'

The security clampdown was the last desperate attempt to keep control by a government that knew its days were numbered. Walter Sisulu and other ANC leaders had been released from prison the previous year and discussions were going on behind the scenes with Nelson Mandela. He could have been free already but he refused the terms, which would have forced him to give up politics and the fight for a truly democratic South Africa. Finally, on 11 February 1990, on his own terms and in front of the world's television cameras, Madiba walked out of prison, hand in hand with his wife Winnie. For Lucas's generation, this was their first sight of the freedom fighter they had been taught to revere. He was now grey haired and frailer than the bold, young rebel they had seen in photographs, but even approaching 70 years old, he was still tall and upright. They were proud. They knew the authorities had not been able to break him, no matter what they tried. The whole Radebe family joined in the celebration that marked the beginning of the end of oppression, and looked forward to a day in the near future when they would be able to cast a vote in the election for a true majority government.

Two months later, just after his 21st birthday, Lucas had a personal celebration. He made his Kaizer Chiefs debut.

Chapter 5
Facing the Lions

Lucas's arrival at Kaizer Chiefs went largely unmentioned in the media. The passionate Amakhosi crowd noticed his long hair when he made his debut in midfield against Bush Bucks, and they began to wonder who the new kid was when he did an excellent marking job on Jomo Sono on his second appearance. It didn't take many games before they were convinced he was an exciting prospect. He scored his first goal for the club against Wits and then really came to the fore as Chiefs won the Castle Cup, coming from behind to beat Moroka Swallows 2-1 in the final in front of 73,000 fans at Soccer City, Johannesburg. Lucas and another exciting young prospect, Doctor Khumalo, were picked out for special mention in the reports.

A few days later, the sponsors announced their awards for the Castle Cup series and the headline in the *Sowetan* told the story: 'Buick's best player award stuns more seasoned stars.' The report read: 'For a player who made his First Division debut for the Chiefs only this season after being signed from the Bopsol League, the R10,000 prize reflects a rise to prominence that deserves to be placed in the meteoric category. What makes Radebe's feat more remarkable is the fact that his natural talent is supplemented by an abundance of composure – an elusive quality among South African defenders.'

Lucas, who was also voted South Africa's Rookie of the Year, was delighted at the recognition and grateful for the R10,000. He knew exactly what he was going to do with it. With the ten Radebe children older and bigger, privacy was becoming a real issue. Johannes and Emily had already taken out a loan to build a couple of extra bedrooms on to their house in Diepkloof, and Lucas insisted they took his prize money to continue the work. He found a builder who erected what amounted to a whole new house around the old one and only charged them R6,000. Like builders around the world, this one insisted on being paid up front and there were times when he disappeared for days on end so that Lucas and his brothers had to track him down. They usually found him working on another job he had undertaken at the same time and received the assurance 'I was coming to you tomorrow.' Eventually their house was complete and the family had never known such comfort and enjoyed so much room to move around.

As the *Sowetan* headline showed, Lucas's Diepkloof nickname had stuck with him in the early days at Amakhosi but it was soon to be replaced. By contrast to the English habit of just shortening a name and occasionally adding an s or y as in Batts, Clarkey, Chappy and Kells, South African stars attract much more imaginative names. Norman 'bites yer legs' Hunter is a rare English example but the game in South Africa is littered with colourful names such as Harold 'Jazzy Queen' Legodi, Thomas 'Who's Fooling Who' Hlongwane, Nelson 'Teenage' Dladla (who kept his name into his thirties), Mulungisi 'Professor' Ngubane and Swallows defender Aaron 'Roadblock' Makathuru. Before long Chiefs fans were chanting 'Rhoo' each time Lucas got the ball. No one was sure how it came about, possibly a variation on 'Lu', and at first he was uncomfortable with it because it sounded as though the crowd were booing him. But it stuck and is still used to greet him today. Meanwhile his new team-mates were impressed by his reading of the game and dubbed him 'Lookaround'.

By February 1991 Lucas had won his second medal, part of the team that beat Jomo Cosmos 4-3 in a thrilling BP Cup final in which Phil Masinga score a hat-trick for Cosmos. By now, Augusto Palacios had handed over the coaching duties to Englishman Jeff Butler, who combined a rare understanding of the African approach to football with the need to instil discipline in certain areas. While he was happy for Amakhosi players to express themselves and do all their tricks in the attacking third, he wanted less dangerous tactics in midfield, and demanded concentration and no frills defending at the back. It not only created a successful Chiefs side, it hammered home lessons that Lucas benefited from for the rest of his career.

Meanwhile, speculation was growing that the release of Nelson Mandela and the progress being made towards universal elections would lead to the lifting of the international sports ban. White rugby fans were concerned they might lose their beloved Springbok emblem, a symbol of oppression to the black majority, but for the mainly black football supporters, the opportunity to see some of the world's best players in Johannesburg, Durban or Cape Town would be a dream come true. You had to be more than 40 years old to have seen the last football international on South African soil, a 2-1 win over Israel by a home team with mainly English sounding names, played in the Rand Stadium, Johannesburg on 1 May 1954. Two generations, starved of seeing their country take on the rest of the world, could hardly hide their anticipation at the thought of watching their modern heroes in a South Africa shirt.

Jomo Sono was one of several people gently hinting that when the time came, South Africa would need one of their own to coach the team and if required, he was ready to answer the call. In an article in the *Sunday Times*, he set out a suggested line-up. 'The motto of my team will be attack is the best method of defence,' he wrote but still found room for Lucas, who was emerging as the best young defender in the league.

South Africa finally heard that its sporting isolation was over in August that year. Cricket was the first beneficiary, able to take part in the World Cup two months later. The first football international was set to be against Cameroon but so far there was no date.

Meanwhile Lucas and his team-mates in the black and gold of Amakhosi were going from strength to strength, closing in on the league title with a 3-0 win over Pretoria City that had *Sunday Times* journalist Sy Lerman enthusiastically describing the opening two goals: The first was scored by Ntsie Maphike - 'a thunderous 25-metre drive'. Then, next to a photo of Lucas, fearlessly diving full-length among the flying boots, Lerman added: 'If Maphike's effort had the 10,000 crowd on its feet, it was nothing compared to the bedlam that followed Radebe's breathtaking headed goal from a Khuse corner in the 36th minute…In the main, City ran out of ideas near goal and were well contained by a defence in which the towering Radebe often caught the eye.'

When the Chiefs finally clinched the title, Lerman praised their team-work in a league where individual brilliance sometimes led to exciting but cavalier football, where enthusiasm at times conjured more improvisation than tactical awareness. And ultra-successful clubs from Manchester United to Real Madrid would have nodded knowingly when he said Amakhosi's championship was 'another triumph in a seemingly unending chronicle of success that will gall many – and delight the rest.'

On the back of Chiefs' success Jeff Butler was appointed as the first national coach but forced to resign before ever fielding a team in a dispute over his qualifications. His assistant Stanley Tshabalala was promoted and 'Screamer' had the honour of naming the first South Africa side of the new era. Lucas had been involved in a South Africa XI for an exhibition match against an All Stars team and was proud when he was named in the squad for a series of three true internationals. South Africa were in for a tough baptism because all three matches were to be against Cameroon, 'the Indomitable Lions' who only two years before had shocked the world when they reached the quarter-finals of the World Cup and then only lost narrowly to England. Lucas was getting used to playing alongside and against big-name players, but the thought of being on the same pitch as the now legendary Roger Milla was something else.

The opening game was held on a wet evening in Durban on 7 July 1992. In *Feet of the Chameleon*, his definitive story of African football, Ian Hawkey described the scene: 'The demographic of the crowd would be a happy mix of the country's ethnicities, and the vast majority raised their right arms and clenched their fists at head height for South Africa's turn at the playing of the anthems. And they heard not the official national anthem, the Afrikaans dirge 'The Stem', but the rousing 'Nkosi Sikelel' iAfrika', God bless Africa. With the crushing emotion of that song on that watershed night, people cried and barely noticed that along the line of 22 men standing to attention on the pitch, the green of Cameroon seemed to measure about a foot taller and appeared twice as muscular as the 11 novices wearing a rather racy gold and white kit designed for the Rainbow Nation, soon to acquire a new nickname that had nothing to do with a Springbok. South Africa became known simply as Bafana Bafana, Zulu for the Boys.'

Lucas and his team-mates had to work hard to contain the Lions but the football gods smiled on them and with five minutes to go, Cameroon captain Stephen Tataw slipped on the greasy King's Park surface and his hand hit the ball. The referee pointed to the penalty spot and Doctor Khumalo fired home the winning shot.

Two days later the action moved to Cape Town. The South African team and support were exultant but were brought down to earth when Cameroon out-played them to win 2-1, despite only having nine men for most of the second half after picking up two red cards. One correspondent noted: 'They played funky, amplified music of the type associated with boxing gladiators entering a ring before South Africa faced Cameroon at the sprawling Goodwood Showgrounds on Thursday. But after two contrasting emotional experiences against the ring-wise, internationally-hardened and abrasive Indomitable Lions, a rendition of Oscar Hammerstein's *Stranger in Paradise* might better have reflected the state of South Africa soccer.'

But the South African fans weren't to be disheartened and 65,000 packed into Soccer City – symbolically halfway between Soweto and Johannesburg - to see the sides clash for the third time in five days. It was the best of the three games and goals from Phil Masinga and Bennett Masinga saw South Africa twice come from behind and earn a creditable draw. The series had been a success on and off the pitch and journalist Shaun Johnson wrote: 'Now hold on a minute: is this the same strife-torn, crime-ridden, race-poisoned South Africa we're all so depressed about? There in the stands, dancing and screeching and hugging each other in paroxysms of patriotism were staidly dressed whites, trendy township teenagers, and a cross-section of just about every other race and clan categorisation you can think of.'

Lucas had played in all three games and could be satisfied with his initiation into international football. Summarising the series a journalist picked him out along with Mark Anderson, Doctor Khumalo and Augustine Makalakalane as the players who had 'passed their baptism of fire' although he went on to voice a criticism that was often to be levelled at the national side in years to come: 'South Africa's tactics in the first two games were too similar to the old-fashioned English style. With individual ball skills which were at least as good as their opponents, South Africa should be striving for more ambitious objectives than massed defence and counter-attacking with speculative kicks.' When it came to a model for their football, South Africa would increasingly look towards Brazil for inspiration rather than the old colonial master.

Nevertheless the big news following the internationals was that English First Division club Crystal Palace were coming to town and bringing players the fans had only been able to watch on TV, like Mark Bright and John Salako. Lucas would be marking them when the opening match of the tour pitted Steve Coppell's side against the Chiefs. The Eagles from south London enjoyed enthusiastic backing at Selhurst Park but they had certainly seen nothing like the scenes that greeted them at Soccer City. A reporter wrote: 'Before 7am women sitting at open fires around the stadium sold food, including sheeps heads, a dish known locally as Smiley. Despite the well-stocked liquor cabinets in the private suites, beer sellers were out in force with tubs of ice to keep their brew cool. Like vultures, touts draped with jewellery and dressed in the latest fashions, were out hunting for floating tickets to keep the black market flowing.'

The Chiefs gave an excellent account of themselves and it was generally accepted that despite the 2-3 final scoreline, they had done South Africa proud. Anyway, Palace's first goal by Mark Bright was disputed because Lucas had acrobatically cleared the header off the line. He was mobbed by his delighted team-mates only for the celebration to be cut short by the sight of the linesman indicating a goal. Shane McGregor equalised and a magnificent, inch-perfect pass from Doctor Khumalo set up Ace Khuse to sweep the ball past Palace keeper Nigel Martyn. The visitors' greater experience started to show in the second half. They eventually clinched the win with a second goal from Bright and one from John Salako. As the two sides shook hands after the match, no one would have predicted that the Palace goalkeeper and Chiefs central defender would one day be team-mates at Leeds United.

Rapidly becoming a nationally-known figure, Lucas found himself more and more recognised in public and often found attractive young women slipping a note with their telephone number into his hand. He enjoyed the attention and occasionally called to invite them out but most of his dates were with a young psychology student Pulane Baloyoi. But even she had to come second to football – he was far too young to think about settling down. He still had a lot to achieve at the Chiefs and maybe he would play abroad one day. Such a move was no longer an unlikely dream. The re-emergence of South African football on the international scene alerted clubs around the world to the talent on show and soon flights into Johannesburg regularly included a number of agents on their passenger lists. Mel Stein, who included England internationals Alan Shearer, Paul Gascoigne and Chris Waddle among his clients, was among the first and admitted that Amazulu's Zambian goalkeeper Shadrak Biembia and Cosmos striker Shaun Donnelly had caught his eye, and that he had 'heard a lot about Kaiser Chiefs' Doctor Khumalo and Lucas Radebe.' Khumalo was hot favourite to be one of the first local players to be snapped up. After his display against Palace he was linked with Turkish club Besiktas, San Lorenzo in Argentina and Sao Paulo in Brazil, while Aston Villa coach Dave Sexton admitted he, too, was an admirer. According to reports Lucas was also attracting attention from Argentina

The vultures were circling, ready to strip the National Soccer League of its top talent and no doubt more would be arriving as Bafana Bafana made their sortie out of the country to face their first competitive challenge, an African Cup of Nations qualifier in Zimbabwe.

Chapter 6

Gunned down

Looking back on those first three Bafana Bafana matches, Lucas admitted they had passed in a bit of a blur. The players felt pride and excitement at being involved in a moment in history, but the full impact of what it meant to be an international footballer hadn't really sunk in. They had just enjoyed the occasion and played in the unrestrained way in which they performed for their club sides. 'We were young and naïve. I remember coming out of the tunnel and looking at the Cameroon players and thinking "they are real footballers",' Lucas said. They travelled to Zimbabwe on a wave of expectation – Bafana Bafana had matched the mighty Cameroon, surely they would qualify for the African Cup of Nations. Hey, they might even win it.

Reality soon hit them. Zimbabwe were two up in the first 19 minutes and even though Sam Kambule pulled one back, Coventry City's Peter Ndlovu scored twice in the second half to crush South Africa 4-1. Lucas missed the next match with injury, a 1-0 home defeat by Zambia, after which the chances of reaching the African Cup of Nations finals looked doubtful. How on earth would they cope in a World Cup qualifier against Nigeria, possibly the best side in Africa?

The answer was not very well. The South Africans were used to playing in front of large, noisy crowds but this was the first time they had experienced 60,000 fans who were all hostile to them. Neil Tovey recalled leading the team out before the match: 'It was just a wall of noise, it hit me like a punch to the body. It was so scary, you could see the fear in the players' eyes.' Nigeria hammered South Africa 4-0 – 'we would have scored many more but we eased up out of respect for Nelson Mandela' taunted one fan. Lucas was almost relieved when he was substituted after 75 minutes, at least it saved him the race to the safety of the dressing room as the delighted crowd swarmed on to the pitch at the final whistle. Bafana Bafana, which eventually became a term of endearment and pride was still a seldom used, affectionate jibe – as in boys among men. After their latest defeat the team arrived home to find they had picked up another nickname – the 4x4s.

The defeat cost Tshabalala his job, temporarily replaced by 'Shakes' Mashaba before SAFA turned to Lucas's former Chiefs coach Augusto Palacios. South

Africa had been back in international football less than a year and already they'd hired four different coaches. The players were in as much shock as the administrators but they were determined to overcome the shortcomings that had been so emphatically laid bare. They notched their first competitive win when they edged out Congo 1-0 in a World Cup qualifier and then beat Botswana 2-0 in a friendly. Both were games they were expected to win, but still it gave them a little more confidence going into the return match against Nigeria.

Although there were these disappointments at international level, 1992 had still been a good year for Lucas. He helped Amakhosi to another league and cup 'double' and just before the second Nigeria clash, he was named as one of six players in contention as South Africa Footballer of the Year. He narrowly missed out to Chiefs team-mate Doctor Khumalo, but the R15,000 for second place was very welcome.

Bafana showed they had learned their lessons when they took on Nigeria in front of 70,000 at Soccer City. With John Moshoeu in sparkling form, they took the game to the visitors and were unfortunate not to grab the winner when George Dearnaley's close-range shot was ruled out for offside. The goalless draw almost certainly meant they wouldn't be going to the USA for the World Cup but Sy Lerman declared: 'At last South African soccer fans held their heads high with pride over genuine touches of class and composure from the talented, if previously immature, local players.'

Lucas was now first choice for both club and country and each passing game gave him more confidence in his ability to play at the highest level. He rapidly learned the tricks of his trade and how to impose his skills on the opposition - when to mark tight or when to stand off a little and use his pace and anticipation to nip in and steal the ball. 'I realised that forwards with their back to the goal liked to be able to feel where the defender was, so I would stay just out of reach. That made them uncomfortable. They didn't know where I was or what I was going to do so I had the advantage,' he said.

He had a short spell on the sidelines following minor surgery, the first of what was to prove countless knee operations, but was still able to return to fire home a match-winning penalty for Amakhosi against highly rated Egyptian club Zamalek in the African Champions Cup. He'd also sparked a lot of media interest when it was revealed that he was on standby to go in goal after the Chiefs named only two keepers in their Champions Cup squad and then transferred one of them to another club.

Politics in South Africa was edging towards a solution that would bring a general election but there was still a rump of mainly extreme Afrikaaners who were hoping to disrupt the progress. On the day Bafana Bafana drew 0-0 with Mauritius in the African Cup of Nations, all thought of football became irrelevant with the news that Communist party leader and anti-apartheid activist Chris Hani had been gunned down in Johannesburg. The savagery of the murder – 'After shooting him twice, Chris Hani's killer calmly walked up to the body and shot him twice more at point-blank range,' read the report – was calculated to incite members of the black population to rise up in revenge and destroy the peace process. Nelson Mandela called for calm; Archbishop Desmond Tutu pleaded: 'Please don't let them manipulate us. Don't let this tragic event trigger reprisals. It is what somebody wants to see happen.' The atmosphere was uneasy for a few days but their followers heeded the pleas and negotiations continued.

In some ways it was incredible that there weren't more shootings. The long years of uncertainty had seen large numbers of people acquire guns. Some had been sought as protection against legitimate fear of attack; but many had fallen into the hands of gangsters who used unsettled times to wage a reign of terror on their fellow citizens for personal gain. In such a volatile climate, no one was immune from danger. The sound of gunfire was not unusual in the streets of the cities and the townships.

That was why Lucas didn't think twice when he heard a shot as he drove along Modisa Street after his mother asked him to buy some cold drinks for the family. His brother Lazarus jumped in beside him, with a friend, Boetie, in the back with Lucas's nephew Mbongeni. He hadn't even reached the end of the road when he heard the crack but it was several seconds before he registered the searing pain. He put his hand to his back and felt the blood. He was losing feeling in his left leg. He had been shot. Lazarus helped his brother into the back seat then drove flat out to the hospital. Lucas was scared. He thought he was paralysed. He thought he would never be able to play football again. Maybe worse. Maybe he was dying. He felt sick.

The staff at Baragwanath hospital gently lifted him from the car and rushed him into casualty. The doctor examined his wounds – a large gash in his lower back where the bullet had entered and another in his thigh where it had come out and buried itself in the car's upholstery. It seemed scarcely possible but the bullet had ripped through Lucas's body without damaging a single organ or even nicking the bone. An inch either way and it might have killed him. It would certainly have ended his career. 'You are a lucky man,' the doctor said. 'You are going to be OK.'

There was plenty of speculation about who shot Lucas and why. Was it a Pirates' fan trying to gun down one of their rivals? Someone from Lucas's

Diepkloof past who still held a grudge from the 1980s? A jealous neighbour? Or, most likely, just a random shooting, not especially aimed at Lucas, just someone aimlessly firing at a passing car? The police didn't bother to investigate so no one was ever caught for the crime and it remains a mystery.

Lucas was out of action for three months. It couldn't have been at a worse time for Amakhosi, who were already struggling and had sacked yet another manager unable to maintain the constant flow of trophies demanded by the fans. It also denied Lucas a chance to play against English champions Manchester United, who were touring South Africa with their new £3.75 million signing Roy Keane. And as he found out years later, it cost him a move to Turkey. Former Coventry and Leicester boss Gordon Milne had taken over as coach of Besiktas and he revealed: 'I went to Africa to look at certain players I wanted to sign. I managed to get Fani Madida and I also wanted Lucas Radebe but he had a non-football injury at the time which ruled him out.'

One potential move Lucas did know about was from Scottish Premier Division outfit Dundee, which appears to have been on the recommendation of former Dundee player Roy Matthews, who was now coaching at Jomo Cosmos. Dundee manager Jimmy Duffy was a bit vague when he was asked about it: 'I've heard about this central defender but I'm not sure of the name,' he said. 'I've heard this guy is very good but I can't elaborate because nothing is definite yet.' And Lucas admitted he knew nothing about Scottish football but he felt the time was right for him to play in Europe. 'I would get a lot of exposure by playing in Scotland and I hope the big teams in France or England will show an interest in me. I would love to play in Europe and with SA players attracting the interest of foreign countries, I hope my dream will come true.'

Kaizer Motaung wasn't too happy at the prospect of losing one of his best players. The Chiefs had finished an unacceptable sixth in the table and a newspaper report predicted a major shake-up with a new team being built around Rudolph Seale, Neil Tovey and Lucas. Questioning the wisdom of some agents' choice of players to take abroad, the article continued: 'Some critics say that Radebe, for example, who is regarded by many as the best central defender in the country, if not in Africa, should have gone overseas instead of national team captain Steve Komphela. There were rumours that Radebe was on the wanted lists of several top overseas teams but Chiefs didn't want to release him as they thought he was too valuable a player.'

To the trauma of the shooting and the turmoil over his future was added a new complication. Pulane gave birth to a son she named Ofentse. He was a fine young boy and Lucas was proud of him but his relationship with Pulane was no longer as strong. The initial reaction, as with so many young men in this situation, was that hc would have to marry, but when he thought about it, he realised it would be the wrong decision. He would make financial arrangements and would keep in touch with his son but marriage would be a mistake.

Lucas could only wait and see what would happen to his career. It was out of his hands. Meanwhile, fit again, he was about to take his first major flight away from the continent, part of the Bafana squad on its way to the USA to play Mexico in Los Angeles. 'My brother Abram told me to be careful because it could be bumpy in a plane,' Lucas said, smiling at the memory. 'I didn't believe him. I could understand how pot holes in a road could affect a car but what could there possibly be in the sky to cause bumps for a plane? The first time we hit turbulence I was very nervous.' Little did he know but over the next few years, bumpy plane rides were to become second nature, though he never grew to like them.

The first international against non-African opposition also proved bumpy with the 4x4s crashing to a 4-0 defeat in the Memorial Coliseum. It was a disappointing end to a difficult year on and off the pitch and Lucas wasn't sorry when it was time to welcome in 1994, a year that was to prove unforgettable in so many ways.

Democracy came to South Africa in April 1994. This was something Johannes and Emily, and millions of others who had grown up under apartheid, had dreamed about but wondered if it would ever come. Many who had fought for this day never lived to see it dawn so while celebrating the biggest day in the country's history, Lucas along with countless others, thought of friends who had died in the struggle to make it possible.

The general election was held on 27 April. There was never any doubt that Nelson Mandela would be his country's first black President, presiding over a government dominated by the African National Congress party. Ten days before the election, Madiba signed an advertisement that appeared in the national newspapers and already his message was peace and reconciliation. 'The time for casting blame is over,' he wrote. 'Now, more than ever, it is the responsibility of every person and every organisation – including the ANC – to ensure that we put an end to violence and get on with building a nation.'

Proudly Johannes, Emily, Lucas and other members of the family over 21 joined the long queues waiting patiently to vote for the first time in their lives. Only those who have been denied the right know how it feels to finally have a say on who will govern you. Along with millions of their fellow countrymen and women, the Radebes had witnessed a miracle. At the Union Building in Pretoria, the new President proclaimed: 'Never, never and never again shall it be that this beautiful land will experience the oppression of one by another...The sun will never set on so glorious a human achievement. Let freedom reign.'

President Mandela was sworn into office on 10 May watched by millions on television around the world and in the presence of a Who's Who of world leaders. As part of the celebrations he attended a football match between South Africa and Zambia. At such a hectic time, it was understandable that he didn't arrive at Ellis Park in time for kick-off, but with the score at 0-0 at half-time, the President entered the South Africa dressing room and was introduced to Lucas and his team-mates. Madiba Magic was born in that instant. Within 90 seconds of the restart, Brendan Augustine and Doctor Khumalo had fired Bafana into a 2-0 lead. Zambia pulled a goal back and Khumalo was sent off just before the end but no one was going to spoil this party.

Clive Barker had recently become the country's fifth coach and after starting with a win in a friendly against Zimbabwe, this maintained his 100 per cent record but he wasn't claiming the credit. 'No doubt the President's presence makes a difference,' he said. 'It's worth a goal start at a home game...if he wants the job as motivator, he's got it.'

Lucas wasn't the only person in awe at being involved in such a momentous event. Journalist Colin Bryden wrote: 'Since Tuesday, I have been trying to think of a sporting occasion that has been as emotional or uplifting as the soccer international against Zambia. Arriving in Australia with the South African cricket team was extraordinary, as was the first World Cup match in Sydney. Rugby Tests and soccer finals have stirred the soul, as did the fervour of Loftus Versfeld when Gerrie Coetzee challenged for the world heavyweight title. Yet Ellis Park was unique, the first time a united, liberated nation has cheered for a sporting team. At last there was a sense of pride in buying a South African flag and in seeing thousands of them being waved in the grandstands.'

Later Bryden added: 'Just as Nelson Mandela had to wake up on Wednesday morning and get to work running a country...so the soccer players dare not dwell on the glories of Ellis Park. Save this. They should be fired with a dream, a sense of destiny, inspired by the reality of what it is like to have a nation supporting them.'

Bafana's next chance to live the dream came the following month in Australia but Lucas was injured and withdrew from the trip at the last minute. What he didn't realise was that he had just caused Englishman Geoff Sleight a long, wasted journey Down Under.

Chapter 7

Strange accents
and Yorkshire pudding

Don Warters, the long-serving Leeds United correspondent of the *Yorkshire Evening Post*, broke the news to the club's anxious fans – manager Howard Wilkinson was looking abroad for talent. Under the heading 'United spread the net', he reported that new chief scout Geoff Sleight had been to South Africa and Australia, looking for players to strengthen the squad. 'He has been running the rule over an international striker and a midfielder,' Warters wrote. 'In addition, United have their eyes on another overseas international, who I understand is a central defender-cum-midfielder.'

United were a club in transition. After the triumph of winning the championship in 1992, they had slumped to 17th in the table the following season, only two points above relegation. Things had improved since and a three-match unbeaten spell saw Leeds finish the 1993-94 season in fifth place. But Wilkinson was frustrated that his side had not done better. 'When you look back over the season we had to scrap for almost every result,' he said. 'We have not had a Shearer, a Wright or a Cole to assist us, unlike our main rivals just above us in the table.' A new striker was a priority.

As ever, the summer was a cauldron of rumours – Manchester United's Brian McClair and Danish international Brian Laudrup were linked with a move to Elland Road. Later Czech Tomas Skhuravy entered the frame. But the transfer market was going mad, with a player like Watford striker Paul Furlong, who had only left non-league football three years before, becoming Chelsea's record £2.3 million signing. Wilkinson had money to spend but he needed several players, so he would struggle to match the fees being demanded for quite ordinary players and would have to look further afield. 'Buying abroad can be cheaper and sometimes it is warranted,' he said.

To get a real bargain he needed to look beyond the players whose prices were about to be inflated in the heat of the World Cup spotlight and on 21 June, Warters wrote: 'Leeds United revealed today that a £250,000 deal to sign a top South African striker has been agreed with the player and his club.' Mamelodi Sundown and Bafana Bafana top scorer, Philemon Masinga, was on his way to Leeds.

It was some time before the name of a second signing – the central defender-cum-midfielder - was revealed to be Lucas and it didn't cause much of a stir. When Wilkinson brought in Rod Wallace two years before, he also signed the striker's twin brother Ray in order to help him settle in the north, and Leeds fans quickly got the impression that Lucas was to be a 'Ray Wallace' figure for Philemon. There was very little mention of his name in the reports, especially as Masinga made such a stunning start, scoring freely in pre-season matches. A feature on what it meant for Chippa to be signed by a top English club hardly mentioned the tall figure photographed smiling beside him in the Elland Road dug-out.

It was only some time later that Wilkinson revealed that he'd sent Geoff Sleight to South Africa to watch Masinga on the recommendation of an old friend Johnny Brooks, a former Sheffield United player. Like all the best scouts, Sleight was always looking beyond the immediate targets and when South Africa captain Steve Komphala told him that Luas was the best player in South Africa, he decided to take a look for himself. 'Geoff phoned and said he was impressed with Phil but that he had seen another player he thought was an even better prospect. That was Lucas. He said South Africa were going to Australia and he'd like to go and take a second look at him so I agreed. As it turned out, Lucas didn't travel so it was a wasted journey but we still decided to sign him on Geoff's say-so.' Of all the signings he made in his life, the £250,000 Wilkinson paid for Lucas was without doubt his biggest bargain.

Chiefs fans were unhappy to see their star defender leave. Brooks along with agent Cliff Durandt and a few other people got involved in the negotiations with Leeds and he later revealed that Kaizer Motaung advised him to keep his involvement in the move a secret or he would be in danger, and indeed Brooks reported that one day when playing golf, 'We were just about to tee-off when I heard this loud bang. Then something whisked past my left ear and I realised it was a bullet. My heart raced as we ducked into the nearest bush and it was only then that the seriousness of the situation hit me.' Lucas left it for others to sort out the deal and in fact it was the Professional Footballers' Association in England who insisted Leeds increased their initial wage offer on the grounds that if they claimed he was eligible to play in the Premiership because of his international status, he should be paid accordingly, and only then would they support his work permit application.

Lucas had mixed feelings about the move. He had already played 155 games for the Chiefs and was well established but he desperately wanted to play in Europe and the new contract would mean an increase in money. He knew it would be painful to leave his family and friends behind, and he had a new love in his life, Itumeleng Mabalane. They both understood it wasn't yet heading towards thoughts of marriage but he didn't relish leaving her behind. He was also concerned about the attitude of some of the people from Leeds who talked to him as though he was a complete novice rather than someone who had represented his country several times, won a load of medals and been runner-up in the Player of the Year awards. He hardly knew anything about his new club and had no idea where Leeds was. He hesitated for a while but then realised this was an opportunity he couldn't turn down.

Johannes, Emily, his brothers and sisters, five girl friends and other friends all turned up at the airport to see him off. There was singing, dancing and tears. Some were saying 'good luck' others begging 'don't go, Ntuba. Why are you leaving us?' Eventually, Lucas had to drag himself free and board the plane. All he can remember of the trip was that it took ages and involved a long stop over at an anonymous airport with nothing to do but wait. Leeds United weren't wasting money on an expensive direct flight for an unknown who might not make the grade.

Finally arriving in Leeds, he found himself in lodgings in Holbeck under the supervision of Kay Jones, a woman who had looked after several generations of young United players. It was supposed to be summer but it was still colder than the winter he had left at home. Even his Bafana team-mate Chippa, who had arrived earlier, wasn't there to greet him because he was in Malaysia with the Leeds team. He was alone among strangers.

Lucas didn't have much time to get to know his new surroundings before being whisked off to Italy on the next stage of Leeds' pre-season. He later admitted that he found former schoolteacher Howard Wilkinson quite forbidding and assistant manager Mick Hennigan even harder to get on with. This was Lucas's first experience of living in a mainly white community and it was difficult to adjust. He revealed: 'I could still feel the gap. I still felt they were 'boss' and I had to abide by what they said. Mick Hennigan was a very critical man. He'd been to South Africa so he knew how things had been. If we made a mistake he'd yell, "is that the way they taught you in South Africa?" as if we were inferior players just because of where we came from. I got the feeling that he thought proper football was played in English stadiums, by English players in front of English fans and everything we had known at home was not of the same standard. I was very quiet.' There was no doubt the criticism hurt and made Lucas wonder if he had made the right decision but he took it without complaint, gritted his teeth and got on with it.

Lucas played two games in Italy but because his work permit had not yet been granted, he was unable to play any of the pre-season matches in England. He was mainly training with the reserve team. It was physically harder than he was used to and the tactics were not those employed by Amakhosi – at Leeds, defenders were encouraged to hit the ball hopefully towards the corner flags for forwards to run on to. He wondered if he and Leeds United were right for each other.

He was desperately home sick, as was Phil, and despite his doubts, Lucas often found himself reminding his Bafana team-mate that this was the opportunity they had longed for and they couldn't give up. The pair vowed to keep each other going. They collected a stash of 50p pieces so they could use the payphone at their lodgings to ring home. They called almost every night, sometimes for a couple of hours at a time. It was expensive and eventually they found a way of prising open the cash box and 're-cycling' the coins. Emily recalls heartbreaking calls where Lucas would be crying and saying he wanted to come home. 'Every day he would call and say he just wanted to hear our voices.'

With his work permit granted, Phil at least had the consolation of playing some football. He scored a second pre-season hat-trick in a match against Boston United and Leeds fans were so impressed they adapted the old Australian ballad and started singing 'Waltzing Masinga!' With the opening match of the season against West Ham fast approaching, Wilkinson said: 'He (Masinga) is in there pitching with the rest of them. He is 25 years old, an international and he will be in with a chance.' But there would be no opportunity for Lucas, the British Home Office were still considering his work permit application.

Phil came off the bench as United drew their opening match 0-0 at West Ham and made his full debut in a 1-0 win over Arsenal in the following game. Next up were Chelsea and after only three minutes, Masinga 'waltzed' on to a Gary McAllister cross and headed his first goal for the club. He was already becoming something of a cult figure and Jason Lumsden, Mrs Jones's grandson, recalled: 'I walked down towards Gran's house and there were hundreds of kids in the street, laughing and kicking a football around. In the middle of them were Phil Masinga and Lucas Radebe, who had just come over from South Africa.'

Light-hearted moments like that were few and far between for Lucas and as he packed his bags ready to return home to meet up with the Bafana squad for an African Cup of Nations qualifier in Madagascar, he wondered if he would ever come back. He wasn't enjoying the football and he knew it would be an enormous wrench to leave the family again. Anyway, the situation might be out of his hands. With no work permit, the immigration officials might not let him back into the country. There wasn't much time to snatch family reunions before the squad set off for the match. It was great to be back among the lads again and to play some South African football. A 1-0 win made it even more enjoyable.

While Lucas felt he was neglected by the Leeds management and found their attitude towards him cold compared to what he was used to back home, Howard Wilkinson and his staff were in fact impressed by the tall, quiet defender. When South African journalist Peter Davies visited Leeds to see how Lucas and Phil were settling, Mick Hennigan told him: 'I really like Radebe. He's got the lot. Pace, strength, skill, vision. Of the pair, he's the one to watch.' Wilkinson was a shrewd judge of a player and had seen enough to know Lucas had a chance of succeeding in England, given time. Behind the scenes he was pulling every possible string to make sure Lucas wasn't turned away at the airport on his return from international duty. According to Johnny Brooks, even Nelson Mandela's name was invoked to break the logjam and it worked. By the time he landed in England, Lucas had permission to work.

At least now he would have a chance to show what he could do and the following day, 7 September 1994, he pulled on a Leeds United shirt for the first time. He lined up alongside Chris Fairclough in a reserve match against Notts County at Meadow Lane. Leeds lost 3-2. Three days later, a bright sub-editor at the *YEP* came up with a headline that was to be repeated countless times over the next decade: 'Lucas Aid'. The report said Lucas had been named in the first team squad for the game against Manchester United, although he was unlikely to play. He was, indeed, left on the sidelines to watch as Leeds beat their arch-rivals for the first time in 15 years in a fiery encounter. Phil had warned him that English football was much more physical than in South Africa and even from the safety of the stand, Lucas could see what he meant. He wondered how he would cope when he finally got his break.

Along with a new environment, strange food and very strange accents from his team-mates - Yorkshire, Irish and Scottish all spoken quickly and laced with slang - he was also having to come to terms with playing conditions. Elland Road had a newly-laid pitch and was an impressive stadium with a giant new East Stand and the old Kop terrace recently redeveloped with seats and dedicated to the memory of the club's most successful manager, Don Revie. Wilkinson also had plans for a Premiership standard, out-of-town, training complex and academy but for the present the players worked on a patch of bare ground opposite the West Stand. It was bumpy and bleak. Some clubs in the lower divisions had better training conditions.

Then there was the Shay. Lucas was picked for the next reserve match against

Sunderland, a home fixture, and in order to protect the Elland Road surface, that meant a trip to neighbouring Halifax and the local club's ground at the Shay. The site was vast but the stadium was very basic. Open on three sides with large, wind-swept terraces on which grass grew through the clinker, there was a single-storey wooden stand on the fourth side, containing very primitive, and usually cold, dressing rooms. The dimly lit, tree-lined car park reminded Lucas of when he used to fetch water at home in Diepkloof. In days when health and safety were words seldom seen together, 36,855 fans had once packed into the Shay to watch an FA Cup tie against Tottenham. But Halifax Town had fallen on hard times and the sad little stadium scarcely saw more than a few thousand these days and they would usually be so muffled up against the cold, they could hardly muster a shout. It was hard to imagine a greater contrast with Soccer City.

Lucas thought back to the huge, colourful crowds who used to follow the Chiefs, singing and dancing amid a cacophony of whistles and vuvuzelas on the terraces, and wondered what the hell he was doing playing in front of a handful of people in Halifax. He recalled the haunting South African song Shosholoza, originally sung by the miners as they were transported to work in the gold mines of the Transvaal. 'Train from South Africa, you are running quickly' they sang, wondering if they would ever see their homeland again. 'At times, when Phil was away, I would sit alone in our room and cry,' Lucas recalled.

The club had moved them into new lodgings, sharing a room in a small semi-detached house in Beeston, owned by Suzanne Humphrey. Peter Davies visited them there and reported that their new landlady was 'the epitome of bustling, northern hospitality, and made it her daily task to ensure the pair were thoroughly fed and watered. At each memorable mealtime during my stay there, every carbohydrate known to mankind would be piled high on the plates – rice, roast potatoes, boiled potatoes, mashed potatoes and, of course, Yorkshire pudding.' Lucas longed for some pap and wors. He would have given anything to be back in Diepkloof enjoying a braai with the family. But he was conscious that as wretched as he felt, this really was a great opportunity. And anyway, if he packed in and went home without giving it his best shot, clubs might decide that South African footballers didn't have the heart to play in England. He had to stick it out. He had to break into the first team. He had to make a success of this.

Chapter 8

Breakthrough and breakdown

Only 7,844 fans turned out to see Leeds take on Third Division Mansfield in the first leg of their Coca-Cola Cup tie on 21 September 1994, the lowest crowd at Elland Road for 32 years. Everyone expected a one-sided affair so it was the perfect game for Wilkinson to give Lucas a taste of English football. He would put him on the bench and then give him a run-out when United were comfortably in front. Good theory but no one told Mansfield. The Stags harried and chased and completely out-fought their big city opponents. Leeds' star international midfielders, Gordon Strachan, Gary McAllister and Gary Speed couldn't get in the game and Mansfield delighted their travelling support by going ahead after only 17 minutes.

Instead of a gentle introduction, Lucas was sent on to bolster a defence under siege, replacing Strachan on the hour. It was a wretched start and the kit man even mis-spelled his name on the back of the shirt – REDEBE. Mansfield left Elland Road with a famous victory, rewarded by their chairman who only charged them 50p for a can of beer on the bus home instead of the usual £1. The only consolation for Lucas was a brief report in the newspaper the next day which read: 'Another plus for United was the confident 30-minute substitute display of South Africa central defender Lucas Radebe.'

Lucas picked up a knee injury and was doubtful for the following match but he recovered enough to be on the subs' bench and his appearance five minutes from the end of a 1-1 draw at Sheffield Wednesday marked his Premiership debut. However, he seemed to be a long way from Howard Wilkinson's plans and it was hard to come to terms with the stark contrasts his life threw up. When he and Phil returned to South Africa for an African Cup of Nations qualifier, with Chippa scoring the only goal as Bafana Bafana overcame Mauritius, he was national hero Rhoo. Four days later the pair were back in action in Leeds reserves against Everton and the small crowd were asking, 'Who's that?'

One of the few consolations was that he had more money in his pocket than he had ever known. He and Phil had started to find their way around Leeds city centre and enjoyed the ability to spoil themselves for a change. One day they found an up-market jewellery shop and Lucas decided it was time he had a watch befitting a Premiership footballer. The shop was owned by David Share who, by coincidence, was the son of the dentist who looked after United players under Don Revie. 'I supplied the gold and Dad put it in their teeth!' David joked. He recalled vividly the day he saw two black, track-suited men peering in his shop window. 'I wasn't sure whether to lock the door or let them in but one of them gave me his broad smile that we've come to know over the years and they came in. Lucas bought a watch and we just hit it off from day one. He started to come into the shop regularly and we'd talk about football and gradually became good friends. I think he appreciated having someone to talk to outside the club.' It was the start of a longstanding friendship.

Lucas and Phil made another trip home for a 1-1 draw with Zambia after which Bafana heard the good news that they wouldn't have to compete in any more African Cup of Nations qualifiers. Because of problems in Kenya, the finals had been switched to South Africa so they were given automatic entry. That was something special for Lucas to look forward to. In fact it all seemed to be going his way suddenly because when he got back to Leeds he was told he would be making his full Premiership debut at Queens Park Rangers that Saturday.

It was not the dream start he had hoped for. He and central defensive partner David Wetherall struggled to hold the QPR attack and powerful England striker Les Ferdinand put his side 2-0 by half-time. Midway through the half, Lucas went into a tackle with Andrew Impey and felt a sharp pain in his knee. Physio Geoff Ladley looked concerned as he treated it, but Lucas assured him he could go on. He limped through the rest of the half and as Wilkinson delivered a searing assessment of United's pathetic first-half display, Ladley again examined Lucas's knee. It was no good; he couldn't go on. David White came into a reshuffled side as Leeds slumped to a 3-2 defeat.

Lucas had to report for treatment the following day and was told that he had seriously damaged his knee ligaments and would probably be out of action for five weeks. Wilkinson said: 'It's bad luck for him, especially as he has waited so long to start a Premiership game. But he should have come off when it happened. He did not do himself or his team any favours by staying on.' It was a message echoed by skipper Gary McAllister, who thought the injury had been brought about because Lucas was still coming to terms with football in England. 'I know Lucas is an experienced international and has played a lot in South Africa but he got his injury in a very English type of challenge. Maybe he was a bit naïve to get caught like he was. He went in fairly and although Andy Impey is not a dirty player, he went into the challenge in a way that he could protect himself. Maybe Lucas went in a bit too fairly.'

No one in South Africa would have been surprised that Lucas had tried to run off a serious injury rather than come off the pitch, especially in his first full Premiership appearance. And equally no one would have raised an eyebrow when he defied the prediction he would be out for five weeks and returned to the bench 16 days later, an unused substitute against Everton.

He tested out his knee in a reserve match on a freezing night at the Shay. Lucas had never been colder. He could hardly feel his legs and every time he tried to call for the ball, nothing came out of his mouth but steam. If he'd known it could be this cold in Yorkshire, he'd have gone to Turkey or South America – anywhere but England! But having come through with no ill-effects, Lucas was back in the first team starting line-up less than a month after the QPR game. If nothing else, Leeds United knew they had a gutsy player on their hands, one who didn't submit easily to injury and pain.

His second start came against Arsenal at Highbury. Wilkinson asked him to play a holding role, patrolling just in front of the back four to help cut off the supply to Alan Smith and Kevin Campbell. It was a role he had performed often in South Africa and it worked brilliantly. Leeds came away with a 3-1 win, with Phil Masinga ending his scoring drought with two goals. Don Warters reported: 'United soaked up a great deal of pressure in a 20 minute onslaught from the Gunners, but their defence - with Pemberton showing the way – battled in great style. Tony Dorigo was in fine form, and had to deal with the right wing raiding of Dixon and Parlour, and in midfield, Radebe shone.'

The outlook was much brighter and Lucas was feeling more settled. He'd persuaded Tumi to come to England and join him and they rented a flat in Bramham, a quiet area outside Leeds. It was the first of many moves with a switch to a new home almost every season over the next few years. With his increased salary, he had also been able to fulfil a long-held dream and bought his parents a house in the Richmond area of Johannesburg. They moved in with the younger children while the older boys stayed in the Diepkloof house.

In addition, Lucas was starting to believe he had the measure of English football. It was certainly more physical and more structured than at home, but he had always been a disciplined player and he felt his ability to read the game stood him in good stead. Wilkinson wasn't so convinced. He thought the game at QPR had passed Lucas by and he felt both South Africans still had a long way to go before they would be completely at home in the Premiership. At this stage, they were back-up to players more experienced in English conditions. For the next game, the Boxing Day visit of Newcastle United, Lucas wasn't even on the bench. It made for a miserable Christmas, even though he had Tumi for company. Lucas was used to the hubbub as the whole family got together at his parents' house but this year Christmas Day included a training session just like any ordinary day.

With Carlton Palmer suspended, Lucas was back in midfield for three games in seven days as 1995 was rung in. It wasn't a happy time at the club. The team and Wilkinson were booed off the pitch after a 2-0 defeat by Liverpool, managed only a goalless draw with Aston Villa and again struggled against minnows in the cup, held 1-1 at Walsall. But Lucas was starting to impress a number of people. After the Villa game, Warters wrote: 'Playing again in midfield, the former Kaizer Chiefs star showed class, and his accurate passing, both long and short, is a commendable feature of his game. His notable efforts against Villa deserved more than to see United end up with just a point.' And under another soon to be familiar headline 'Cool hand Lucas', Wilkinson was reported as saying: 'Lucas looks to be some player. He is very composed. He always seems to have time. He wins headers. And he is an excellent passer of the ball.'

Lucas was replaced at half-time by Phil as Leeds vainly tried to unlock a 0-0 draw with Southampton, and he found himself on the bench for the FA Cup replay against Walsall. With inspirational, championship-winning skipper Gordon Strachan announcing he was bringing forward his plans to retire at the end of the season, the match was played in an end-of-an-era atmosphere. And the new order didn't seem to hold much promise. By the time Lucas came on in the 70th minute of one of the most extraordinary FA Cup ties seen at Elland Road, Walsall had twice come from behind to level at 2-2 and if anything, they were looking the more dangerous. The game went into extra-time and Wilkinson played his final card, sending on Masinga in place of Rod Wallace. Soon after the restart, Lucas hit a raking pass to the wing, the ball was crossed and Phil steered it home. Within ten minutes he had completed a hat-trick, Leeds were through and quiz book compilers had a novel question with which to challenge football fans for years to come. Having only played half an hour, Phil found himself back in the reserves two days later but even more deflating, his place in the first team was thrown into greater doubt after Leeds beat the German transfer deadline by minutes and agreed a £3.5 million fee with Eintracht Frankfurt for Ghanaian striker Tony Yeboah.

Lucas smiled sympathetically when he saw United's latest African recruit struggling to come to terms with Yorkshire. Yeboah's welcome to Leeds photograph was taken under an umbrella and within a couple of days, the Ghanaian went down with a throat infection and cold. It was hardly surprising. Soon afterwards the *YEP* reported that snow storms had forced people to abandon their cars and they had still been struggling home at two o'clock in the morning.

Conditions were so bad, Leeds were not even able to switch training to the all-weather pitch at Wakefield prison because it was frozen. After the initial novelty of seeing snow wore off, Lucas just wondered what on earth he was doing in a country with a climate like this.

Omitted from the visit of QPR and the FA Cup tie against Oldham, Lucas came on for the injured David Wetherall at Blackburn and returned to midfield in the usual physical battle at Wimbledon. But frustratingly, he wasn't even on the bench for the FA Cup defeat at Manchester United. It was as though Wilkinson didn't think he could handle the big occasions, apparently unaware that Lucas had several times played in front of larger and more fervent sets of fans than the 42,744 at Old Trafford. Perhaps there was a hint at the reason for Wilkinson's unwillingness to take a chance in an article about the Premiership's decision to cut its size by relegating four clubs and only promoting two. Although Leeds were comfortably near the top of the table, Wilkinson admitted: 'The Premier League at the moment is full of fear, without a shadow of a doubt. Nine Premiership managers have gone already, the number of transfers is up, and the number of clubs due to be relegated is up too. This is a situation that creates hysteria and generates fear. And fear is never the best environment to work in.' With many disgruntled Leeds fans wanting a new manager, Wilkinson tended to rely on people hardened to the English game.

When Lucas ran out to face Coventry at Elland Road on 13 March it was his tenth start and his first for a month after picking up an ankle ligament injury in training. With David Wetherall and John Pemberton injured, he had a rare chance to play in the centre of defence alongside Carlton Palmer but the game was only a few minutes old when he went down clutching his knee. As before, he persuaded the physio that he could run it off, but when he collapsed again in the 23rd minute, he couldn't even stand. The stretcher was called for and he was carried off. Surgeons performed an exploratory operation that same day and gave him the bad news – he had ruptured the cruciate ligaments in his right knee and would need major surgery. It was an injury footballers dreaded. At one time, it automatically meant the end of your career and while medical techniques had improved a lot, and in recent years Paul Gascoigne, Alan Shearer and John Salako had all made successful comebacks, recovery was always slow. Lucas was warned that he had little chance of playing again before Christmas.

A fortnight later, Lucas had reconstructive surgery and started the long haul back to fitness. It was one of the most frustrating times of his life and often he would admit to Tumi that he thought he would never play again. Why would Leeds United bother to stick by him, he wasn't even a regular member of the team? At first he was in a plaster from hip to ankle with a hinge at the knee to restrict movement. It was very uncomfortable and often painful. At night he would lie awake sweating, unable to move easily. He desperately wanted to take a bath but had been told he mustn't until the plaster came off. One day he could take the itching no longer. He wrapped black plastic bin bags around the plaster and eased himself into a deep, hot bath. What bliss! But the water quickly seeped into the gaps around the plastic bags and the plaster turned mushy. Lucas was horrified. He phoned physio Alan Sutton and sheepishly said: 'Al, something's happened.' He was immediately taken back to the hospital for a new plaster to be fitted and had to suffer a stern lecture from Wilkinson.

United had enjoyed a good end to the campaign and booked a spot in the UEFA Cup next season. It also meant they were given several invitations for overseas tours and Lucas couldn't believe it when he heard that Leeds would be going to South Africa but he would have to stay at home. They were due to play Amakhosi but he would be back in Yorkshire receiving treatment. Even worse, Wilkinson and the physios told him he couldn't go home at all. He had hardly seen his family in the last twelve months and he'd been through hell. At times the only thing that had kept him going was talking to people back home and planning to see them again during the summer. He was horrified at the thought of not getting to Johannesburg. He begged and begged until finally they relented. He could go home - for just one week.

It was an unbelievable relief to be back with the family and he even took in a Chiefs game, where he was paraded round the ground on crutches to a hero's welcome from the fans. 'Rhoo!' they yelled. 'Rhoooo!' The seven days raced by. He phoned the club to try and get an extension – just one day would be better than nothing – but they wouldn't give in and after another tearful airport farewell, he was back in Leeds.

He was the only player at the club. Each day Tumi drove him to Elland Road for treatment, then picked him up again in the evening. Instead of being in South Africa to celebrate one of the greatest moments in the country's post apartheid story, Lucas watched on television as Joel Stransky dropped the goal to win the Rugby World Cup for South Africa and Nelson Mandela, wearing a Springbok shirt, presented the gold trophy to Francois Pienaar. It was the perfect symbolism for the Rainbow Nation.

Lucas could hardly bring himself to read the reports from home as Leeds lost 1-0 to Mamelodi Sundowns and were then beaten on penalties by Benfica, so missing out on the chance to play against the Chiefs.

United was a club under a cloud and there was speculation that a takeover was imminent. Richard Thompson, the chairman of QPR was reported to be ready to quit the London club and make a £20 million bid for Leeds. Wilkinson was an even-money bet to be among the first managers to get the sack when the new campaign got under way. But United started the season strongly with three straight wins and after ten matches they were fourth in the table, only two points behind leaders Newcastle, and had knocked Monaco out of the UEFA Cup.

The club went into mourning in September when they heard that Albert Johanneson had been found dead. It was particularly poignant for Lucas and Phil. Albert had joined Leeds in 1960 from the South African township of Germiston and was the first black player to appear in a Wembley cup final when he played against Liverpool in 1965. On his day, he was a stunning player, quick and an elusive runner, but opposition defenders who struggled to beat him fairly, discovered they could intimidate him into going into his shell. Albert regularly suffered racist abuse on and off the field and, having grown up as a second-class citizen in South Africa, never managed to make the transition to feeling he was the equal to his white team-mates or any other white man. At his peak he had earned £200 a week – a huge amount then - but when his playing days were over he gradually sank into poverty, alcoholism and depression, and despite several efforts by former team-mates to help him, he became a sorry figure around the city. In a final tragedy, he died alone in an anonymous towerblock flat and it was five days before anyone found his body. He was only 55 years old.

Albert had died unnoticed but his funeral was attended by ex-team-mates, other big names from football and hundreds of people who had enjoyed watching him play. Lucas stood at the graveside alongside Albert's daughter Yvonne and spoke for many South Africans when he said: 'He was an inspiration to us.'

As the season went on, Lucas concentrated on getting himself fit. He spent hours in the tiny treatment room situated just off to the side of the players' tunnel at Elland Road. The physios were very encouraging, always trying to keep up his spirits and eventually he was allowed to start running, at first just gently lapping the pitch at Elland Road then, as his knee grew stronger, running up and down the concrete steps in the stand. Finally physio Alan Sutton would time him in a gruelling series of 12-minute runs around the track with only a short recovery period between them. In time he was allowed to try twisting and turning as he ran and at last he was told he could kick a ball again. Once again Lucas's grit and determination saw him beat the odds and he started a tentative, 45-minute come-back in the reserves at the Shay on 20 November, a full month ahead of schedule. The African Cup of Nations finals in South Africa were only a few weeks away. He hardly dared hope that he might be ready in time.

Chapter 9

Champions of Africa

In November 1995 Bafana Bafana emerged unbeaten from the Simba Four Nations Cup, drawing 2-2 with Zambia and beating both Egypt and Zimbabwe 2-0. It took coach Clive Barker's unbeaten run to 12 games but while Sy Lerman was impressed by the form of some of the players, the South Africa *Sunday Times* correspondent was far from convinced that the squad was yet looking up to scratch for the African Cup of Nations which was now only weeks away. Lerman was especially concerned about the defence. 'Steve Crowley has performed yeoman service for South Africa but current form decrees there is no room for him at this stage,' Lerman wrote, adding that he was also worried that 'Steve Komphela's qualities as an off-the-field leader have long blinded Barker to his on-the-pitch shortcomings.'

Bafana Bafana looked at their best, Lerman thought, when they played with their most inventive midfielders – Doctor Khumalo, Ace Khuse, Augustine Makalakalane and John Moshoeu. The trouble was that of the four, only Makalakalane did any defending, which left the guys at the back unprotected and vulnerable. The solution, Lerman concluded, lay with a return to fitness and form of Lucas. That would allow the coach to play three central defenders – Lucas, Mark Fish and Neil Tovey – and two attacking full backs. Even more important, 'with a fit, in-form Radebe, South Africa could afford to use three inventive, predominantly attacking midfielders.'

The flaw in the plan was that Lucas had been out of action for eight months and the omens weren't good. Bafana Bafana were clinging to a hope raised by an optimistic headline in the *YEP* the day they tackled Zambia. 'LUCAS IN FROM THE COLD FOR UNITED - Forgotten man is back in the running,' it read over a story that told of a 'surprise' 45-minute appearance in Leeds' reserves against Birmingham City.

A great deal hung on that match, possibly even Lucas's career. He was nervous. It was like starting all over again but he was determined not to flinch from the tackles. For once playing at the Shay was to be relished and after coming through this first test, he told journalist Don Warters: 'My injury was a bad one and it was worrying. Eight months is a long time to be out but I kept on going. All the time I was positive about it. I kept my mind on getting fit again and I worked hard to do so. Now I think everything will be all right after another couple of games. I hope to be challenging for a first team place soon – before Christmas.' And he clearly hadn't given up hope of taking his place in the historic tournament in his homeland. 'I have been looking forward to the finals and it would be good for me if I could play in them.'

The next day he wasn't so sure it would be possible. The knee was swollen and sore and he was anxious as he made his way to the too familiar surroundings of the treatment room to get it checked out. The physios reassured him that he was bound to get some reaction but Lucas couldn't help worrying. He didn't have time for setbacks. Once more he forced himself to run lap after lap of the track around Elland Road, willing the pain to go away. It was two weeks before the physios felt he was fit enough for another reserve outing, 75 minutes on a bitterly cold night against Manchester United, followed a week later by a full game at right-back against Liverpool. Lucas was beginning to feel strong. But reserve matches were one thing – ideally he needed to test the knee in the intensity of a Premiership clash.

Phil flew back to Johannesburg to play in an international friendly against Germany in front of Nelson Mandela. The Germans were preparing for Euro 96 and fielded a strong side but Bafana matched them impressively and managed a goalless draw, thanks to some superb goalkeeping from Andre Arendse. Phil reported back that fans' expectations were starting to grow at home.

At face value, things looked quite promising for Lucas. Training was going well and whenever he read quotes from Wilkinson about the African Cup of Nations, his name was always included along with Chippa and Tony Yeboah. Both he and Phil were mentioned when the Leeds boss expressed his delight that Clive Barker wasn't going to insist on FIFA's rule by which he could call up players two weeks before the first match so instead of flying out on New Year's Eve, the pair would travel straight after the Coca-Cola Cup game against Reading on 10 January, only three days before the opening match of the finals.

But privately Wilkinson was expressing doubts about Lucas's ability to stand up to the rigours of a schedule that could possibly see South Africa involved in six games in a little over two weeks. Lucas needed a chance to prove his fitness. He was called up to the squad for the big Christmas Eve match against Manchester United but sat on the bench as joyful Leeds fans watched their side win 3-1. Three days later, he was again on the bench at Bolton but this time he came on in the 89th minute, replacing recent signing Tomas Brolin. He was only in the action for 112 seconds but it felt good. Surely he was going to get to SA now?

Not if Wilkinson had his way. Lucas recalls: 'Towards the end of December, Howard told me that I hadn't played a full game where I was tested, so he was going to withdraw me from the squad. I was devastated. I begged him to change his mind. I said I would do anything to prove to him that I was ready to play. I tried to explain to him just how important this was to me – this was South Africa hosting the African Cup of Nations for the first time. I asked him to let me go back for a week, to train with the squad to show what I could do. But he wouldn't budge.

'Clive Barker sent Victor Ramathesele, the team doctor, over and I paced up and down outside Howard's office at Elland Road while they had a meeting but it was no good. Victor sat me down and said: "They are worried you will break down again and that might mean another long lay off or even the end of your career. I'm sorry, there was nothing I could do." I was shattered. The finals were so close now that it seemed hopeless.'

But behind the affability and ready smile, the willingness to put himself out for others, there is a steely resolve within Lucas that kicks in when the going gets tough. He simply wouldn't give up. He kept pleading with Wilkinson and phoned Clive Barker, begging him to try again. Finally the coach called back and said: 'It's OK, Howard has said you can come over but that we have to be very careful and only play you gradually. At the first sign of any recurrence of the injury you have to go straight back to Leeds.'

Barker was taking a massive gamble, going against the warnings of Wilkinson and the instincts of his own team doctor, but he told the press in South Africa: 'Those 112 seconds against Bolton were the crucial factor. Leeds are sure to have set stringent fitness tests before fielding him in the first team – and it's worth taking a chance on a player with his ability.' For Lucas it felt like Christmas had come all over again.

As ever, the welcome home was warm but there was no escaping the realisation that expectations were soaring. South African sport was on the up. Two years before the cricketers had completely outplayed England at Lord's, humiliating Mike Atherton's side by 356 runs in the first Test between the nations for almost 40 years. The Springboks had won the World Cup, beating the mighty All Blacks only seven months before. Surely if the rugby players and cricketers could do that, Bafana Bafana should stroll away with the African Cup of Nations? Who was there to fear, especially now Nigeria had withdrawn after a dispute between the two governments? In fact some South African sights were already being set higher, encouraged by FIFA's President Joao Havelange confirming that he expected the 2006 World Cup finals to be played in Africa.

It seems Barker agreed with Sy Lerner's assessment of Steve Komphela and he dropped the skipper, giving the armband back to Neil Tovey, who had been skipper for the first few games after South Africa were re-admitted to the international scene until pressure had been applied to pass the honour to a black player. It was a symbol of just how far the Rainbow Nation had come that there was now no protest when a tall, blond, white guy, who looked as though he could easily be a Springbok wing forward, replaced a black captain.

South Africa made the perfect start to the tournament. Three days after playing in front of just over 20,000 at Elland Road, Philemon produced one of the best displays of his career to the delight of a sell-out crowd in Soccer City in Johannesburg. With his President looking on, Masinga led the charge as Bafana showed no signs of the pressure on them. 'The Indomitable Lions' didn't know what hit them. After only 14 minutes Phil latched on to a cross from Doctor Khumalo and hammered the ball past William Andem for the first goal of the tournament. He was involved again as Eric Tinkler set up Wolves' striker Mark Williams for the second just before half-time and then took a pass from John Moshoeu and back-heeled it into his team-mate's path for 'Shoes' to stroke home the third. The exuberant singing, dancing fans were in ecstasy.

Lucas watched delighted, if a little frustrated, from the stands. Clive Barker had stuck to his word and not even named him on the bench but training was going well and when the team was announced for the second match against Angola, Lucas was included as a substitute. With 77 minutes gone and South Africa leading 1-0 thanks to a goal from Williams and some world-class saves from Arendse, Lucas entered the tournament, replacing Khumalo. Persistent rain had made the pitch wet and slippery but he put in a few tackles and felt no ill-effects. He was OK.

With South Africa already qualified for the knock-out stages, Barker made four changes to his line-up for the third match against Egypt, including starting Lucas in central defence. Still mindful of his need to protect the knee – and of his promise to Wilkinson - the Bafana coach took Lucas off with 14 minutes to go. They lost the game 1-0 - the first defeat at home since August 1992 - but no one was particularly concerned. The camaraderie and optimism in the camp were high. Lucas recalls: 'I give a lot of the credit to Clive Barker. He was a good coach. He trusted us and treated us like adults. He never restricted us. No one took advantage. We grew as a team and we had a great spirit and togetherness.'

Heavy rain reduced the crowd to 50,000 for the quarter-final against Algeria and their singing was sometimes as much to steady nerves as to celebrate during a hard-fought match that had all the tensions and changes in fortune that can make football such a gripping spectacle. Lucas was part of the three-man central defence with little to do early on as South Africa battered at the Algerian goal while their opponents rallied men behind the ball and fought to keep them out. With half-time only a couple of minutes away, Bafana Bafana were awarded a penalty but the normally reliable Khumalo shot tamely and it was comfortably saved. It was a subdued bunch who listened as Barker urged them to maintain their shape and keep playing as they had because the breakthrough would come. And come it did, midway through the second half, in the unlikely form of defender Mark Fish who gambled forward, beat three defenders to the ball in a melee of legs and rammed it home. The Algerians suddenly had to attack and they were so effective, neutrals wondered if their initial tactics had been misguided. Only a brilliant, trademark interception by Lucas denied them a quick equaliser.

Eventually South Africa took the sting out of the response and they looked as if they had done enough but with six minutes to go, Algeria won a corner and defender Lazizi Tarek headed past Arendse. Extra time looked inevitable but there was to be one more twist. Helman Mkhalele and Shaun Bartlett worked the ball to John Moshoeu at the corner of the penalty area, he made himself half a yard of space and fired an unstoppable, angled shot into the corner of the net. There was no coming back from that.

Ghana, from the outset the strong favourites to take the title for a record fifth time, beat Zaire 1-0 with a goal from Tony Yeboah and would now face Bafana Bafana in the semi-final. Lucas would have the job of marking his Leeds team-mate, one of the most powerful and deadliest strikers in the game. Wilkinson's cut price bargain would be head to head with the United manager's record signing. The odds against South Africa were increased because they would be without their star marksman – Chippa had picked up a second yellow card of the tournament against Algeria and was suspended. The match was billed as 'the real final' with scant notice taken of the other semi-final where in-form Zambia were expected to cruise past Tunisia.

Around the country and in the media, little else was discussed in the couple of days between the quarter-finals and the semis and Yeboah sounded confident when he told the press: 'It is disappointing that this game is not the final. I believe they are the best two teams in the tournament and I think whoever wins will go on to lift the cup. But we are confident we will win.' Nervous South Africa supporters tried to ignore his words, although many feared he might be right. Back in England, Wilkinson and Leeds fans were much more concerned because he'd also said he'd be joining the celebrations in Ghana if they won the competition. With an FA Cup tie against Bolton coming up and Leeds already struggling to put together a team because of injuries, this was not what they wanted to hear. Their concern was echoed in the report of the semi-final clash. Bafana Bafana's thrilling 3-0 win was greeted with joy, not for Lucas and Phil, but the fact that it meant Yeboah now had no excuse to delay his return to Leeds. 'Yeboah's loss is United's gain,' ran the headline in the *YEP*.

The semi-final met with a different reaction in South Africa. In front of a noisy, deliriously happy and excited crowd, the home team were just unstoppable although it might have been different had it not been for a rare squandering of an early chance by Yeboah. Lucas tried to switch play across the pitch but was horrified when he saw his pass intercepted by his United team-mate. With only the keeper to beat, Yeboah looked certain to put his side ahead but the Ghanaian, who had cracked in unforgettable goals from all kinds of angles at Leeds, somehow shot wide. Lucas recalls: 'As we walked out for the match Tony said "You ok, man? Take it easy, you don't want to hurt your knee again." I clattered him early to let him know I was fully fit and he had a game on his hands. My heart stopped when he intercepted that pass but after he missed his shot, I stuck so close to him for the rest of the match, he didn't get a kick. Ghana were definitely the best side in Africa at the time but we played them off the pitch. We were great – we could have beaten any team in the world that night.' Man of the match was John Moshoeu, who opened the scoring with a spectacular overhead kick in the 23rd minute and rounded things off with brilliant solo effort two minutes from the end. Any hopes of a Ghanaian comeback had been killed off within seconds of the start of the second half when Shaun Bartlett made it 2-0.

There was another shock in the other semi-final when Tunisia halted Zambia's run and made all of South Africa more confident they must now go on and win the tournament. Messages of support poured into the team's hotel and Deputy President Thabo Mbeki reflected the optimism felt throughout the country when he said: 'We now have one short mile to go. I urge Bafana Bafana to move relentlessly towards capturing the African Cup of Nations on Saturday. The rainbow warriors have sent out a clear message: Nothing, not even Tunisia, will stop us.'

The weight of expectation and the hullabaloo that surrounded the squad had been high throughout. Now it knew no bounds. The pressure might have fazed some players but this group, still relatively inexperienced in international football, managed to take it in their stride and focus on the game. It wasn't easy. Lucas remembered: 'The atmosphere in the country was amazing. I don't think anyone went to work. All they could think about, all they talked about was football. The team hotel always seemed to be heaving with people. Even on the day of the final the place was seething with media wanting interviews and pictures, and sponsors wanting us to do things. But we were strong as a team. Come the final, we were really up for it.'

As the teams emerged into the sultry heat of Soccer City, they were met with a wall of noise that took the breath away. It was estimated around 15,000 more fans had found a way in than the stadium's 80,000 capacity and they were determined to sing and cheer their side to success. The slightest advantage – a goal kick or a throw-in won – was acclaimed, and moments of high skill brought pandemonium. Lucas was having a tough personal battle against Tunisia's talented striker Mehdi Slimani but he stuck to his task with determination – the characteristic tongue sticking out in concentration – and the longer the game went on, the less of a threat his opponent became.

All over the field, Bafana players were winning their personal battles and getting on top but it wasn't until the second half that their domination paid off. Phil picked up an injury and was replaced in the 65th minute by Mark Williams, a move that changed the game and wrote the Wolves' striker's name into the history books. He'd only been on the pitch 12 minutes when he rose above a goalmouth scramble to meet Moshoeu's floated cross and headed his team in front. And two minutes later, he took a perfectly weighted pass from Khumalo and fired home with his left foot. A fleet of jumbo jets could have flown over the stadium at that moment and no one would have been able to hear them for the roar of the crowd.

The tumult reached a crescendo as Nelson Mandela, wearing a Bafana Bafana shirt, presented the cup to Neil Tovey. Amid the hugging and dancing, the singing and laughing, many tears of joy and sheer emotion were shed. Moshoeu revealed that when he threw his shirt into the crowd 'A white person came and asked me for my autograph. It was the first time in my life that had happened. I felt tears in my eyes.' The nation was ready to party.

The symbolic significance of the victory was not lost on Lucas and he had even more reason to celebrate – less than a year after his career looked as though it might be over, a mere six weeks since Wilkinson had told him he wasn't fit enough to play, he had come through three full games in a week and picked up a winners' medal as an African champion. He was tired, but he, too, was ready to celebrate.

He wasn't supposed to. Before the semi-final, when logic told everyone that his tournament would probably end with the third-placed play-off, it had been agreed with Leeds that he and Phil would catch a plane at 8.10 the morning after the final, ready to play in the third round FA Cup tie against Bolton.

After the victory over Ghana, returning early had looked optimistic. Now it was inconceivable. Lucas turned his phone off in case Wilkinson called and threw himself into the celebrations. He laughs at the memory: 'It was a massive party. The country never slept that night. There were people singing in the streets and cars driving around sounding their horns, the national flag flying from their windows. Nelson Mandela came to the hotel to congratulate the team. Leeds rang Clive Barker and asked where I was but I stayed out of the way.'

Wilkinson saw things from a different perspective. 'Given the importance of the Bolton cup-tie, the least we were entitled to was for the players to be home on Sunday,' he said. 'We pay their wages. They have, in effect, been on loan to South Africa.' The phrase 'we pay their wages' was one Lucas was to hear many times over the next few years and he found there was a price to pay for disregarding the paymaster. 'I eventually got back on the Wednesday,' he said. 'Howard was really angry and threatened to throw the book at me. I knew he liked Mandela and said that the President had insisted we all had to stay, but it did no good. He fined me two weeks' wages. The worst thing was that the party was still going on back home. The next week the whole team was invited with partners to Sun City for a free weekend. I wanted to be there so badly and to crown it all, after all the fuss, Leeds played in the semi-final of the Coca-Cola Cup that weekend and I sat on the bench, and only came on for the last minute. I hardly remember the game – my mind and my heart was in Sun City.'

Chapter 10

Under the Twin Towers

Howard Wilkinson was struggling. His squad was badly depleted with John Pemberton, Tony Dorigo and Richard Jobson on the injury list and Mark Ford, Paul Beesley and on-loan Lee Chapman all suspended. The last thing he needed was three players on duty in Africa. He had some important games coming up including the Coca-Cola Cup semi-final against Birmingham and, before that, a fourth round FA Cup tie against Bolton three days after the African Cup of Nations final.

In contrast to Johannesburg, back in Leeds the weather was freezing and six inches of snow on the Burnden Park pitch caused the FA Cup tie to be postponed for a second time. That was nothing compared to the icy reception Lucas and Phil faced after they failed to turn up on Sunday evening as planned. Wilkinson was already annoyed because reports had been circulating about a bust-up between himself and Tomas Brolin. And his mood wasn't improved when Tony Yeboah arrived back from the African Cup of Nations a day late and with a thigh injury.

Wilkinson was not a happy man but even his famed temper and the drop to below-zero temperatures couldn't wipe the smile off Lucas's face at the memory of the triumph at Soccer City and he and Phil were photographed happily playing snowballs. Ever the diplomat, he realised it was important to show he understood the club's view and told the press: 'I have not been able to play many games for Leeds United since I came here so I feel I owe the club something. The injury I got was very serious but the club have taken good care of me and now my goal is to get back in the side.' Leeds captain Gary McAllister was struck by how much winning the tournament had lifted the spirits of his two team-mates. 'In the few training sessions they've had since they returned to Leeds they have looked very buoyant,' he said. And even Wilkinson could see the advantages of Lucas having come through some games and proved his fitness. 'Before his injury, he was just beginning to find his feet in the English game. He has returned ready to play for us and that is a bit of a bonus.'

There was another reason for Lucas to be smiling so much. During the African Cup of Nations he had met Feziwe Ngqobe. She was different from all the other women he had known, quieter, almost diffident. But she was special.

It had taken him some time to persuade her to let him have her phone number but they met a few more times before he returned to England and now he was calling her regularly. He knew this was a special relationship but of course it wasn't straightforward because Tumi was still with him in Leeds.

It was something of an anti-climax when Lucas only made two one-minute substitute appearances as Leeds beat Birmingham 2-1 in the first leg of the semi-final and then overcame Bolton 1-0 in the much delayed FA Cup tie. Phil wasn't even on the bench for either match. For all the hype about how important it had been for them to hurry back, nothing much had changed, or it certainly must have seemed that way to Lucas when he found himself playing in freezing, torrential rain in front of a handful of people as Leeds reserves took on Sheffield United at Bramall Lane. It was hard to find any reason to be optimistic and he desperately wanted to get away but wasn't sure how easy that would be. He just hoped that the advice he'd received from Gary Blumberg turned out to be true.

Blumberg was a South African lawyer who gained some of his experience of sports management when working with Mel Stein in London. He first came to Leeds to handle the negotiations when young goalkeeper Paul Evans joined the club. It was Evans who introduced his fellow countryman to Lucas and the pair hit it off straight away and started a personal and professional relationship that became very important in Lucas's career. Blumberg and other colleagues built a structure that allowed Lucas to concentrate on his football, knowing that the business side of his life was taken care of. 'Our business relationship was sealed by nothing more than a handshake,' said Blumberg, who remains chairman of Lucas's company. 'We quickly realised that we were dealing with a unique person, especially in the context of South Africa, and that has guided our actions ever since. We have always taken the long-term view – sometimes turning down lucrative short-term deals that didn't fit comfortably with Lucas as a man, as a footballer or as an important figure in South Africa.'

At that time, Blumberg was a near neighbour of QPR chairman Richard Thompson and former Arsenal manager George Graham, who was serving a suspension for taking cash in a transfer deal, and the South African had become aware of rumours that things were likely to change at Elland Road. 'Don't do anything hasty,' he advised Lucas. 'If you hang on, things might turn out much better.'

The same didn't look true for Chippa, who knew his chances of renewing his work permit were in peril. Lucas had been given special dispensation because of his long injury but Phil was running out of time to get in the 75 per cent of first team games he needed to qualify. However, the striker was a surprise replacement for Brolin in the Coca-Cola Cup semi-final second leg and vindicated Wilkinson's selection by scoring the first goal as Leeds brushed Birmingham aside 5-1 on aggregate to book a place in the final against Aston Villa. The Birmingham match was also a turning point in Lucas's season and the start of a remarkable roller-coaster period. He was, as usual, warming the bench but after 20 minutes Tony Dorigo went down injured and, after a quick assessment, physio Geoff Ladley signalled to the bench that the Australian couldn't continue. Wilkinson told Lucas to warm up. 'Before he went on I asked him if he'd ever played left back before. He said he hadn't but that didn't stop him producing a polished display,' the Leeds boss admitted to the Press after the game.

Leeds fans were not convinced that Wilkinson and the board of directors were on the right path but with the certainty of the club's first trip to Wembley in 23 years and the growing anticipation of a second visit after shrugging off Port Vale's challenge in an FA Cup replay, the mutterings of discontent heard in the lead up to the New Year were at least put on hold. Lucas, too, was able to put the memory of those bleak days of his injury to the back of his mind as he began to be a regular name on the team sheet either at left-back or in the centre of defence. With the confidence instilled by being an African champion and at last feeling he was a recognised member of the team, he started to show United fans something of his true ability. Don Warters, who had always gone out of his way to praise Lucas in the early days, wrote after Leeds went down 1-0 to Blackburn: 'Lucas Radebe further enhanced his claims for a Wembley place with another polished performance last night...The South African defender had turned in solid and unruffled displays in United's last two games and he again looked the part... Such is his composure that he looks at home whether playing in a three-man central defensive line-up or the more usual back-four.'

The games were piling up. A goalless draw with Liverpool in the FA Cup meant a replay at Anfield had to be fitted in five days before the Wembley final. But Lucas wasn't concerned; he was relishing being in the thick of the action and even allowed himself the dream of picking up three cup-winners' medals in less than six months. He had been Leeds' man of the match in the first game against Liverpool, keeping the double threat of Stan Collymore and Robbie Fowler quiet - Fowler joked later, after he'd moved to Leeds, 'that's when I christened him 'Rash' because he was all over me' - but Liverpool's England international Steve McManaman took control of the replay and lacklustre Leeds crashed out 3-0.

Despite that, there was plenty of optimism in the camp and the city in the build-up to the final. Even though Leeds had been thumped 3-0 by Villa only six weeks before, the army of fans heading down the M1 with scarves flying from car and bus windows could see nothing but glory ahead. The service stations rang with the singing of 'Wem- berley, Wem- berley, we're the famous Leeds United and we're off to Wem- berley.'

Lucas understood the importance of the historic stadium in the English sporting psyche. He had watched FA Cup Finals on television in South Africa and appreciated that only a few people were fortunate enough to show off their skills in that arena. He recalled: 'When I was playing at the Chiefs, Kaizer Motaung, the owner, used to go to England for the Cup Final every year and he would come back and tell us about Wembley. He told us how big it was, about the great atmosphere created by 100,000 people, and what a privilege it was to be there even as a spectator. We could imagine how much more special it must be to play there, and in my mind I always hoped I would one day get there as a player.' He had finally made it.

The team coach drove through the giant gates at one end of the stadium and parked in the long tunnel outside the dressing rooms built deep below the stands. The stroll on to the pitch was relaxed, giving the players time to take in their surroundings and the fact that they were under the famous twin towers. The warm-up wasn't too different from usual, a chance to get a feel of the pitch and run off some of the nerves. But the enormity of the occasion really hit home as they left the dressing room just before kick-off. They walked up the slope of the Wembley tunnel towards the light and a growing awareness of the noise created by 77,000 fans, which became a roar as they strode out into the full glare of the arena. In single file, they made their way across the sanded area behind the goal and on to the lush turf, to stand anxiously below the royal box for the preliminaries, desperate to get started and shake off the tension.

The Coca-Cola Cup final coincided with the Oscars where Mel Gibson's *Braveheart* swept the board, picking up five golden statuettes. How the Leeds followers must have wished their team had shown a little of the William Wallace spirit. Instead the players seemed to freeze. The fans were already concerned before the kick-off, trying to fathom out the reasoning behind Wilkinson's team selection. He started with three central defenders, including Lucas, a ploy he'd used to good effect before, but the surprise was putting winger Speed at left back. But the biggest concern was up front where, of Yeboah's usual partners, Deane and Brolin were on the bench while Masinga was up in the stands. Instead, the manager had opted for Andy Gray, the son of former Leeds player Frank and nephew of Elland Road favourite Eddie. As it turned out the 18-year-old winger, who had only made his first team debut earlier that month, took the fight to Villa and was the only Leeds player to emerge from the game with credit. But the fact that his selection turned out to be a good one didn't stop the fans turning on Wilkinson for the woeful display they were witnessing. Deane came on at the start of the second half for young Ford, who looked out of his depth, but made little impact. Leeds were already a goal down and Villa soon doubled their lead following a mistake by Lucas. Henry Winter described the goal in the *Daily Telegraph*: 'Wright's awkward cross placed great pressure on Lucas Radebe. With Milosevic lurking, hungry for any scraps, Radebe cleared hurriedly, his scissors kick flying straight to Taylor. His first-time volley, combining accuracy and velocity, disappeared into the net. The sight of Wetherall, diving full-length to no avail, represented a graphic image of Leeds' plight. Overstretched and overwhelmed.'

By now the Leeds fans were thoroughly miserable. 'Why is Brolin on the bench?' they yelled and finally Wilkinson sent the Swede on in place of Lucas. It made little difference and United conceded a third as the fans' mood turned to anger, booing the team and especially the manager all the way down the tunnel after they had picked up their losers' medals. Although the match was a major let-down for Leeds United and the fans, with hindsight, Lucas said: 'Of course the result was a big disappointment, but for me it was still a big thing to get to the final and to play at Wembley.'

A shell-shocked Wilkinson faced the press afterwards and admitted: 'We didn't do the fans or ourselves justice. We didn't cause Villa any problems. We just didn't perform.' One of the most astute managers in football, the Leeds boss knew that the pain and the recriminations would go on for some time but even he couldn't have foreseen the turmoil that was about to hit the club.

Chapter 11

Keeping his hand in

The backlash from the Wembley defeat soon destroyed any pretence that Leeds were on the way to the glorious future that had been hoped for when they won the championship in 1992. Splits were showing in the camp and being aired publicly. Predictably Tomas Brolin had refused to travel back with the rest of the players after the final, saying: 'If I cannot play in a big game like that, then I have to think about my future. I think I will have to try to find another team to play for.' Tony Yeboah made all the right noises about being happy to stay with Leeds but at the same time his agent let the Press know his client would be thinking about moving on because he wanted European football.

The most devastating intervention came from Carlton Palmer who, in the guise of defending Howard Wilkinson, claimed: 'I can understand the fans' point of view but yesterday was nothing to do with the manager. It was down to a group of players, quite a few of whom just did not perform on the big occasion. In my opinion, the lack of effort shown by professional footballers in as big a game as the Coca-Cola Cup Final was nothing short of a disgrace.' Admitting that he had not played well, Palmer however added: 'I competed - I tried and if people can come off at the end of a game and say that, then fine. But I don't think there were too many yesterday who could say that.'

Ever the realist, Wilkinson said: 'I know we have to make changes. We need a fresh impetus going into our last nine games, which prepare the ground for the next season. The players now face a big test of character. They have to redeem themselves and regain some pride. Wallowing in self pity is not the answer. We only want players who are desperate to play for Leeds United and who take pride in owning and wearing the Leeds shirt.'

The next match was against Middlesbrough at Elland Road and to no one's great surprise Yeboah cried off, having picked up a back injury in a friendly for Ghana, and Brolin was struck down with tonsillitis. Wilkinson took the opportunity to give a run out from the bench to a 17-year-old Australian who had been impressing in training and the reserves, thus marking the start of a stellar Leeds career for Harry Kewell. This also turned out to be an important game for Lucas although it started badly when his third-minute challenge on Nick Barmby had the referee pointing to the penalty spot and Graham Kavanagh smashed his shot past John Lukic. Wilkinson must have felt he'd upset every god known to man when his medical staff told him at half-time that Lukic had concussion from a kick in the head and could not continue. With no keeper on the bench, Wilkinson turned to the only other player with any experience between the posts and threw the jersey and gloves to Lucas.

When they saw Lucas trot towards the Kop goal at the start of the second half, Leeds fans sat back waiting for the inevitable hammering. But as Don Warters reported, 'Radebe was beginning to settle down remarkably well between the posts and he turned up trumps with a fine display, making several stops of note, two of them to deny former United winger John Hendrie.' United's forwards were unable to salvage anything at the other end but there had been plenty of effort from the side and everyone was impressed by Lucas who now only needed a chance to play centre forward to show he could fill every position on the pitch.

Leeds picked up what was to be their final victory of the campaign, beating Southampton 1-0, but then the season went into free fall, on and off the pitch. Lucas was praised for his marking of Denis Bergkamp at Highbury but couldn't prevent Arsenal winning 2-1, and like the rest of the team, he appeared tired and dispirited playing at right-back when they crashed 3-1 at home to Nottingham Forest.

Next up would be Chelsea but before that the front pages of the *YEP* reported another bombshell at Elland Road - chairman Leslie Silver had stepped down after 14 years at the head of the club. The 71-year-old paint multi-millionaire decided it was time he took his doctor's advice to slow down. He retained his shareholding but speculation that his resignation would spark a takeover bid quickly ciruclated. Managing director Bill Fotherby was immediately put in place as the new chairman and tried to calm talk of a takeover, preferring to hint at a cash injection from someone like Paul Sykes, the multi-millionaire who had built Meadowhall shopping centre in Sheffield, Barry Ruberry who had created Pace, a massively successful electronics company near Bradford or, once again, QPR managing director Richard Thompson.

Lucas was replaced by John Pemberton in the starting line-up against Chelsea but came on after 37 minutes when Pemberton was injured. It was another bad day at the office for the whole team and they went down 4-1. The next match was a midweek visit to Manchester United who, while Leeds were in chaos, were sweeping all before them, well on the way to overhauling the ten-point advantage Kevin Keegan's Newcastle had built up by Christmas. Lucas was again on the bench at Old Trafford but called into action after only 17 minutes when goalkeeper Mark Beeney, who had been preferred to Lukic, was sent off for deliberately handling the ball outside his area. Wilkinson again had no sub keeper, so called off Mark Ford and told Lucas to don Beeney's sweater and gloves.

Once again he summoned up the experience of those now distant games in the heat and dust of Bophuthatswana and produced a remarkable performance. David Wetherall, who was centre-half for Leeds that day, recalled: 'When Mark was sent off we thought we were in big trouble but Lucas did magnificently. Those of us in front of him were feeling nervous but every time we looked round there was that big, re-assuring smile and it filled us with confidence.' Lucas turned aside a shot from Brian McClair and took a fierce volley from Ryan Giggs as though keeping goal against the best side in England in front of more than 48,000 people was an everyday occurrence. With the defenders working their socks off to protect him, he looked set for a second goalkeeping clean sheet until Roy Keane took a pass from Eric Cantona, twisted and turned on the edge of the area to create some space and fired into the far corner. At the final whistle, players from both sides and even the referee went over to Lucas and congratulated him. Ironically, after struggling to stand out as more than just a squad player since arriving in Yorkshire, he had finally won special recognition from the Leeds fans with two displays as goalkeeper.

Leeds put up another battling performance against Newcastle - Lucas hitting the bar with a 20-yard shot and Shaka Hislop producing a stunning last-minute save to deny Wetherall - but the Geordies kept their title hopes alive for a few more days thanks to a goal from former Manchester United winger Keith Gillespie. Lucas found himself back on the bench for the final home match against Tottenham Hotspur, which Leeds lost 3-1, taking their run of defeats to six, the worst sequence since 1947. The usual end-of-season lap of honour was somewhat subdued. Everyone at Elland Road was relieved to see the campaign come to an end and while the goalless draw at Coventry didn't set the pulses racing, Lucas and recalled Phil Masinga were both praised for their performances. At least the dreadful losing streak was halted.

As Lucas packed his bag, eager to return to South Africa and the chance to see Feziwe and his family, he could look back at a season where he had made progress as a player, shown his versatility and won the hearts of many Leeds fans by his willingness to play anywhere, including in goal. But it had not been a good season. The childhood dream of playing in a cup final at Wembley had turned into a nightmare and he wasn't looking forward to coming back for the next campaign, especially as it looked certain that Phil wasn't going to get a renewed work permit and would have to move abroad. This was not how Lucas had envisaged life would be as a professional footballer in England. Little did he know that events in Leeds while he was away, would bring about changes that would re-ignite his career.

Chapter 12

Sharp suits and promises

Leeds United was owned in equal shares by three men, outgoing chairman Leslie Silver, Bill Fotherby, who had joined the board in 1981 and gone on to become the highest paid managing director in the Premiership, and Peter Gilman, a property developer, whose company had built the new East Stand at Elland Road. They had gained complete control the previous summer when they persuaded the small shareholders that it was important to create a simpler, executive shareholding to enable the club to be run more efficiently. It was that shareholding that was now up for grabs.

The era of a self-made millionaire taking over his home-town club and usually losing money in return for local kudos was coming to an end, certainly at the highest level. And it would still be a few more years before Russian oligarchs and middle-east billionaires indulged their fantasy by owning an English club. In the mid-1990s the buzz around football was that there were fortunes to be made. Corporations and the stock market were to be the next big thing. The arrival of subscription TV in the form of Sky Sports meant big money for top clubs - while Leeds United's future was in the balance, a new £743 million deal with Sky and the BBC was announced - and the popularity of Premiership football around the world on the back of TV sales had entrepreneurs sitting up and taking notice.

Supporters weren't happy. It felt as though their clubs were becoming part of corporate conglomerates run by people who had no feeling for the traditions, nor much interest in the performances. Fans could see the advantages of being able to compete for the best players but were wary that the new breed of owner had an eye more to the bottom line than the glory. The smart young men with city backgrounds acknowledged that success on the pitch was necessary for profit off it, but they were less likely to take a gamble on a new striker or creative midfielder when a struggling manager decided he just needed 'a couple more players to complete the jigsaw'. Football was now an investment. The era of football club as a brand had arrived.

Back in South Africa for the summer, Lucas had some anxious moments. He was aware that he was starting to make his mark in English football, just as the sport was changing beyond all recognition. For players at the top it was to become lucrative beyond their wildest dreams but it also made clubs more ruthless. Top teams would soon be able to afford the best talent from round the world and if you weren't in that few percent, your prospects were much less enticing. He knew that he still had some way to go to convince Howard Wilkinson that he could make it in the top flight and had some concerns that the manager's summer signings might see him move even further down the pecking order. His career was at a crossroads and the correct path wasn't at all clear.

It was against this background that Leeds United came to be taken over. As long rumoured, Richard Thompson was involved following his resignation from the board of relegated QPR. Thompson didn't bid for United as an individual but as a member of the Caspian Group, a media company in which he held a minority stake along with Chris Akers, described as a corporate financier. The company was thus far famous for having the rights on children's TV cartoon favourites The Wombles and Paddington Bear, but saw Leeds United as the first step towards creating a massive, stock market-quoted sport and leisure company.

Their bid, which would pay each of the three current shareholders £5.5 million, take on the £10 million debt and make another £12 million available to buy players, was supported by Silver and Fotherby. Gilman, on the other hand, supported a bid by a rival group from Yorkshire. Their offer was said to be worth more money but Silver and Fotherby stuck with the London offer, which was finally announced as successful on 3 July.

While the wrangling over ownership was going on, Chippa Masinga's appeal against his work permit not being renewed had failed and he began contract talks with Grasshoppers of Zurich. Wilkinson made his first signing, picking up legendary Liverpool and Wales striker Ian Rush on a free transfer in the hope that some of the old magic could be rekindled on the pitch, while a future coach and maybe manager developed behind the scenes. To underline that the end of the season hadn't removed the discontent, Gary Speed let it be known that he wanted to leave and, soon after, crossed the Pennines to join Everton, the side he had supported as a boy.

Meanwhile there was the distraction of Euro 96 with Elland Road the venue for three matches hosted by Spain. Leeds United fans may have been disappointed when England went out on penalties to Germany in the semi-final but at least they could console themselves that with new owners in place, at last there would be enough cash to ensure United had a team to be proud of this season. They should have known better. It all started brightly enough. Within hours of the takeover going through Wilkinson announced he'd signed a highly-rated teenage midfielder from Charlton Athletic, Lee Bowyer, snapped up for

£2.5 million. And Lucas arrived back for pre-season training, knowing that he had more competition for a central defensive slot because Richard Jobson had declared himself fit.

Leeds looked to be on the up at last. Akers, rather than Thompson, was turning out to be the main player at Caspian and he and his fellow directors had big ambitions for the club. Top of the list was a successful football team, able to compete with Manchester United and Liverpool. There were plans to buy back the Elland Road ground from Leeds council and there would also be a new arena with a multi-screen cinema, concert hall and home to ice hockey and basketball franchises. This was to be Britain's Madison Square Gardens. It was heady stuff.

Cannily, the new board left Bill Fotherby in place as chairman. The fans had something of a love-hate relationship with Fotherby - his extravagant 'leaks' that big signings were around the corner just as season tickets were going on sale, only for them to come to nothing once the tickets had been sold, were legendary. But his presence helped give a sense of continuity. In reality, though, this was a revolution and very much of its time. It was less than a year before Tony Blair, backed by spin doctors Peter Mandelson and Alistair Campbell, swept into 10 Downing Street on a landslide of optimism for New Labour. It was at the start of a new era for the city of Leeds, transformed from a dying industrial base to a vibrant regional centre growing wealthy on services, especially in the financial sector. Over the next few years, Leeds was to become a trendy, 'ab fab' city of nightspots, cafes, top-priced restaurants and a shopping Mecca that flourished with the arrival of stores like Harvey Nicholls and designers like Vivienne Westwood. Caspian were of their time. They were to football what New Labour were to politics - sharp suited, confident, ambitious and just a little liable to promise more than they could deliver.

Ironically, they initially found their ambitions thwarted by an old-fashioned football director, Peter Gilman, and while it was only a hiccup on the inexorable corporate advance, it proved costly to the team and deadly to Wilkinson. Gilman's High Court challenge to the takeover was unsuccessful but while it was in progress, all transfer activity was blocked and several key targets joined other clubs. Just as bad, the uncertainty was causing problems in the United camp. Brolin had failed to turn up for pre-season training and McAllister was lured to join Gordon Strachan, now manger at Coventry, for £3 million. The last member of the midfield, so influential in the 1992 Championship triumph had departed. *YEP* columnist Mike Casey wrote a scathing piece under the heading 'Trouble at Disunited,' claiming that McAllister's move 'does more than punch a great hole in the team. It sends out the message that Leeds United, less than a month away from the new season, are in a sorry state…While their rivals have their plans well in place, United are in a state of flux…If anything the team is weaker than the one that finished last season.'

When Wilkinson was finally able to move into the transfer market, he quickly bought goalkeeper Nigel Martyn from Crystal Palace for £2 million and it is somewhat ironic to note that in Martyn and Bowyer, he had probably made two of his best buys since signing the likes of McAllister and Strachan. But he had missed some important players, and even though he also paid a club record £4.5 million for former Manchester United wonderkid Lee Sharpe, there were still big holes in the squad. Wilkinson needed time to fill them but time was something he didn't have.

Lucas couldn't help contrast the turmoil at Elland Road with the atmosphere back home where Bafana Bafana were still enjoying the heady feeling of being champions of Africa and continuing to raise fans' expectations that this was a team for the future. The first game since the historic final had been played in April. It saw the world champions Brazil arrive at Soccer City for a friendly to mark the second anniversary of President Mandela's inauguration and such was the desire to witness the champions of two continents go head to head, kick-off was delayed for 20 minutes while everyone was accommodated. South Africa made a dream start, Doctor Khumalo putting them 2-0 up in the first half, but Brazil hit back after the break through Falvio and Rivaldo curled a superb shot into the top corner for the equaliser. It looked as though Bafana would be rewarded with the draw their play deserved but six minutes from time Bebeto hung in the air and produced a brilliant scissor kick to fire home Za Maria's right-wing cross. But 'the Boys' had performed well and since then Lucas had featured in two World Cup qualifying games, home and away against Malawi, helping his side keep two clean sheets as they picked up victories that brought the dream of being involved in France '98 a little closer.

The internationals left only a short time to spend with family and friends at home before heading back for the hard slog of pre-season training. Lucas got a fair amount of game time as Leeds played pre-season matches in Germany, Dublin and back in England, and he was in central defence with Richard Jobson for the opening league match at Derby's Baseball Ground. Things went well initially - Jacob Laursen turned the ball into his own net after 18 minutes and teenager Ian Harte came off the bench and lashed in his first goal for the club midway through the second half. But Derby hit back with two goals in as many minutes. With minutes to go Lee Bowyer marked his debut with a goal that looked to have clinched the points for Leeds but a slip by Lucas allowed

Sturridge to grab his second and earn his team a draw. It was great entertainment for the crowd but Lucas felt wretched that his error had denied Leeds a winning start.

The mistake seemed to affect his performance in the second game, a 2-0 home defeat by Sheffield Wednesday in which he was described as lacking confidence by the *YEP*. The home fans showed their discontent by booing the players off at half-time, and Lucas's match finished early when he had to leave the field after a clash of heads with Andy Booth opened up a gash that needed four stitches. The next two games saw him make cameo appearances as a substitute and in between he found himself back in the reserves and back in midfield. Although he was praised for his performance, things still looked bleak for him. The coaching staff didn't seem to rate him – there were rumours they were desperate to sign Spanish international defender Miguel Angel Nadal - and he again started to think his career might pick up if he moved away from Elland Road, maybe to another English club or by following Chippa to Europe.

Even though they were sixth in the table, Leeds was a club in crisis. Rush had not scored in a competitive match since signing and in some desperation Wilkinson had brought in another veteran, Mark Hateley, on loan. Everyone had a theory about what was wrong, including a former student of heraldry, John Cook, who suggested it was because the club badge had the white rose of Yorkshire upside down. 'The way Leeds has the badge is more in keeping with them on the other side of the Pennines,' he said. So disillusioned were the fans that less than a week before the match against Manchester United – always the biggest game of the season at Elland Road – 2,000 tickets remained unsold.

In the end the game was its usual sell-out but Leeds fans must have wished they had saved their money. It was an afternoon to forget from the third minute, when Harte's goal-line clearance hit Martyn and rebounded into the net. Not even the sight of former Leeds stirker Eric Cantona blasting wide a penalty could cheer the home supporters as they watched their team torn apart by the slick Reds. Lucas came on as part of a three-man substitution with Hateley and Andy Gray in the 56th minute but there was no stemming the tide. Goals from Nicky Butt, Karel Poborsky and Cantona, completed the rout and the team were booed off the pitch.

Monday morning's *YEP* carried a banner headline: 'WILKO SACKED!' It is a measure of the man that he attended the press conference that announced his dismissal. Clearly shaken yet with the utmost dignity and no trace of malice, Wilkinson said: 'I am very disappointed, very sad and obviously very shocked.' He was left to return to his home in Sheffield and wonder what might have happened if the court case hadn't blocked his signings and if he'd been given more time to develop the young talent he knew was coming through the academy. Meanwhile, in the unsentimental world of football, everyone else's attention was turning to who would take over in the manager's office. It was to turn out to be a turning point in Lucas's career.

Chapter 13

George's long lost love child

The day after they sacked Howard Wilkinson, Leeds United announced that George Graham was their new manager. The speed of the appointment immediately sparked a conspiracy theory that the former Arsenal boss had been paid £100,000 to turn down other jobs until Caspian's directors found a way to get rid of Wilkinson. After all, people like Gary Blumberg had heard rumours as far back as the previous April that a job was waiting for Graham at Elland Road as soon as he completed the ban imposed on him for taking money as part of a transfer deal. It was common knowledge that Graham was a neighbour of major Caspian shareholder Richard Thompson and was it coincidence that he had recently turned down the chance to manage Manchester City? Graham and Caspian fiercely denied any payment.

Superficially the two men were very different. Wilkinson himself recognised he had something of the schoolteacher about him and could come across as dour. Anticipating the age of celebrity by a few years, he once reflected on the media's preference for the views of some of the more colourful but less learned managers by saying:'Next time I'm coming back as a personality.' Graham was more urbane and relaxed but in many ways the two men had much in common, especially in a shared view that the only place success comes before work is in the dictionary

Born in Bargeddie, a small mining and industrial village not far from Glasgow, Graham was the youngest of seven children, raised by his mother after his father died of TB when George was only a month old. It was a tough childhood, marked by the sectarian conflict that remains a feature of Scotland's second city.

But the youngster showed early talent as a footballer and was snapped up by Aston Villa when he was just 17. Later 'Gorgeous George' became part of Chelsea's 'Swinging Sixties' team along with people like Terry Venables, Bobby Tambling, John Hollins and a young Peter Osgood, but the turning point in Graham's career came when Arsenal manager Bertie Mee paid £75,000 to take him to Highbury. After a couple of seasons in which the Scot was leading scorer, Mee switched him from striker to midfield and even though he lacked a yard of pace – his nickname was 'Stroller' – Graham more than made up for it with his skill and intelligent reading of the game. Not only did he enjoy enormous success, including being part of Arsenal's double winning side of 1970-71, he was also introduced to the Arsenal ethos, far removed from the glamour-boy image of Stamford Bridge. Mee was a motivator who saw discipline and hard work – 'stopping mediocrity being perpetuated' - as the secret to winning. It was drummed into everyone at the club that Arsenal was no run-of-the-mill outfit. It was a club with tradition and status, part of football's aristocracy. When you entered Highbury Stadium, you walked through marbled halls. In stark contrast to Chelsea, no one from Arsenal was allowed to be late, no one broke curfew, no one even appeared in public less than immaculately dressed and groomed. While Graham remained an amusing and popular social companion away from the game, professionally he was a changed man. He had found a philosophy that was to guide the rest of his career.

Graham carried this work ethic and discipline into management when he entered the notorious Den at Millwall. He inherited a team at the bottom of the old Third Division, saved them from relegation, turned the place round and led them to promotion. It seemed only natural that Arsenal turned to him when they changed their manager in 1986. The directors were desperate. Standards had dropped and so had results - it was almost ten years since they had won a trophy. Graham had a clear-out and rebuilt, reintroducing the Highbury ethos. Success followed, starting with the League Cup in 1987. That was the beginning of a magnificent eight-year period in Arsenal's history which included two Championships, a second League Cup win in the same season as they took the FA Cup, and the European Cup Winners' Cup.

It may seem strange that such a stellar career, built on discipline and strict values, should falter in the grubbiness of a scandal over an illegal payment by an agent. But any judgement should be tempered by consideration of football's culture at the time. It was an open secret that such payments were a regular occurrence. It may have been against the rules but it was accepted that it was just part of the business. Graham was the only manager picked out for punishment by the football authorities, who have singularly failed to uncover a single other wrongdoer. He served a sentence for several of his colleagues and he did so with dignity when many in his situation would have sold a lurid story to voracious Sunday newspapers.

Something else often overlooked when Graham's career is discussed is that he was responsible for signing creative and exciting players like Ian Wright and Anders Limpar and giving David Rocastle and Paul Merson a chance to shine. However, it is true that, especially in his later years at Highbury, he built his side around the talents of a back four that is possibly the best defensive unit seen in league football. Lee Dixon, Tony Adams, Steve Bould and Nigel Winterburn were as well-drilled as any crack military unit. But their success was established on more than just the ability to step forward, put an arm in the air and catch the opposition offside. They each understood defending, took pride in it, and saw a goal conceded as an affront to their professionalism and dignity.

Graham's arrival at Elland Road lifted the fans, especially when he promised to bring back the glory days. He relished being back in the spotlight and was determined to do things his way. The players were given notice that life was going to change: 'I've got to stamp my way of working on to my staff and players and if I get it right we can join the giants of football. Sometimes people get a bit stale and you need new blood,' he said.

Lucas only knew of the Scot by reputation but he was delighted with what he heard at the first team meeting, held the day the new 'gaffer' took charge. Graham made it clear that everyone started with a clean slate and would be given a fair chance to show what they could do. Their success or failure depended on what they did for Graham, not what had gone before. Lucas remembered: 'That was just what I needed to hear. I wanted a fresh start, an opportunity to prove myself.'

The new manager added that, just as at Arsenal, he was going to build from the back and true to his word, when they went out on the training pitch for the first time, the whole session concentrated on defence. Lucas felt renewed optimism. He was determined to work as hard as he could to win over the new manager with his ability. His fellow central defender David Wetherall recalled that the South African made a good start: 'George Graham's first session was one-to-one marking. Lucas didn't give the strikers a kick of the ball.'

It was too much to expect instant change in his fortunes and Lucas didn't play any part in Graham's first four matches in charge. But he was encouraged by the way the new manager spoke to him and also from the attention he received from David O'Leary, who had taken over as assistant manager from Mick Hennigan. Lucas had known O'Leary briefly during the Irishman's injury-wrecked spell as a United player and realised the former Arsenal centre-half had a lot he could teach him. He also knew that O'Leary was convinced Lucas was ready and urging Graham to give him a chance in the team.

That finally arrived when he came off the bench against Leicester, only to find himself straight back in the reserves, but on 12 October, and with Carlton Palmer suspended, the new manager gave him his first start, part of a back three with Wetherall and Richard Jobson, against Nottingham Forest. They kept a clean sheet and United won the match 2-0.

Lucas was aware that almost a quarter of the season had passed and so far he hadn't played in the 75 per cent of matches he would need by the end of the campaign to get his work permit renewed. But he did well in the Forest game and it marked the start of his first long run of matches – 14 before missing out because of international duty - since he joined the club. He was enjoying his football again and each training session saw him grow more confident as he polished his defensive skills under the tutelage of Graham and O'Leary.

There were a few hiccups along the way. He was struck down with gastro-enteritis in the middle of a match against Aston Villa and had to race for the sanctuary of the dressing room toilet to avoid major embarrassment, a story he told against himself amid gales of laughter in later years. And he was guilty of a mistake for one of the goals when Graham's first return to Highbury saw his new charges crushed 3-0 by his former team. But on the whole Lucas was starting to blossom under Graham. He was instrumental in keeping a clean sheet at home to Sunderland and even had a hand in one of Leeds' three goals; and he impressed in a 2-0 defeat by Liverpool after Graham switched him to do a marking job on England winger Steve McManaman in the second half. 'Lucas was my man of the match,' Graham said afterwards. 'He was outstanding on McManaman, who had caused us problems in the first half.'

Graham was increasingly impressed by the South African and started to use him regularly in a man-marking role to snuff out the opposition's key player. He shut out Matthew Le Tissier in a 2-0 win at Southampton and the ploy worked again as Leeds beat Chelsea 2-0 with Lucas denying Gianfranco Zola any space – 'Zola is one of my favourite players,' Graham said, 'but Lucas showed he was equal to the task. He has been outstanding in our last three games.'

Lucas was overjoyed. Even when Graham let it be known he was looking to strengthen his defence with new signings, there were no more thoughts of going home, only of making his mark in the English game. 'It was going quite badly for me earlier in the season when Howard Wilkinson was here and when the new manager came I was not in the side straight away,' Lucas admitted to the *YEP*. 'But suddenly everything has opened up in front of my eyes. I have got a new lease of life and I intend to make the most of it.'

Following the loss against Liverpool, Leeds went five matches undefeated without conceding a goal, only for the run to grind to a halt with three defeats in a row over the Christmas holidays. Leeds fans soon started to get restless about the defensive football served up by their team. One survey claimed they were the most disillusioned in the country. While Lucas may have been relishing the new regime and growing in confidence and stature with each game, there were still major problems in the camp. Graham was unhappy that some of his most highly paid, senior players - Ian Rush, Carlton Palmer, Tony Dorigo, Tony Yeboah and Tomas Brolin became known as 'the famous five' - were not contributing as he thought they should. Several players who thought a mid-week 'groin strain' could mean skipping training discovered that under the new regime, that meant also coming back to the treatment room in the afternoon and being released just in time to get caught up in the rush hour traffic.

Graham wanted to begin rebuilding the squad. He signed Norwegian Gunnar Halle from Oldham and with a budget of only £5 million at their disposal, he and his new chief scout, Ian McNeil, started to scour the continent for inexpensive recruits. One of their first signings was a central defender, a threat to Lucas's place in the side. Burly Dutchman Robert Molenaar arrived from FC Volendam determined to win a regular spot in the starting line-up and got his chance early in January while Lucas was playing for Bafana Bafana in a goalless World Cup qualifier in Zambia. Molenaar was voted the man of the match on his debut and the fans were so impressed by the ferocity of his tackling that, much to the player's embarrassment, they instantly nicknamed him 'The Terminator.'

The Dutchman wasn't eligible for the FA Cup tie at Crystal Palace so, as so often in his career, Lucas was straight on a plane after the Zambia match, and arrived back in London to join up with his team-mates. There was no time to feel exhausted. He needed all his wits about him to contain lively Palace striker Bruce Dyer as the south London side took the game to Leeds. The match was locked at 2-2 with a few minutes to go when referee Roger Dilkes ruled that Lucas had tripped Dyer in the penalty area. The whole United team thought it was a dive but their protests were waved away and Dyer stepped up to take the kick. But Nigel Martyn, making his first return to Selhurst Park since his move north, pulled off a brilliant save and clinched a replay, which Leeds won 1-0.

The arrival of Molenaar allowed Graham to field a three-man defensive unit that included David Wetherall and Lucas, but the South African was back on man-to-man duty in a goalless draw against Arsenal, marking the mercurial Paul Merson out of the game. However, flu meant he missed the trip to Highbury three days later when Graham rejoiced in a 1-0 FA Cup win over his former club.

Any dreams of FA Cup glory were dashed in the next round when they were knocked out by lowly Portsmouth, managed by Graham's old friend Terry Venables. That was followed by a 4-0 defeat by Liverpool and angry fans, who couldn't understand why Yeboah wasn't back in a side that was struggling to score goals, turned on the new manager. As Liverpool's third goal went in, they chanted 'Yeboah on, Georgie out;' and they sang 'Are you Wilko in disguise?' as the fourth hit the net.

Graham understood the fans' frustration over Yeboah but he wasn't convinced the Ghanaian was working hard enough in training to get fit and he had been angered that the striker had played in a World Cup qualifier and picked up another knock. Their simmering differences came to a head in March when Yeboah objected to being substituted at Tottenham. Ripping off his shirt as he left the pitch, he threw it in Graham's direction. His later apologies fell on deaf ears in the manager's office and among the fans. His days at Elland Road were numbered.

Yeboah wasn't the only problem. Graham needed a clear-out but that couldn't be done overnight. It was a matter of getting through the season and then making changes but it was an uncomfortable time for everyone at the club and there were few good headlines. When Leeds played a goalless draw against Aston Villa at the end of April – their 24th clean sheet of the season - the *YEP* fitted supporter Jeremy Bridge-Butler with a heart monitor and proclaimed that it had shown he was more excited by the prospect of eating a meat pie than by any of the action on the pitch.

New Labour stormed to power with a landslide victory in the May Day, 'sleaze-busting' election to the strains of the D:Ream anthem 'Things Can Only Get Better' and even Tory supporters among the Leeds fans hoped that was true. With only one goal scored by Leeds in their last five games, the supporters showed that while they may be weary they hadn't lost their sense of humour by changing the first line of Vera Lynn's classic war-time hit song to 'We'll score again, don't know where, don't know when.'

The season ground to a halt with a 1-1 draw at home to Middlesbrough, a match that saw the Teesside club relegated. United were 11th in the table, having conceded a meagre 38 goals, nine of which had been scored before Graham arrived. It was fewer than all but three of the sides above them, including champions Manchester United. But Leeds had only scored 28, the lowest in the league and the smallest total ever by a side who were not relegated.

United fans traipsed off towards their summer in somewhat melancholy mood, but behind the scenes there were some good things happening. Ian McNeil had spotted a striker playing in Portugal called Jimmy Floyd Hasselbaink, who he reckoned would be a more than adequate replacement for Tony Yeboah, and under the guidance of Eddie Gray and Paul Hart, Leeds youth side had romped away with the Northern Intermediate League and also won the FA Youth Cup with a team that included Paul Robinson, Alan Maybury, Harry Kewell, Jonathan Woodgate, Stephen McPhail and Matthew Jones, all of whom were to go on to become full internationals.

Despite the turmoil at the club, Lucas had never felt more settled. He had cemented his place in the team, playing in 35 of the club's 46 league and cup games, and to his delight, in February Graham had prevailed on the directors to give him a new, improved three-year contract.

A bond of mutual respect had quickly grown between the two men, so much so that the rest of the squad joked that Lucas must be George's long-lost love child. Lucas smiled at the memory and said: 'From the first day I knew I would get on well with George. He treated me with respect and the same as any other player. There were no references to the fact that I was a low-cost buy from South Africa as there had been with Mick Hennigan. If I got something wrong, he explained it and helped me get better.'

For the manager, Lucas was an ideal person to coach. Perhaps, as South African writer Graeme Friedman suggests in *Madiba's Boys*, the pair's shared experience of growing up in a large family with not much money and in a place where prejudice was an everyday experience, played a part in their friendship. Certainly Graham looks back on their time working together with true affection: 'Lucas had a nice personality and was a joy to work with,' he said. 'He had a great attitude and he loved training. Coaching is teaching, imparting knowledge, and as any teacher will tell you there are some pupils who are good at absorbing information and some who are not. Lucas was one of the best. He listened carefully to everything he was told, took it in and tried to incorporate it into his game. He was a quick learner.'

Graham rates Lucas on a par with Tony Adams and great modern defenders like John Terry, Nemanja Vidic and Ricardo Carvalho. He explained: 'People go on about ball-playing centre halves who can come out of the back four with the ball, but their first job is to defend. That's what I liked about Adams, Bould and Keown at Arsenal – their first priority was to prevent goals being scored. Great defending is an art. It's not just a matter of going out and kicking someone up in the air. There's an art in knowing when to challenge and when not to challenge, when to go to ground and when to stay on your feet. Lucas loved the art of defending. He gave centre-forwards nothing. He was up there with the best.'

To have someone believe in him to that extent meant everything to Lucas and he soaked up every bit of knowledge offered to him, determined to push on and become even better. And he had received another boost. Out of the blue, he heard the shock news that he had been chosen to replace Neil Tovey as captain of South

Africa and was about to lead his country into one of their biggest games yet, against England at Old Trafford. But first he had to sort out a few problems that were troubling the Bafana squad.

Chapter 14

Bonjour Bafana

Lucas could hardly believe the changes that had come over his life. It was as though he was being showered with rewards for coming through all the anxieties of the past few years. And it was not just professionally that everything was coming right. In January, Tumi had given birth to a little girl, 'a Yorkshire lass' they named Jessica Lesedi. 'I was very nervous at first, afraid that I would drop her,' the proud new dad admitted. 'And I couldn't stand her crying but now it's no problem.' Lucas experienced the awe and protective instincts so familiar to fathers of daughters, emotions so profound they were difficult for him to articulate beyond the almost inadequate 'love'. But the word that sprang to his mind when Clive Barker phoned to offer him the South Africa captaincy as they stepped up their World Cup qualification campaign was one that he'd picked up in Yorkshire – 'gobsmacked.'

He was deeply honoured and proud but also a little concerned. He was following in the footsteps of Steve Komphela and Neil Tovey, big characters and natural leaders while he was much quieter, less assertive. Lucas knew he was popular with his team-mates and that they respected him as a player but would that be enough? Barker had no such reservations. He said: 'Radebe leads from the front. He is likely to captain South Africa for many years and he is the right man to lead the country to France.' But still Lucas knew the armband carried a much more onerous burden than just leading out the team and tossing a coin.

The days of innocence in the Bafana Bafana camp were over. While the team had exceeded expectations, it was generally regarded that SAFA, football's governing body in South Africa, hadn't kept pace. They were mocked in the press when they virtually closed their offices for the annual holiday and so failed to see a letter from FIFA saying that Mark Fish was suspended for the Zambia match after picking up two yellow cards. Even more damning was the fact that they seemed to have no method of keeping track of something as basic as players' bookings. It was as though they were still in the amateur days before being re-instated to international football. Fish, who was playing for Lazio at the time, flew home only to be told by embarrassed officials that he should return to Rome.

Lucas knew some of the squad, especially the home-based players for whom international fees were an important supplement to low wages, had been muttering that the bonuses for winning the African Cup of Nations had not been fairly divided and it seemed to almost all the players that while their skills drew the crowds and created the cash that poured into the Association's coffers, they were still being woefully under paid. Before the next World Cup qualifier in Congo, they were astonished to read in the newspapers about what seemed to them inadequate bonuses for qualifying for the finals in France. More importantly, there had been no negotiation, so before setting off to Pointe Noire to face the 'Red Devils', the players and technical staff were locked in a long meeting with SAFA chief executive Danny Jordaan, thrashing out a better deal, which would give each player R60,000 for qualifying.

Pointe Noire was not a place the players looked forward to. They knew from their previous visit four years before that they were in for an uncomfortable time and so it proved. Congo, who currently led the group, were a tough, physical opponent and in good form so Bafana Bafana would need to be at their best but preparations were far from ideal. Their first hotel was so inadequate, they quickly moved to another where the lack of rooms meant some of the accompanying journalists camped in the lobby. The training pitch was bumpy and below the standards most village teams would play on but when they tried to switch practice to the match stadium, Congolese soldiers armed with AK-47s persuaded them it wasn't a good idea. Almost inevitably, South Africa lost a bruising encounter 2-0.

The dreamed of trip to France '98 was starting to fade and by the end of the month, when Bafana played Zaire, Barker had made three changes to his starting line-up, including dropping Tovey from the team and giving Lucas the armband. Because of the civil unrest in Zaire, the match was played in Togo and it couldn't have been a starker contrast from Pointe Noire. Their luxury hotel overlooked the stadium and SAFA had flown in a chef to make sure the food was just right. The game coincided with both South Africa's Freedom Day and Independence Day in Togo – perfect for a party. Lucas started his captaincy with a vital, if unimpressive, 2-1 victory but Barker's changes couldn't have worked better with two recalled players, Masinga and Khumalo, on the score sheet. Chippa's winning effort took him to 11 for his country, equalling the record of Donald Wilson set in 1947.

The only thing that threatened to undermine the squad's progress was the continuing discontent about money and it came to a head when they assembled in Manchester towards the end of May to prepare for a clash with England. The resentment that was already simmering boiled over when the players saw how many officials were on the trip. They dubbed it the 'soccer gravy plane' and

'Lucas loved the art of defending. He gave centre-forwards nothing. He was up there with the best.' – George Graham. (© Press Association)

Growing up in Diepkloof 4.
The characteristic smile was there even as a baby. (centre).
Lucas on the ground with elder sister Elizabeth and brother Abednego. (top left).

By the age of six, Lucas was used to helping look after his dad's cars. (top right)
13 year old Lucas striding out. (below left)
Mr Cool, 17 year old Lucas with a friend. (below right)

Lucas with his parents Emily and Johannes.

Diepkloof Wolf Wanderers – Lucas is in the goalkeeping kit in the back row.

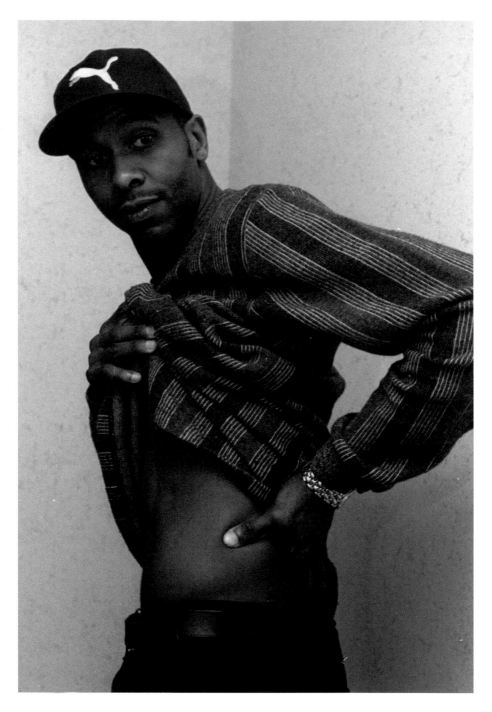

Another inch… Lucas shows the scar where the bullet entered his back while driving through Diepkloof. (© Andrew Varley)

It wasn't long before the tall skinny kid started to impress in the Kaizer Chiefs' defence. (© Sunday Times)

Bravely diving among the flying boots, Lucas heads a goal against Pretoria City to help Amakhosi on the way to the championship. (© Sunday Times)

(left) Lucas and Philemon Masinga give Howard Wilkinson a lift soon after arriving at Elland Road (right) Have you heard the one about the English summer? Lucas shares a joke with Tony Yeboah, team-mates in England, opponents in Africa. (both © Yorkshire Post)

Confident keeping – Lucas makes a save against Middlesbrough, one of two occasions he went in goal for Leeds. (© Yorkshire Post)

Top class defender – Lucas gets above Derby's Deon Burton (top) and snakes out a long leg to deny Dwight Yorke (below). (both © Yorkshire Post)

All those childhood overhead kicks pay off as Lucas challenges
Newcastle United's Laurent Robert. (© Yorkshire Post)

(top) Lucas dispossesses Tunisia's Adel Sellimi as South Africa triumph in the 1996 African Cup of Nations final. (© Press Association)

(below) Proud Lucas leads Bafana Bafana in their first World Cup campaign in France 1998. (L-R standing) Doctor Khumalo, Mark Fish, Philemon Masinga, Andre Arendse, Sizwe Motaung, Neil Tovey. (L-R front) Mark Williams, John Moshoeu, Lucas, Innocent Buthelezi, Eric Tinkler. (© Press Association)

Always smiling – in training with Tony Yeboah and David Wetherall. (© Yorkshire Post)

Chairman Peter Ridsdale, captain Lucas and manager David O'Leary share a joke in the optimistic days when everything seemed possible. (© Yorkshire Post)

Lucas and Lucas Hugo try their hand as shepherds at Lineham Farm, a charity Lucas supported near Leeds. (© Yorkshire Post)

Working for the community

(Top left) Lucas launches the Leeds United Book Challenge with Ceit Brown from Robin Hood Primary School. (© Yorkshire Post)

(top right) Education Leeds presented Lucas with an award to acknowledge his work in challenging racism and his contribution to schools in Leeds. (© Yorkshire Post)

(Below) Lucas was always happy when he was making children smile. (© Yorkshire Post)

Lucas used much of his time at home in South Africa encouraging young people. Here he is with FIFA president Sepp Blatter on a visit to an SOS Children's Village in Cape Town. (© Press Association)

(top) Ready for the cold of Moscow. (© Yorkshire Post)

(below) Lucas had to get over his fear of flying many times to answer the call of club and country. (© Yorkshire Post)

(top) Protected by riot police shields, Lucas leads out his team-mates for the ill-fated UEFA Cup semi-final against Galatasaray. (© Yorkshire Post)

(below) Feziwe brushes away a tear as she, Lucas and Lucas Hugo visit the flowers laid at Elland Road in memory of the two Leeds fans murdered in Istanbul. (© Yorkshire Post)

Lucas and inspirational cancer fund-raiser Jane Tomlinson switch on the Rothwell Christmas lights. (© Yorkshire Post)

decided enough was enough. These negotiations were usually handled by a small committee, as they had been before the Congo game, but this time, almost as though they were testing his credentials as captain, the players left Lucas to go into the meetings alone. In many ways he was in a no-win situation; if he satisfied SAFA he would lose credibility with his team-mates, but if he went too far the other way, SAFA might re-think his position as captain. There was no personal gain for Lucas. He was one of the fortunate overseas players to whom international payment was a bonus. It was the South African-based players who needed it to bolster their wages. In the end he decided to follow his instincts and agreed with his team-mates that it was time to stop paying players 'peanuts' while officials enjoyed lavish perks. Each player was being paid R5,000 plus R200 a day expenses to play against England. Given the money SAFA would get from the match, that was far too low.

The negotiations were long and hard. Danny Jordaan and Irvin Khoza accused the players of being greedy mercenaries and argued that their match fee was far less important than the opportunity to impress all the scouts from clubs in England and across Europe who would be at Old Trafford looking for new talent. Knowing that most of the home-based players were hoping to follow the likes of Mark Fish and Lucas to the more lucrative European leagues, they threatened to cancel all future friendly internationals thus depriving them of opportunities to show their skills. At one stage during the seven-hour wrangle on the day before the match, the SAFA chief decided to play hard ball and declared that the R5,000 was all there was, take it or leave it. He, like others before and since, underestimated the tungsten core behind Lucas's smile and affability. The new captain refused to be bullied. He knew the strength of feeling in the camp and informed the Association that if that were the case, they would leave it. The players would pack their bags and refuse to play. He convinced SAFA this was not an idle threat and the Association finally gave in and agreed that the match fee would be split among the players, giving each man R20,000.

Lucas's brinkmanship was pulled off in the knowledge of the deep significance of the match and the repercussions if a strike had been called. As well as the very real desire of players to showcase their talent in a big spotlight, many other people had their own reasons for focusing on this game in a way they wouldn't any other friendly international. While Bafana Bafana looked to Brazil for their football inspiration, and most of their great rivalries were with other African sides, a fixture against England was of deep symbolic significance. It was the home of football, the place whose countrymen had brought the game to South Africa. It was the newly emerged Rainbow Nation against the old colonial oppressor, and many white South Africans who showed no interest in the domestic game, followed soccer in England. They too would watch this match, some not sure which side to support. 'It is hard to overstate just how big this match was at that stage of Bafana Bafana's development,' Gary Blumberg said.

A protracted, head-to-head confrontation with the country's ruling body was not the ideal preparation for an international match. As well as being team spokesman in the negotiations, Lucas found himself in great demand from the press both as captain and the most recognisable face to English journalists. In truth, they saw the match mainly in terms of the preparation it provided for the World Cup qualifier Glenn Hoddle's men faced the following week in Poland. Lucas understood that but was determined to add another perspective. Full of praise for English football and the players, he nevertheless reminded the media of the progress African football had made in recent years. He also pointed out that Bafana Bafana too were preparing for a World Cup qualifier, one that could be argued was even more significant than England's. 'If we qualify for the finals in France it really would give the people back home something to celebrate,' he said. 'Football is one of the things that has helped black people in my country. It is known as a black sport, but its popularity is growing all the time. These days there is as much interest in soccer in the press as there is in rugby and that never used to be the case.'

He also advised the journalists not to be too confident that England only had to turn up to win. Don't underestimate 'Madiba Magic' and the talent of the players, he warned. 'Every game we play we want to win for Mr Mandela. And when you look at the players in our squad and the ability we have, we can make England sweat. They don't know our style of football. We won't be nervous, this is an opportunity for us to shine and show what we can do.' And sounding very much like 'the son of George', Lucas added: 'We've got skilful players. If we can mix that with a bit of hard work and commitment, I don't see anyone stopping us in the future.'

There were 52,676 people in Old Trafford for the match, among them a healthy following of exiled South Africans, many draped in the new national flag. South African journalist Peter Davies was there and in his book *Chasing the Game* he pointed out: 'It was surely the first time that white South Africans had outnumbered black ones at a game involving Bafana Bafana.' While God Save the Queen was, as usual, sung without much passion, N'kosi Sikelel' iAfrika was sung mightily as was 'Shosholoza' although Davies noticed, 'whiteys showed no particular mastery of the lyrics.'

The match wasn't a classic. Hoddle rested several of his first-choice players and the new unit took a while to find any cohesion. For South Africa, the slippery conditions underfoot were not conducive to their normal style of play. England took the lead when Phil Neville set up Rob Lee to fire past Andre Arendse but just before half-time, Nigel Martyn made a rare mistake and John Moshoeu acrobatically lifted the ball back into the area with a bicycle kick for Phil Masinga to head the equaliser. It looked as though the match would end in an honourable draw, but as against Brazil, Bafana were denied their share of the glory when Ian Wright scored the winner with help from his hand, an infringement seen by everyone apart from the referee.

The major talking point of the match came in the final minutes when Linda Innocent Buthulezi put in a crunching tackle on Paul Gascoigne that saw the slimmed-down midfielder stretchered off with what looked to be a bad injury. The English press, who before the match had been amused by the fact that a footballer was named Linda, now turned on him for the tackle, even though the injury turned out to be far less serious than it had appeared. Buthulezi was unimpressed and insisted 'I am an aggressive player, a hard player, but not a dirty player' and without a trace of irony he added: 'My message to Paul Gascoigne is that he can become a great player if he changes his attitude.' Clive Barker was generous in his praise of England but wistfully added: 'we'd like to get them on a hot afternoon in Soweto.'

The next World Cup qualifier was only two weeks away, but four days before they lined up against Zambia, South Africa faced the annual Nelson Mandela inauguration challenge against the Netherlands and Barker made several changes. Lucas was struggling with a recurring back injury but Barker was keen to team him up again with Tovey to provide some much-needed experience. Between them the pair had 75 caps, more than the rest of the starting line-up put together. As might be expected, the Dutch rang rings round Bafana, easing to a 2-0 win that could easily have been far greater.

Although logic told them it was a result to be expected from such an inexperienced team, the home fans and the media were jumpy. Xollie Mtshazo spelt it out in the *Sowetan*: 'Never before has Barker been under so much pressure as after South Africa's dismal showing against Holland. His priority should be to avoid a repetition of Wednesday's near massacre.' But once again the coach had got his tactics exactly right. He brought back his seasoned, rested players to face the team known as 'Chipolopolo' or 'the bullet' after their fans' battle cry, and Monday morning's headlines, below a picture of dancing, rejoicing supporters, read: 'BAFABULOUS Barker's Boys blitz Zambia 3-0 as

World Cup dream comes closer.' Now they only needed a draw against Congo in August to make it to the World Cup finals.

Back in Leeds, United made a solid start to the new season, Jimmy Hasselbaink scoring on his debut in a 1-1 draw with Arsenal. But the match against Congo was at the back of Lucas's mind throughout pre-season and straight after the Gunners match, it became his main focus. As he flew back to Johannesburg he felt that familiar mixture of anticipation, tinged with nerves. And on getting home there was no escaping the importance his countrymen attached to the result - it seemed as though no one was talking about anything else.

The hours between getting up on the morning of a game and kick-off are always the most frustrating for players. For a big match, that is multiplied many times. No matter how often you look at your watch, the hands hardly seem to move. No matter how much you try not to think about the game, it is always on your mind. But South Africa had discovered a new secret weapon for overcoming the tension: Nelson Mandela. Two years before, Madiba Magic had worked for the Springboks when the President walked in their nerve-taut dressing room just before the Rugby Union World Cup final. Morné de Plessis recalled: 'Suddenly the players saw him and everybody was laughing, smiling, clapping. The tension just fell away.' Bafana Bafana had experienced something similar during the African Cup of Nations, and now on the morning of arguably the most important game in the country's history, it happened again. Footballers are not renowned as early risers, especially on match day, but on the morning of the Congo clash there was no time to lie around in bed. Lucas and his team-mates didn't even have time for breakfast. At 8am the President's motorcade swept into the hotel forecourt and Mandela stepped out to greet the players. Like almost everyone else who has met Madiba, Lucas has been struck by the statesman's ability to put people at their ease and once again the whole squad relaxed in his presence. Assistant coach Phil Setshedi told the *Sowetan*: 'The President told the players to go out and represent the nation in grand style as they've done in the past. It was motivating, the tension that had earlier prevailed was gone by the time we posed for pictures with him.' The Mandela effect had worked again and the atmosphere on the bus going to the stadium was relaxed as the players sang and joked.

The match was always going to be tight and so it proved, the teams separated by a single goal, almost inevitably scored by Phil Masinga. But it was enough. 'Bonjour Bafana' read the headline the following day as, once again, work was put on hold and the country came together to rejoice with another exuberant party. Congratulations poured in from all sides, including from the President, who said 'the boys have done the country and its people very proud.'

There was also a message from South Africa's first football superstar, Steve 'Kalamazoo' Mokone, who now lived in America. An international at the age of 16, Mokone became the first black South African to play in European football when he signed for Coventry City in 1955. Later he played for Cardiff, Barcelona, Marseille, Torino and Valencia. Mokone told his country's latest heroes: 'It is certainly the proudest moment of my life to see South Africa go to the World Cup finals and if I die now, I will die happy. Oh how I wish was 40 years younger!'

Chapter 15
Club v Country

The city of Leeds continued to boom. The first million pound apartment had recently been sold and the reputation of the burgeoning night-life was attracting affluent, party-seeking visitors from all over the country. It wasn't the complete story, of course. Local Labour Party MP Derek Patchett pointed out that on the way to their lucrative jobs in the city, commuters from out of town 'drive past thousands of people for whom work has become a totally unknown way of life. For those families, the presence of the Harvey Nichols store in Leeds is no more than a reminder of their own exclusion.'

But the directors of Leeds United were concentrating on the affluent sector of the city. They held a special evening for local businessmen where Chris Akers outlined his vision for the club and tried to sign them up for one of the many sponsorship packages on offer, or to persuade them to commit to taking an executive box for match days. His plans reached far beyond a successful football team. The new arena would go ahead the following year, but before that there would be a series of subsidiary companies established to provide services for the fans and general public. They would soon be able to buy books and magazines from Leeds United Publishing, invest their cash through Leeds United Financial Services and book their holidays through Leeds United Travel.

It also emerged that the club had a new chairman. Bill Fotherby, who ironically was the man who introduced corporate hospitality at Elland Road when he disguised Portakabins as luxury executive boxes in the South Stand, was stepping down. The day-to-day running of the club now fell to managing director Jeremy Fenn, one of the original Caspian directors, but he didn't want to be the public face of Leeds United. They needed someone the fans would trust, someone to convince the faithful that their club wasn't being snatched from them by a load of London city slickers. The ideal candidate was already a junior member of the board. Leeds-born Peter Ridsdale had supported United since he was a small boy. On leaving school, he'd started out as a clerical assistant in the personnel department of a car showroom and eventually worked his way up to become managing director of retail at the Top Man chain of stores owned by retail giants Burton. In the 1980s, when clubs were first allowed to carry advertising on their shirts, Ridsdale persuaded Burton to emblazon their logo on the second division outfit's kit, a deal that earned United £50,000 and him a place on the club board. His credentials were perfect. He was comfortable with the financiers, businessmen and people Roy Keane described as 'the prawn cocktail set' who were becoming so important to United's ambitions, while the ordinary fans thought of him as one of their own.

Caspian had their management team in place and were ready to implement their long term plans to see Leeds become one of the biggest clubs in Europe. What they couldn't anticipate was that in Ridsdale they had appointed a man who wasn't prepared to be a mere figurehead. He also wasn't willing to wait for the long term and his fast-track strategy was to provide Leeds United with some of its most exciting years, and also lead to its downfall.

All of this, especially Ridsdale's appointment, was eventually to impact in a big way on Lucas's life but at the time it was only of fleeting interest. He liked the idea of being at an ambitious club who wanted to compete for trophies with the likes of Manchester United, Arsenal, Chelsea and Liverpool and he could see the logic of a strongly based company that created the cash to achieve that. He understood that as captain of South Africa, he had an important role to play in raising United's profile in his country. But of necessity, footballers' perspectives tend to be short term. They know they can influence the here and now but with the transfer market, they can never be sure they will still be around in a year or two. So Lucas was much more concerned with thoughts of South Africa's forthcoming World Cup qualifier against Congo and what George Graham was doing to improve the Leeds squad before the new league campaign.

While the directors talked an expansive and ambitious game, there wasn't a great deal of cash for Graham to spend on players. But he made some astute signings, including striker Jimmy Floyd Hasselbaink, midfielders David Hopkin, Alf Inge Haaland and Bruno Ribeiro, and full-back Dave Robertson. Perhaps even more important were the players who left the club in a wholesale clear-out that saw fees collected for Paul Beesley, Tony Yeboah, Brian Deane and Carlton Palmer. On top of which, Ian Rush moved to Newcastle and Tony Dorigo to Torino on free transfers and Tomas Brolin went out on loan. Graham's famous five top earners had gone and, when the fees for selling fringe players like Mark Ford were included, he'd built a new squad for around £5 million net.

Lucas got to know his new team-mates in a pre-season training camp in Sweden and by the time Leeds played their annual matches in Ireland and back home at Bradford City and Nottingham Forest, it was clear that the dressing-room atmosphere had improved from last season. Hopkin was made captain, which meant Lucas had to get used to an even more pronounced Scottish accent and acquire a new word, 'mingin', a sexist term the red-haired midfielder used whenever he found anything that didn't please him.

Leeds picked up four points from their first two games with two of the new signings, Hasselbaink and Ribeiro on the scoresheet. But three straight defeats followed and Graham sought to lower expectations, pointing out that whereas managers at some clubs could spend huge sums on a single player, like the £15 million Newcastle splashed out for Alan Shearer, he wasn't in a position to bring big names to Leeds. Rebuilding, he claimed, would take some time. This provoked his new chairman to respond in the press, a practice which was to become so commonplace. Ridsdale earned the nickname 'Publicity Pete', with one wag claiming, 'every time the fridge door opens and the light comes on, Peter is there, ready with a quote.' In what was seen as a rebuke to his manager, Ridsdale said: 'I don't want anyone to feel that we as a club will accept being tucked in behind the top few clubs in the Premier League. We are a top six club in everything from the point of view of stadium, the supporters and the city and that is where we expect to be.' Graham noticed wryly the chairman's list of assets didn't include cash.

Lucas was playing with the confidence that comes from knowing the manager rated him and that, as long as he did his job, he was likely to be one of the regular names on the team sheet. He felt at home, one of the boys, no longer an outsider. It had taken him a while to get used to English changing rooms after the singing, clapping and dancing that often marked the pre-match warm up back home. In England there tended to be much more aggression, more up and at 'em. The United dressing room was certainly no place for shrinking violets. With people like Gary Kelly around, you had to be prepared to take practical jokes with a smile and newcomers soon learned not to wear anything they valued to training because it might end up with the sleeves chopped out before you went home.

Press officer Dick Wright often found himself the butt of the practical jokers, including having his mobile phone hidden and his reading glasses taped to the roof of the Portakabin where he made his office at Thorp Arch. An amiable former schoolteacher, Dick went far beyond his media duties, helping arrange charity work, player public appearances and even assisting the players with their correspondence and household problems. Lucas grew to rely on him to help keep his increasingly busy life in order and Dick received a number of phone calls on the defender's behalf. But he wasn't sure if it was yet another joke when he picked up the phone and a voice said, "This is President Mandela's office, would it be possible to speak to Lucas Radebe?" Fortunately Dick didn't respond with an expletive because it really was Madiba wanting to speak to Lucas.

As the team's form picked up, they took 22 of the next 30 points, including a 1-0 win over Manchester United that saw Lucas's central defensive partner Dave Wetherall head the winner on the day his son Adam was born, and Roy Keane suffer a serious, self-inflicted injury when he tried to kick Alfie Haaland. Lucas's reputation continued to grow. In the *YEP*, Simon Stone wrote: 'The charismatic South African skipper has been the star of the show so far this season with a string of superb performances at the heart of United's defence.' And George Graham said: 'Lucas has been outstanding. His partnership with David Wetherall is getting more impressive all the time.'

Lucas had fitted in a couple of friendlies for South Africa, against France and Germany, without missing any United fixtures, but there was a match coming up against Brazil at the start of December followed quickly by three games in the Confederation Cup in Saudi Arabia and, of course, the defence of the African Cup of Nations was only weeks away. The fast improving teenager Harry Kewell was also due to go back home to play in a series of internationals and Graham was already frustrated that he would soon be without two of his in-form players. The Scot accepted the need for international coaches to have their best players for major competitions, but he was unhappy that his plans were being thwarted by what he considered to be an unimportant jamboree like the Confederation Cup. And while accepting that Clive Barker had every right to call up Lucas for the African Cup of Nations, Graham said: 'It would be lovely if South Africa paid Lucas his wages. They are going to have him for three weeks in February, so why shouldn't they pay his wages?' Graham increased the pressure by claiming he was tempted to put a block on all future signings outside the European Union. 'I am seriously considering never signing a South African player because of the excessive international demands placed on them. And that goes for South American players too and any players outside the EEC.'

Lucas was once again trapped uncomfortably in the middle of a fierce club v country tug of war. Things were going so well at Leeds that, as much as he wanted to play for South Africa, he tended to agree with Graham about the Saudi Arabia tournament and said he would prefer to miss that but go to the African Cup of Nations. He was growing tired of the way SAFA ignored the fact that his living was made with Leeds United. It was as though they felt that they owned him and that his first loyalty should always be to South Africa no matter how meaningless the match. SAFA exerted enormous emotional pressure, playing on his patriotism and his loyalty, and at times seemed determined to make him play in friendlies where he could have been excused almost as if to prove a point. Gary Blumberg, who found himself accused of bias by both sides, was regularly involved in negotiations between club and country and commented: 'I don't think people realise to this day the strain that was put on Lucas over the years. While he knew how important Leeds United was to his career and he felt enormous loyalty to them, especially after George Graham took charge, he found it difficult to say no to his country. And I know from being in the meetings, just how much pressure was put on him.'

In the end United thrashed out a compromise with Barker that saw both sides gain something but which, as ever, would put an immense strain on Lucas. They decided he would play for Leeds against Everton on 6 December then take the flight to Johannesburg where he would arrive five hours before the friendly against Brazil in which, it was agreed, he would only take part for 45 minutes. He would miss the opening game of the Confederation Cup so that he could return to England and face Chelsea at Stamford Bridge before dashing to be in the Bafana line-up two days later for the game against United Arab Emirates followed by a match against Uruguay. That would allow him four more days to get back to Leeds to face Bolton.

'We definitely want him for the Everton and Chelsea matches, but it will depend what his physical condition is like as to whether we play him in the Bolton game,' Graham said. With something like 18,000 miles travel and five football matches in ten days, the odds seemed against it. As it turned out the situation was eased when Lucas picked up a booking that saw him suspended for the Bolton game and the Boxing Day visit to Liverpool, and a mix-up over arrangements meant he and Barnsley's Eric Tinkler missed their flight to Saudi Arabia so were unable to play against UAE.

Even with those reprieves, it was an exhausting schedule that would have seen most players wilt. But if Lucas resented being treated like a package that could be air-mailed around the world to suit other people's ends, he kept his frustrations to himself. He smiled his winning smile and played out of his skin. He was star man in a goalless draw against Everton and the following day shone again as South Africa were narrowly defeated by Brazil. Graham was relieved his defender had returned uninjured but apoplectic that Barker had gone back on the agreement and played Lucas for the whole 90 minutes instead of just one half. The Scot revealed that Leeds had almost pulled Lucas out of the trip: 'He carried an injury against Everton after getting a kick on the calf during the first half,' Graham explained. 'We could have taken him off at half-time but he is so important to us. He has been excellent this season – outstanding.'

Leeds players wore black armbands for the match against Chelsea to honour the passing of Billy Bremner, who had captained the side through Don Revie's glory years and was considered second only to his mentor among the club's most influential figures. London journalists, never the greatest admirers of the Revie style that combined flair with naked aggression, gleefully pointed out how apt it was that in the first match since the feisty Scot's death, United had Kelly and Haaland sent off in the 'Battle of Stamford Bridge.' That changed the tactics dramatically. One report read: 'At the heart of the defence David Wetherall reigned supreme, ably supported by Lucas Radebe, who started out man-marking Gianfranco Zola but ended up marking anyone who came hear him.' A gutsy, leg-wearying display by Leeds saw them come away with an unlikely goalless draw.

Back in Saudi Arabia, Barker was under pressure. His side had lost three friendlies since the World Cup triumph over Congo and so far been less than convincing in the Confederation Cup with a draw against the Czech Republic and defeat by United Arab Emirates. The consensus seemed to be that if Bafana Bafana didn't beat an inexperienced Uruguay side, Barker's days as coach were numbered. They made a good start when Lucas headed his first goal for his country but things then fell apart. Trailing 3-1 they pulled back level with two goals in seven minutes only to fall to an effort in the closing minutes. Bafabulous was now replaced by Bafumblers and the coach resigned.

Saddened by the departure of Barker, a man he rated highly, and concerned about the effect it might have on South Africa's defence of the African Cup of Nations, Lucas dragged his exhausted body back to Leeds where, thanks to his two-match suspension, he was able to get some much needed rest over Christmas. The time seemed to fly by and with Robert Molenaar having done well as his replacement in the heart of the defence, Lucas found himself back in midfield in another draw against Aston Villa. The next match saw the visit of Oxford United in the FA Cup and another landmark for Lucas although, as Stephen Brenkley pointed out in *The Independent*, not reached in particularly spectacular style: 'Gary Kelly's corner to the near post found Radebe. The increasingly accomplished South African did not have to go to the trouble of jumping to head past Phil Whitehead, his first goal for Leeds in 93 appearances.' Skipper David Hopkin admitted he and the other players had given Lucas some 'stick' about his lack of goals but added: 'I was delighted for him because he is such a wholehearted player and good to have in your team.'

A man-of-the-match display against Arsenal was even more remarkable when it was revealed that Lucas was suffering a recurrence of a back injury that made twisting and turning painful. He was spending more time on the treatment table than on the training pitch but he was determined to battle on, not least because the African Cup of Nations was now imminent. However, after struggling against Sheffield Wednesday he was admitted to hospital because of the back problem and missed the FA Cup tie against Grimsby and South Africa's Castle Cup match in Namibia. Ironically his services in those two matches had been the subject of another heated exchange between SAFA and Leeds United and in the end, both missed out.

The hostility between club and country was barely hidden these days and even though he was unable to get official clearance from South Africa, Graham decided he would play Lucas against Crystal Palace on 31 January, even though the match fell within the 14-day period before the African Cup of Nations in which Bafana had the right to demand players joined the squad. 'As far as I am aware Lucas says all the South African players are meeting on Monday. Fish is available to play for Bolton, Phil Masinga is apparently due to play for Bari this weekend. And as long as he is fit, Lucas will play against Palace,' Graham said.

Lucas's back stood up to the test reasonably well and he had the satisfaction of snuffing out the the threat of Tomas Brolin, who had moved to Selhurst Park and had been determined to put one over on his former club. United won 2-0 and once again the fans were impressed by the South African who was starting to become something of an icon. They admired the way he had handled a gruelling schedule without complaint and without lowering his high standards in matches. They noted with approval that he had the guts and commitment to play through pain and not let injuries affect his play. They recognised that he had played a key part in Leeds' climb to seventh in the table, in with a chance of securing a place in Europe next season.

Lucas felt weary but excited as he headed home to link up with the national squad. He knew expectations would again be high, perhaps unrealistically so in view of recent results and Barker's resignation. But, as always, he was determined to give the cause 100 per cent.

Chapter 16

Sent off on a stretcher

The African Cup of Nations was held in Burkina Faso, a mainly agricultural country about half the size of France. Yet somehow the gamble of taking Africa's major tournament to one of the poorest countries on the planet was vindicated – it was well run and produced some exciting football. While SAFA waited for their first choice coach Philippe Troussier to fulfil his obligations with the host nation, Jomo Sono took over from Clive Barker. However, his reign didn't get off to a good start when his nominated list of players arrived after the deadline and was cut from 22 to 20 as a punishment.

Bafana Bafana's start to the tournament wasn't too encouraging either. They only managed draws with Angola and the Ivory Coast in their opening group games and had just one goal, a penalty, to show for their efforts. Unless they showed a marked improvement against Namibia, the defending champions would be going home early. Fortunately for them, Benni McCarthy, playing only his seventh game for his country, opened his international scoring account with four goals inside 21 minutes. South Africa were runners-up in their group and now faced Morocco in the first knock out match.

The win lifted the squad's spirits and the relaxed atmosphere encouraged by Sono helped create some momentum. McCarthy was on target again against Morocco and with a late goal by David Nyathi, they booked a semi-final spot – another tough clash with Congo. Their rivals took the lead early in the second half but McCarthy just couldn't stop scoring. He equalised on the hour and then with the game on a knife-edge, grabbed the winner in the first half of extra-time. South Africa had recovered from a shaky start and now only Egypt stood between them and retaining the trophy.

But the extra half hour had sapped extra energy from the team and three days later, in a hot, steamy cauldron of a stadium in Ouagadougou, the Burkina Faso capital, South Africa never recovered from conceding two early goals. The Egyptians then shut up shop and John Moshoeu said: 'We could not break them down because they packed their defence in numbers. Frustration then set in. Had we scored a goal it would have changed the complexion of the game completely.' Bafana Bafana had discovered a new star striker and reached the final for the second tournament in a row but there was no hiding their disappointment at falling short of their goal. They would have to regroup before the World Cup.

Lucas was again a few days late arriving back in Leeds, though this time it wasn't parties that held him up but talks with SAFA about the appointment of a new coach. When he finally arrived he had Feziwe with him. He knew she was the woman for him and steeled himself to tell Tumi that their relationship was over. He wasn't proud of himself but he could see no other way. He could no longer go on pretending. He was heartbroken when Tumi took Jessica back to South Africa but determined that he would not lose touch with his daughter. Feziwe started to study at Leeds Metropolitan University and the couple found a house in the picturesque village of Linton, where several Leeds players lived because it was near the Thorp Arch training ground.

United were still in seventh place in the league after five matches that had brought two wins and a draw. But if Lucas hoped the club was in for a period of stability with everyone pulling in the same direction, he was to be disappointed. Relationships between George Graham and his board were still uneasy as the rows over the gap between ambition and investment rumbled on. The club's share price had taken a hit in the autumn with the publication of a report from accountants Deloitte & Touche that suggested several football clubs' losses were starting to spiral out of control. As the Leeds board scrambled to find new institutional investors, they continued to make optimistic noises about the club's rightful place among the top sides in the country so they were not best pleased when Graham announced to the world that he was 'fed up with having to shop in the bargain basement. I can't go out and buy £6 million and £7 million players and we could never afford their salaries. We are not in the same bracket as some of the other big boys.' Graham knew he was on firm ground because his was a success story. Although results might not have improved as much as fans had hoped when the takeover took place, they were better. And a study of Leeds' financial situation by a local academic said the best news in the figures was that the players bought by the Scot had vastly increased in value.

Peter Ridsdale felt it necessary to go into print once more. In an interview with the *YEP* he pointed out that the company had been forced to pay generously to buy out the former directors, had to reassure the bank about the overdraft, had invested in a large number of players and 'at a time when everybody would accept that a change of manager was required, we brought in one of the most successful trophy winners in recent times.' In other words, Graham had not come cheaply.

Lucas was happy to let the manager and directors argue about the money. He just wanted to re-establish himself quickly in the team because while he'd been away Robert Molenaar had put in some top-class performances and United's latest 'bargain basement' signing was Austrian international defender Martin Hiden. Not wanting anyone to have doubts about his commitment, he issued a statement apologising for his late return from South Africa, but also came as close as he had thus far to pleading with the authorities to take action to improve the club v country situation for players outside Europe. 'We had a very hard tournament, played under difficult conditions and we came back late from Burkina Faso on Sunday night,' he said. 'I was tired and I had some other things to do concerning the team – but I'm not using that as an excuse. Leeds pay my wages and that's where I'm making my living. It needs to be sorted out much better in future.'

Lucas needn't have worried too much about his place in the team. Graham might have been angry at his late return but he wasn't going to let that cloud his football judgement. Lucas was at the heart of the defence in the FA Cup quarter-final against a Wolves side that was a shadow of its former glories. The home fans reckoned they had a clear path to the semi-finals, and possibly then on to Wembley but Wolves went ahead and when Hasselbaink's late penalty was saved by Hans Segers, Leeds were out.

The Cup exit proved to be a blip in a successful final few weeks of the season. A 4-0 win over Blackburn was followed by a 5-0 thrashing of Derby County in which Lucas was named as United's star player. He also picked up a booking, which meant he would miss the next two games, and for once that turned out to be a lucky break. The first match of his suspension was at West Ham, after which the team's plane crashed with an engine on fire seconds after take-off from Stansted airport. Cool-headed work by the pilot, Captain John Hackett, brought the British Aerospace 748 back down safely and quick thinking by David O'Leary forced a door open so everyone escaped unhurt. But it was a shaken group of players that returned to Leeds in the early hours of the morning, several of whom felt dubious about ever climbing on board a plane again. Despite all his trips between South Africa and England, Lucas had never been that keen on flying and was relieved not to have been aboard. Hearing some of his team-mates' descriptions of what had happened was bad enough and didn't help his peace of mind the next time he was strapped in ready for take off.

Lucas was back in the side for the visit of Chelsea, which Leeds won 3-1 to go fourth in the table but he found himself the subject of unwanted headlines after the next game, played at relegation-threatened Everton on the day before his 29th birthday. Referee Uriah Rennie booked him for an innocuous looking foul on Nick Barmby after a quarter of an hour. Two minutes later, Lucas lunged into a full-blooded tackle on Don Hutchison but it was the Leeds man who was left gasping as pain shot through his knee. A quick glance told the physio that Lucas couldn't carry on and he was lifted on to a stretcher. His first thought was that he hoped it wasn't a bad one, not with the World Cup just over a month away. He hardly noticed that as he was carried from the field, Rennie flourished a second yellow card in his direction followed by a red. It was the first time he had ever been sent off. Fortunately, when his knee was examined back in the dressing room, the damage wasn't as severe as he'd feared and he was able to limp to the team bus and contemplate the disciplinary blot on his record. Like most players, he felt hard done by. 'I thought the first booking was a bit harsh,' he said. 'And I don't think my second challenge was reckless. I saw the ball and thought it was 50-50 and that I could make it. But when I went in he pushed the ball a little too far and I caught him with my knee.'

The injury recovered quickly enough for Lucas to play against Bolton the following weekend. His red card meant he would miss the following match and he travelled to Switzerland for a World Cup training camp with South Africa. As usual, George Graham was unhappy with the arrangement, complaining that SAFA had not even had the courtesy of informing Leeds about the session. But it was a storm in a tea cup and Lucas returned fit and well to play in the last two games of the Premiership season, ending with a man-of-the-match display against Wimbledon.

Leeds finished fifth in the table, which meant Graham had achieved the target set by his board and booked a place in the UEFA Cup the following season. The United boss could look back with some satisfaction. Hasselbaink had proved a shrewd signing, hitting 23 goals in all competitions as in stark contrast to the previous season, Leeds notched 57 league goals while still maintaining a strong defence. What's more, the *YEP* had re-run their heart monitor experiment during the season and this time the football proved much more exciting than the meat pie.

To his delight Lucas received a phone call to tell him that he had been voted as the fans' Player of the Year, beating his central defensive partner David Wetherall by one vote. It put his name on a list of players that included people like Norman Hunter, the first winner back in 1971, Eddie Gray and Peter Lorimer. Supporters' Club secretary Eric Carlile said: 'Lucas is one of those people who always turns up at our functions and he is a very popular character with the fans and a deserving winner of the award.' It meant a lot to Lucas that the people who paid their cash week after week to watch the team had chosen him for the accolade. The uncertain, unhappy person of his early days in Leeds had won their acceptance and admiration by hard work, talent, courage, dedication and a constant, uncomplaining smile. Now he would need all those qualities in the small matter of leading his country into the World Cup for the first time.

Chapter 17
Bumpy road to France

Thoughts turned to the World Cup the minute the final whistle blew to mark Bafana Bafana's unsuccessful defence of the African Cup of Nations. Given the turmoil from which they started and the fact that Jomo Sono had stepped into the breach as coach at the last minute, a silver medal was not a bad achievement and many felt South Africa could build on that foundation in the run-up to France in June. The players were in no doubt that in Sono, they had the right man to lead them. When they arrived back from Burkina Faso, Lucas held a press briefing at Johannesburg International Airport and against raucous chants of 'Jomo! Jomo! Jomo!' from the likes of Mark Fish and Phil Masinga, he announced: 'Jomo is a great coach. Hopefully he will also take us to France.'

SAFA were in a difficult position. They had already given the job to Philippe Troussier and Sono was only a stop-gap while the Frenchman fulfilled his earlier obligations. Faced with hundreds of fans chanting Sono's name, the ruling body's chief executive, Danny Jordaan uncomfortably pointed out: 'This cannot be an emotional decision. We understand and appreciate the feelings of the people but we are looking for a man who will take Bafana Bafana to France and beyond. Sono and ourselves know he will be committed to his club and will have to review his own situation.'

In many ways, the appointment of itinerant Parisian Troussier made sense. He was very knowledgeable about African football, having coached in the Ivory Coast, Nigeria and Burkina Faso, and he had experience of South Africa after a brief spell at Kaizer Chiefs just before Lucas left for Leeds. However, he had the reputation of being something of a martinet in his approach, an example of which Lucas described to Ian Hawkey in an interview for *Feet of the Chameleon*: 'He thought we needed to be tougher but he went too far. One day he was dragging my team-mate "Bricks" Mudau around the ground by his feet.' While some thought the Bafana Bafana squad needed more discipline, others were concerned that the two cultures would end up at odds. It was a sensitive time in South Africa's history for a white man to think he could bully and at times physically abuse black players.

All this was happening when the country probably needed the fillip of sporting success more than at any time since majority rule. As in the rest of the world, the economy was struggling and the initial euphoria of Nelson Mandela coming to power was slowly being eroded by more everyday concerns. Hoped-for reforms were slow in materialising, the conditions in which many of the poor lived were still less than adequate, and it seemed to some people that the Truth and Reconciliation Commission was providing former oppressors with an easy way out. The President recognised the mood of the country in his New Year address: 'If the early years of our democracy brought celebration of our very freedom and common humanity; if these first three years of freedom meant the outpouring of national pride in the prowess of our sporting teams, in our new constitution and more; then this past year has been one in which slowly but surely, we are all coming to better appreciate the difficulties of change, as well as the sweat and toil required to improve our lives and forge our unity as a nation.' Emphasising the progress that had been made in many areas, Madiba nevertheless conceded: 'We know that the numbers of people reached in service delivery are not nearly enough; the quality still needs much improvement; the crime rate is still too high; and the divisions of the past still play themselves out in many areas. We know that our tasks will take years to complete…Our achievements so far have shown what can be done when we set aside petty differences and together pursue the common good. By working together we can build the South Africa of our dreams.' Those final two sentences should have acted as a reminder to all those – coaches, officials and players - about to represent South Africa in France.

Troussier didn't start work until 1 March, less than three months before the opening ceremony in Paris. One of his first duties was to take his squad to meet Nelson Mandela at his official Pretoria residence Mahlambandlopfu. Lucas introduced each of the players to the President who had delayed a trip to Geneva to make time for the visit. 'To show you how much I appreciate your efforts, I had to put all my engagements on hold to be with you,' Madiba said. And he showed he understood the enormity of the challenge ahead of the players when he added, 'I know we have a first class team which is ready to compete with the best in the world. It is not so much the victory that we expect, but the spirit in which you compete should be exemplary.'

Lucas also made a short speech, thanking Madiba for his kind words and encouragement. 'We know we have a huge responsibility and we will not let the nation down in France. We hope to come back with honours. We have faith in ourselves and the coach,' he said.

Not everyone in the country shared Lucas's apparent belief in Troussier but if the Frenchman was concerned about the opposition to his appointment, he didn't show it and certainly didn't go out of his way to court popularity. He immediately upset the South African media by refusing to talk to them after his first training session with the squad. And, shortly after, he was in a fracas with journalist Dominic Chimhavi that raised the spectre of the old black-white divide in South Africa. It was pointed out in the *Sowetan* that five years before, when black coach Stanley Tshabalala struck a white journalist, he had been sacked. 'Now Troussier has manhandled a black journalist, the public is waiting anxiously to see what kind of treatment is meted out against the so-called "white witchdoctor",' the paper said. And when SAFA did nothing, columnist Sello Rabothata wrote: 'Let us be fair and face facts. We still live in a divided country and whether some people like it or not – colour still plays a big part in how matters are approached. In South Africa white still remains right and black is always wrong.' That may have been an over-simplification and unfair on the progress made during South Africa's recent history but it resonated with a lot of people. Troussier had not got off to a good start.

He also created a stir when he announced his initial 28-man training squad, which would eventually be reduced to 22 for the tournament. The main criticism was that he had picked too many debutant 'foreigners' in Hans Vonk, Albert Phiri, and Pierre Issa, who had played little of their football in South Africa. The selection played into fears that the Frenchman was going to change the team's style to a European model and he admitted he had leaned towards players with European experience because of the challenge ahead of them. To some this was sabotage.

The country's apprehensive mood didn't improve with South Africa's first warm-up game against Zambia, which ended in a 1-1 draw. Damning with only a hint of praise, *Sunday World* journalist Xolile Mtshazo wrote in his match report: 'It is clear that Troussier has the material to work with but he needs more hard work to blend his team into a cohesive unit for the more demanding challenge against Argentina in Buenos Aires on Monday.'

That was the next stop on a hectic schedule and despite any doubts they might have had, the fans turned out in huge numbers to wish the squad good luck as they left Johannesburg. South Africa had caught World Cup fever. In just a month they bought 100,000 copies of Shibobo, the specially-recorded song which had Benni McCarthy rapping with popular band TKZee. Now the fans lined the streets of the city, waving the national flag as the team bus headed towards the airport, and hundreds more crammed into the terminal. The familiar cries went up every time a player was spotted: 'Feeesh!' 'Shoes!' 'Rhoo!' As Lucas and his team-mates disappeared through the check-in, the fans burst into a spontaneous singing of N'kosi Sikelel' iAfrika.

The squad had three days' training in Buenos Aires before tackling the two-time world champions in the last match before heading for their next training camp in Stuttgart. The team gave a good account of themselves in the first half but appeared to run out of steam after the break and lost 2-0. In their report, the *Sowetan* continued to raise doubts about the coach whose presence they claimed was looming over the shoulders of the players: 'The element of joy is gone and it was evident that some players were scared to make even the slightest mistake.'

Many of the squad, especially those who played their club football in South Africa, were finding it hard to come to terms with the coach's attitude. It seemed to them that they were second-class citizens compared to those with European experience. The Frenchman certainly believed in driving everyone hard. The mixture of 'kick up the pants' with 'a comforting arm round the shoulder' favoured by so many coaches, didn't seem to cross his mind. With him it was stick, more stick and even more stick with little sign of carrot. More than one player was reduced to tears by the ferocity of his criticism.

Not everyone thought the Frenchman was on the wrong track. In the *Sunday Times*, Sy Lerman was encouraged by what he saw: 'A gritty, resourceful performance against Argentina began the process of restoring and reshaping morale, with controversial French-born coach Philippe Troussier finally gaining widespread acceptance and recognition for his uncompromising methods.' For his part, Troussier was sounding unconcerned about his largely negative reception: 'It is nothing new for me after ten years coaching in Africa to be confronted with hostility. If anything it is an incentive to work harder and do my job better.'

The team arrived in Stuttgart on 27 May, 16 days before their opening Group C match against host nation France. Working mainly behind closed doors, this was a chance to finalise tactics and set pieces. It should have also been the time to build the camaraderie that would carry the group through an intensive tournament but Troussier's acerbic style made that harder and it was a rather subdued bunch who played a couple of games against local club sides and a drab 1-1 draw with Iceland.

Lucas had agreed to provide the South Africa *Sunday Times* with a weekly column during the World Cup and in the first of these he wrote: 'I feel an overwhelming sense of destiny as South Africa's first captain to lead a team to the greatest sporting event on earth.' He clearly felt the hand of history upon him and with a mixture of pride and perhaps a little anxiety about the contrasting mixture of gloom and expectations at home, added: 'It is very difficult to control the hype surrounding the performances of the national team. We all know that football, throughout its history, has had the ability to both unite and divide nations, towns and villages – and it is no different at home. However, no other sports team in South Africa can claim to be as representative of the people as Bafana Bafana. The players are very aware of this and believe me, are desperate to do well every time we step on the field. As long as the feverish level of support is accompanied by a degree of realism, I think people will be able to accept our performances and results in France.' His pledge for the opening game could have come straight from the George Graham coaching manual: 'We aim to be positive, committed and aggressive against the French and will make them work hard. Like all South African teams before us, we would also want to play good football, but not at the expense of defensive discipline and organisation.'

He was soon to get the opportunity to test those aims in the heat of battle.

Chapter 18

Turmoil in Vichy

Five days before their opening World Cup game, Bafana Bafana left their hotel in the Black Forest for a seven-hour coach trip to France. Lucas reported that it was a tiring ride with players mainly trying to snatch some sleep but he also confessed: 'It was a long journey but for many of us, Doctor, Shoes and myself included, it was preferable to flying. I have never been fond of flying and the recent incident involving Leeds United has made me more nervous.' They were headed for the small town of Vichy in the centre of France, which was to be their headquarters throughout the tournament. To the players' surprise, they were met by crowds lining the streets waving French and South African flags and were welcomed with bunches of flowers by several thousand people at the sports arena where they were to train. Vichy had decided that the visit of Bafana Bafana was the ideal way to promote an image of their picturesque town that wasn't connected with wartime collaboration with the Nazis.

The warm reception they received helped raise morale as did the sight of many fans who had clearly made the trip from South Africa to support the team. There was an added bonus with a relaxing visit to the glittering Vichy Opera House where legendary South African singer and anti-apartheid campaigner Miriam Makebe, 'Mama Afrika', was performing. The hotel, which was only a boat ride across Lake Allier from the training ground, was inundated with letters and faxes of good wishes and each player received a personal, note from Nelson Mandela, wishing him well.

The first major setback in their preparations came with the injury in training to Andre Arendse. The experienced keeper had lost his place in recent months to Brian Baloyi or Hans Vonk but he had been one of the stars of the team that won the African Cup of Nations and had done as much as anyone to help Bafana Bafana reach France. It was cruel that he would not be able to take any part in the finals and every player was chillingly reminded that no matter how talented you are, the difference between joy and despair in football can be as close as the next tackle. Troussier called up Paul Evans, the lad who had spent two years on the staff at Leeds without getting a competitive game before moving to Bradford City and then back to Supersport United in Johannesburg. He, too, was struck down in training, snapping his cruciate ligament, and had to be replaced after the opening match by Simon Gopane, the first World Cup player to carry the number 23.

The team flew to Marseilles the day before the game against France and trained that evening in Stade Velodrome where the match would be played. Once again they were heartened by the sight of so many South Africa fans mingling happily with the French in the streets, cafes and bars of the famous port. Kick-off was set for 9pm so there was a long wait for the players to contemplate what lay ahead. They strolled round the hotel, tried to rest, and attempted to distract themselves. Like great golfers, Lucas liked to visualise events before they happen, believing it helps the body react when a similar situation arose in reality. 'I play the game in my mind beforehand, making sure I get all the tackles right. Then I can put it all into practice on the pitch. I try to visualise the players I'm going up against, their movement and things like that.' But some of his team-mates didn't want to dwell too much on the quality of their opponents. France were among the favourites to lift the Jules Rimet trophy thanks to the presence in their team of superstars like Marcel Desailly, Thierry Henry, Youri Djourkaeff and World Player of the Year Zinedine Zidane. Best to think of other things until later.

Nelson Mandela couldn't be at the game but his deputy Thabo Mbeki went into the South Africa dressing room just before kick-off to pass on the President's good wishes. They would need every ounce of Madiba Magic if they were to get anything from this one but they were up for it. The dressing room was filled with music, excitement, nerves and enough adrenaline to get a jumbo jet off the ground. This was it. The moment they had imagined when they were small boys but which had then seemed impossible, the goal they had worked so hard to achieve in recent years, their place in history was finally here.

Lucas had never felt more proud than the moment he led Bafana Bafana into the cool night air for their first taste of World Cup football, then stood with hand on heart as the strains of N'kosi Sikelel' iAfrika filled the stadium. He said later: 'Hearing the national anthem always arouses a sense of patriotism in me but that night it was something really special and a feeling I will never forget.'

Like the rest of his team-mates, Lucas looks back at the match itself with less fond memories. France simply outplayed South Africa. Zidane was like the conductor of a world-class orchestra at the height of its powers. No matter how much Bafana Bafana tried to pin him down, he continued to conjure chance after chance and the match was as good as over in the 34th minute when Christophe Dugarry rose above the flailing arm of Vonk and headed home Zidane's in-swinging corner. To their credit, South Africa kept battling away and the hosts didn't double their lead until 13 minutes from time when the unfortunate Issa, on the ground where he played his club football for Olympique Marseille, deflected Djorkaeff's shot out of the grasp of his own keeper. And hard as he tried, Issa was unable to prevent the injury time coup de grace after Henry, at pace, exquisitely clipped the ball over the advancing Vonk. The distraught South African defender, who had been one of the side's best players up to the final few minutes, left the pitch in tears. He was not alone in feeling distraught.

Lucas described the match as 'a harsh introduction for us'. He was honest in what proved a prophetic assessment: 'The French were superb – it is going to take a horrible loss of form or an excellent team to stop them winning the World Cup. But we did not play to our true potential. We are all disappointed but we know we can only improve.' The team made its way back to Vichy the next day where Lucas received a phone call from the President, urging the squad to keep their heads high. 'There is still much to play for,' Madiba said.

Lucas's mood was lifted by the arrival of his parents, bursting with pride after seeing their son lead his country into the World Cup. But Troussier's men needed to regroup and prepare themselves for their next match against Denmark, a game they must not lose if they were to have any chance of reaching the knock-out stages. The odds against them were growing, with McCarthy struggling after picking up an ankle ligament injury in the closing stages of the France match. Even more concerning were the growing ripples of unrest about Troussier's regimental style. His was much stricter than the approach adopted by Clive Barker, under which the players had flourished and there were mutterings when two incidents of curfew-breaking brought the players fines. An incandescent Troussier threatened to quit and Lucas found himself as the middle man, trying to patch things up between an unmoving coach and an unhappy group of players.

But the real dispute was over the style of football the Frenchman wanted them to play. It was alien to their natural, free-flowing game and while rumours of a player revolt were denied, a clear-the-air meeting was held in which Lucas and some of the senior players put their views to Troussier. Whatever the coach's shortcomings or mistakes, rebellion was not going to help the cause. Lucas had worked with Troussier before and knew he was a good coach who had sound ideas to pass on. He also knew how much his own game had benefited from the disciplined defending instilled by George Graham so his weekly *Sunday Times* column hinted at some frustration when he wrote: 'At no time has the team ever threatened to "do it our way" as was quoted in one of the papers. Group dynamics are always complex and Philippe, especially, has had a relatively short time to get to know all the players. Likewise, they have had to get used to his regime.

Much has been made of him establishing strict discipline in the camp. From a personal perspective, the sooner all South African players realise that this is part of professionalism at this level, the better. The players here have accepted this. We are here with a common goal: to do well at the World Cup. And there is no doubt that Philippe is the man in charge.'

It was time for any differences to be set aside and for everyone to focus on the Danes, who were no longer the force that won the European Championships in 1992 but still had some top class players in brothers Brian and Michael Laudrup, and one of the world's best goalkeepers in Peter Schmeichel. But they had been unimpressive in scraping a 1-0 win over Group C's weakest side Saudi Arabia, so all was not lost and being realistic, Troussier told his players: 'Nothing has changed. The match against Denmark was always going to be the decisive one.'

The game was played in the Municipal Stadium, in Toulouse. Bafana Bafana were given a lift when McCarthy passed a late fitness test and was able to play and as they prepared for the 4pm kick-off, they felt confident the considerable late afternoon heat would give them an edge. In fact the Danes settled quicker and Spurs striker Allan Nielsen put them ahead after only 13 minutes. They soon had chances to put the game beyond South Africa's reach: Martin Jorgensen hit the post with a swerving free-kick and Brian Laudrup's diving header put the rebound straight at Vonk. Just before half-time Ebbe Sand crashed in a shot from the edge of the area that smacked against the same post.

At half-time, Troussier pushed John Moshoeu further forward and persuaded his players to press the Danes more. The tactics paid off and Lucas and his team-mates had much the better of the second half. They got their reward in the 52nd minute, when McCarthy darted on to a back heel from Shaun Bartlett, burst between two defenders and fired the equaliser between Schmeichel's legs. There were ecstatic celebrations both for the 20-year-old striker's skill and the country's first World Cup goal. And there was still time to go after the winner.

Unfortunately for Bafana Bafana, the rhythm of the game was constantly interrupted by the over-fussy referee John Toro Rendon. All the officials were under pressure because FIFA President Sepp Blatter and World Cup co-President Michel Platini had castigated them for not issuing enough red cards for foul tackles. Rendon was determined not to fall foul of his masters again and, after showing two yellow cards in the first half, he issued another five in a 15-minute spell after the break. Not content with that, he also handed out three red cards. First to go was Miklos Molnar for a foul on Lucas. It looked much worse than it was because Lucas was writhing in agony but as he explained afterwards: 'The sending-off seemed harsh. I went down in a tackle, which was awkward for both of us, and I got caught in that most painful of areas! I certainly was not looking to make a meal of it, as the Danish fans seemed to think. That is not my style.' Two minutes later. Albert Phiri's World Cup came to an end when he, too, saw red, and with five minutes to go, Dane Morten Wieghorst was given his marching orders for a foul on McCarthy. 'The guy didn't even touch me and the referee gave him a stupid red card,' the striker said.

The drama didn't end there. Bafana Bafana kept pushing forward and as the match went into added time, Quinton Fortune blasted a shot from the edge of the area that hit the bar and flew over. A few inches lower and things would have looked so very different.

The coach gave the players a night off after the Denmark game with strict orders to be back in the hotel by 1am. But once again the curfew was broken and Troussier went ballistic. Brendan Augustine and the aptly-named Naughty Mokoena stayed in a Vichy disco into the early hours and having threatened stern action after the first two breaches, Troussier ordered them to pack their bags and go home. The camp was in turmoil. Many believed the punishment was too harsh, another example of the coach over-reacting, and there were tearful farewells as Mokoena and Augustine left the hotel on the Monday morning. Augustine, especially, would be missed, for as Lucas pointed out, 'He has a lot to offer at international level. He is very experienced and has become an important player for Bafana Bafana.' But the skipper backed his coach's decision: 'Both players knew that it was important to retain discipline and focus. I think if you gave them the time again, they would have done things differently. We really need to pull together now if we are to progress.'

Apart from the natural desire to get through to the knock-out stages, there was an extra incentive because it would mean a match against arch rivals Nigeria, who had already qualified at the head of Group D. Players like Lucas were sick of hearing from Super Eagles' fans that their 1996 African Cup of Nations victory was hollow because Nigeria didn't take part. Mark Fish relished the prospect of finally thrashing out the continent's bragging rights: 'In effect it would be for the championship of Africa,' he said. 'We've heard a hundred times that a game against Nigeria was in the offing, it would be funny if it comes about in the World Cup.' Troussier had his own reasons for wanting to come up against Nigeria. He had been the coach that led them through World Cup qualifying only to fall out with the officials in Lagos and get the sack. 'I have dreamt of this game,' he said.

The equation was simple: South Africa had to win their match against Saudi Arabia while France beat Denmark, and between them they had to overcome

Bafana's four-goal inferior goal difference. It needed a fine balance in tactics. While South Africa had to go looking for goals, they couldn't afford to concede so Troussier moved Lucas forward to strengthen midfield and brought veteran Willem Jackson into the back line. Meanwhile, the opposition camp was in some disarray, having sacked coach Carlos Alberto Parreira after a 4-0 defeat by France ended their hopes of advancing. As South Africa bade farewell to Vichy and made for Bordeaux, Lucas wasn't sure whether to expect an opponent with nothing to play for or one whose spirits had been lifted by a change of coach.

The match turned out to be something of an anti-climax. South Africa were on top for most of the 90 minutes but had to make do with a 2-2 draw after Saudi Arabia were awarded two penalties, both against Issa, and both harsh.

It was a subdued party that made its way back to the team hotel, ready to pack up and head home. Lucas reflected that the turning point of their campaign may well have been the third French goal, the one Issa almost stopped going over the line but then helped into the net as the ball ricocheted from one foot to another. 'Had we managed to keep the score down to 2-0, we would not have been under such pressure in terms of goal difference,' he explained. 'To have gone into the Saudi game needing a win, but not a big win, would have made a difference. Even at 1-0 we had to keep committing men forward and were in danger on the break.'

That night Lucas received another call from Nelson Mandela, asking him to pass on to the squad that he was proud of their efforts. And the flagging team spirits were raised once again when they received a hero's welcome at Johannesburg International Airport. 'I was very proud to be a South African and Bafana Bafana captain, There is no place like home,' Lucas said.

Inevitably, Troussier's contract was not renewed. He had probably been unrealistic to try and impose a different style on the squad in his broken English only a few months before the tournament started, and Clive Barker's more softly softly approach would have suited the players temperament better than the Frenchman's strict regime. SAFA had a lot to think about before announcing the next coach. There were also lessons for Lucas. As so often in his life, he had found himself at the centre of a tug of war, this time between the coach and the team. With a camp that was often unhappy and divided, he had tried to keep the various groups together. To his surprise, he found himself being criticised from both sides after the event.

Troussier claimed: 'The team lacked a true captain who could liase with the management. At times I took issue with the indiscipline that reigned in the side.' Presumably referring to what Graeme Friedman identified in *Madiba's Boys* as a difference in approach between European-based and home-based players, the Frenchman added: 'It is hard to work with a divided squad, one that suffers from class differences, and is constantly distracted by outside influences.' Lucas, as ever, tried to give a balanced response: 'I read what Philippe Troussier had to say about the lack of leadership and I was surprised and disappointed,' he told the Leeds United matchday programme. 'I thought his comments were a bit harsh. He wanted someone to blame because we didn't go further in the tournament. But despite what he has said, I still rate him a great coach, even though we didn't get the results we wanted.'

Even more hurtful to Lucas was when Phil Masinga told the press that he didn't think Lucas had the leadership qualities to be captain and should be replaced by Mark Fish. If Chippa had something to say, why did he not say it to his face rather than go to the papers? But once again, Lucas decided he had to rise above personal pain for the sake of the team. He and Phil would have to play together again, so when asked for a reaction, he said: 'Initially I was disappointed because of the good relationship I had with him. But I am not the kind of person who holds grudges. Although I have never had the opportunity to speak to Chippa after the statements he made about me being a bad captain for Bafana Bafana, I have forgiven him.'

Perhaps it was easy for Lucas to be magnanimous with both men. After all, George Graham, a man whose opinion he valued more than either Masinga's or Troussier's, had just made him captain of Leeds United.

Chapter 19

Are you going or staying?

The first hint that George Graham was considering Lucas as a possible new captain came in pre-season. Possibly urged on by David O'Leary, he gave the defender the armband for a number of matches, including a tournament in Ireland that involved Lazio and Liverpool as well as local favourites Shelbourne. David Hopkin had been plagued by injuries in the previous campaign and struggled to win a regular place in the side. In his absence, the armband passed around between David Wetherall, Nigel Martyn and Gary Kelly but with the new season just a couple of weeks away, Graham wanted to settle on a leader. He admitted that Lucas wasn't the obvious choice but decided that by appointing the South African he could achieve two goals with one move: 'Making Lucas captain will, I hope, show the confidence I have in him and how much I rate him,' Graham said. 'I also hope it will bring a little bit more from him as a player and make him a bit more demonstrative on the field. I shall be looking for a bit more from him, not just in his performance but in trying to draw more out of other players in the side.'

Lucas was surprised and delighted. 'When George made me captain for the friendlies I thought he was just trying to give my confidence a boost. But when the pre-season was over, he called me into his office for a chat. It was then he told me that I would be his new captain. I was speechless. He said that I had leadership qualities and an exemplary attitude. He also said I had been here long enough and that from what he had seen, I was up to the challenge. That was great, not only for me but for the players back home who can see that there are opportunities to be exploited over here. Who would have thought that a player from Soweto would one day join a club like Leeds United, let alone become captain!'

Naturally, Lucas was a little apprehensive. He was aware he'd be in the spotlight more than before and he knew he couldn't be a captain who would shake his fist and gee people up with rousing rallying cries. He'd have to do it his way, setting the right tone and having a quiet word of encouragement or, where necessary, criticism. He was about to start his fifth season at United and even he was surprised how far he had come after such a shaky start. He said: 'I am greatly honoured to have been made captain of the team and I am proud of the respect the people of Leeds have shown to me. Since I arrived here, I have always given 100 per cent to whatever I have done and it will be no different now. I'll be giving my new job my best shot.'

Compared to recent summers, this had been relatively quiet for Leeds with Graham only bringing in two players, striker Clyde Wijnhard and full-back Danny Granville. But, of course, being Leeds United, a degree of turmoil was never far away. For some time there had been rumours of boardroom rows and they seemed to be confirmed when Chris Akers, one of the driving forces of the original takeover, quit the company. New directors were appointed but most significantly, Peter Ridsdale was more firmly in control than ever, becoming executive chairman.

But boardroom shuffles were to seem minor compared to the upheaval to come. Tottenham Hotspur chairman Alan Sugar wasn't too happy with the performance of manager Christian Gross and sacked him two games into the new season. Graham was immediately tipped as a possible successor along with Ruud Gullit and former Spurs full-back Joe Kinnear. Ridsdale issued a 'hands-off' warning over the Leeds boss but he and many others were aware that if one of the main purposes in Graham's life was to prove to Arsenal how wrong they had been to sack him, there could be no better place than at their biggest rivals Spurs.

Leeds' season started promisingly – three draws and two wins in the opening five games, with only one goal conceded, saw them at the top of the Premiership for 24 hours and in fine shape as they prepared for their UEFA Cup tie against Portugese League side Maritimo. Lucas was delighted that some of the targets he had set at the start of the campaign were being achieved: as well as a string of clean sheets, United had a 100 per cent home record after squandering too many points at Elland Road last season, and the number of yellow cards, especially for dissent, had dropped.

Maritimo have a remarkable record in European football despite playing in a stadium that holds fewer than 10,000 fans but when Leeds watched videos of the team before their first leg tie at Elland Road they felt the high-paced English game would prove too much for the Madeira-based side to cope with. In the event, Maritimo matched fire with fire, erected a strong defensive wall and Leeds were happy to get away with a 1-0 win thanks to a powerful 84th minute strike from Jimmy Hasselbaink. The Portuguese had plenty of reasons to believe they were still in the tie, as their Canadian international Alex Bunbury kept telling Lucas during the game. 'There was a bit of banter flying around with Bunbury telling us to enjoy our bit of success in the first leg because they were going to put one over on us when we got over to Madeira,' Lucas said afterwards. 'He was saying we would be in for a hot time over there and he wasn't meaning the weather!' Lucas finally got tired of Bunbury's boasting and retorted, 'Let's get this game over first then we'll let our football do the talking at your place.'

The Leeds skipper was less concerned with Bunbury's bravado than over the increasing number of reports linking Graham with Spurs. It was clear there was more substance to the stories than mere speculation and every day a bit more fuel was added to the flames. All the indicators seemed to point in one direction and finally Ridsdale admitted Alan Sugar had approached him for permission to talk to the United manager.

By one of those twists of fate so frequent in football, a trip to White Hart Lane was next up for Leeds, after a goalless draw against Aston Villa. Speculation grew to fever pitch, with the London media confidently predicting Graham would be in the home dug-out rather than the away. Apparently relishing being in the eye of the storm, a smiling Graham said: 'All I know is that the chairman told me Spurs have made an inquiry to ask if I was available and it was turned down. So it's business as usual for me. I just carry on. I'm looking forward to going down to Tottenham on Saturday.'

Lucas felt anxious and helpless. Graham had been so important in his career that he hated the idea of losing him. And if the Scot went, who would come in and what would he make of Lucas? Would he still want him as captain? Would he still rate him as player? Asked for his views, Lucas said: 'George is a great manager and has done well for us here. When he came to the club we were struggling and he managed to pull things round. I think we would all love to see him stay here and finish the job he has started.'

As match day approached, it became clear Graham would still be in the Leeds camp but would soon be joining the opposition. He knew he faced a crowd united in hostility at White Hart Lane – Leeds fans calling him Judas for quitting, Spurs fans not entirely happy to see a man who had brought so much triumph to their north London rivals, taking over their club. The players also faced an unusual situation, both sets out to impress the same man.

There can have been few more bizarre Premiership matches. Leeds went ahead after three minutes through Gunnar Halle and in his book *United We Fall*, Ridsdale notes: 'If ever you needed a photo to tell its own story, it appeared in the following day's papers: there's me leaping up, both arms in the air with unrestrained joy. And there, rooted to his seat next to me, is a glum looking George Graham, motionless, expressionless.' Leeds went on to take a 3-1 lead before Spurs hit back to claim a point. Graham brushed aside questions about his future and said: 'I'm very happy with the result.'

As the team set off from Leeds-Bradford airport for Maritimo on the Monday morning, Graham finally admitted publicly that he wanted the Spurs job, explaining, 'It's a personal thing. I want to get back to family life again. I'm engaged and she has been very understanding but if there's a chance for me to get back to London she'll be ecstatic. Also my son, daughter and grandchild live in London.' Behind the scenes Ridsdale had agreed a £2 million compensation package with Sugar, who had also agreed to reimburse Leeds the £1 million bonus they had paid to Graham. The match in Madeira would be the Scot's last as United manager.

Despite a 9pm kick-off, conditions were still very humid and Maritimo cranked up the atmosphere before the game with blaring music, dancing girls and a fire-eater. All the hours of conditioning that had made Leeds one of the fittest sides in the Premiership would be needed if they were to prevail. With a 'what we have we hold' strategy, Graham left Wijnhard on the bench, preferring Haaland as an extra man in midfield. It appeared to be working well and with Lucas and Molenaar in superb form at the back, Maritimo were struggling to create any chances. But just before half-time, former Benfica defender Jorge Soares went up for a free-kick and headed past Martyn. The tie was locked at 1-1 and neither side was able to make a breakthrough; even an energy sapping, half-hour extra time didn't produce a winning goal. It would be decided on penalties. Haaland fired home Leeds' first, matched by one from Bunbury. Harte was as sure as ever from the spot and United gained an advantage when Maritimo hit the bar with their second. Granville was next up for Leeds. Having not played a first team game since his £1.6 million signing from Chelsea, this was his debut and he had only left the substitute's bench in the final minute of extra-time. He scored with his first touch of the ball for Leeds. A second Maritimo miss, left Sharpe to finish things off. Leeds were in the next round and Lucas was off the hook. If the shoot-out had reached 5-5 he was next up to take a penalty for Leeds.

With the match finishing close to midnight, the team flew back to Leeds the next day. Graham left the airport without talking to the journalists and headed straight for talks with Sugar in London where he shook hands on a deal that night. Leeds asked David O'Leary and Eddie Gray to step into the breach as caretaker bosses while they decided who they wanted as their new manager. It was the hot story on the back pages and the media quickly speculated that Lucas and Nigel Martyn would be the first two players Graham would try to sign. If it were true, it would give Lucas a dilemma. He was close to the Scot, admired and respected him, and would love to keep playing for him. On the other hand he felt enormous loyalty to Leeds United who had given him his chance in England, stood by him when he had been injured and where he felt very much at home. Much would depend on who took over at Elland Road. 'You never know what your future is going to be until a new manager comes. For players it will be like starting all over again,' Lucas said. He just hoped the directors would make up their mind quickly and he let them know via Gary Blumberg that he thought David O'Leary would be a good man for the job. There were only three weeks until they were due to face a star-studded Roma side in the next round of the UEFA Cup. Any delay would be unsettling and could jeopardise the good start they had made to the season.

Chapter 20

Set in cement

The gods who control the Premiership fixture computer were in mischievous mood again. After their little joke with the Spurs game, they had now set it up so that Leeds' next match would be at home to Leicester City, managed by Martin O'Neill, the man Peter Ridsdale had decided he wanted as the new manager. The scene was set for another bout of frenzied speculation. Fortunately for Lucas he was going to get a break from it because he was needed back home for Batana Bafana's first African Cup of Nations qualifier against Angola.

Not that the pressure was going to let up in South Africa. A large number of people were still dissecting the World Cup lessons and arguing over the way ahead. *Drum* magazine carried an article by S'busiso Mseleku headlined 'Let's play African soccer again!' in which he sought the views of several senior South African figures. Clive Barker had no doubts that a local approach was needed. 'Anyone who coaches South Africa must know the feel of South African soccer,' the former coach said. 'It must be somebody who's been in the townships and felt the emotions that accompany South African soccer. You can't teach a Ronaldo, Maradona, Shoes, Doctor or Benni. These players possess natural talent that just needs to be nurtured. We must return to our kind of soccer.' Former Kaiser Chiefs star Zacharia 'Computer' Lamola agreed: 'Our style revolves around keeping possession,' he explained, adding that he had been taught that players should treat the ball as they would a girlfriend: 'You don't let anyone mess with your girlfriend, so you mustn't let anyone take the ball from you.' SAFA appeared to take notice. They turned to Troussier's number two in France, 42-year-old Trott Moloto, a former player with Kaizer Chiefs and Moroka Swallows. As well as working with the players in France, he had coached several of them when he'd been in charge of South Africa's under-17 team. The visit of Angola was his first match as boss of the national team and he made three changes in his starting line-up from the side that finished the World Cup. It was noted that all the newcomers played their club football in South Africa.

Once again the country's expectations were soaring and they left Lucas in no doubt what was required of him. The day before the match, a massive picture of him filled the front page of the *Sowetan* and beneath the headline 'BATHATHE RHOO!' (Take them Rhoo) he read: 'There is only one soccer match to watch tomorrow. And one man is tasked with bringing glory to Bafana Bafana – Lucas "Rhoo" Radebe.' He didn't let them down. It was a tight match and South Africa had to wait until the 84th minute before Shaun Bartlett fired in the winner but it was a good start.

The news from Leeds wasn't so encouraging. United had suffered their first defeat at the hands of O'Neill's 'Foxes', adding urgency to the directors' desire to persuade the Leicester boss to join them. But things weren't moving as smoothly as they might have hoped. The Leicester board simply refused to let Leeds talk to O'Neill and there had also been an unexpected reaction among the Leeds fans. David O'Leary's decision not to jump ship with George Graham but to stay on as caretaker even though he knew he wasn't the board's first choice and might face the sack if O'Neill took over, struck a chord with the supporters. As he took his place on the bench for the Leicester match, they rose to their feet and started to chant: 'O'Leary! O'Leary! O'Leary!' It was completely unexpected and the Irishman said: 'After 25 years in the game you think nothing will surprise you any more but that certainly did.'

An international weekend brought a break in fixtures that would have been the ideal time for a new manager to work with the squad but instead there was deadlock. Leeds were confident O'Neill wanted to join them but couldn't talk to him because Leicester dug in their heels. Lucas felt it was all dragging on too long and for once he showed a glimpse of public irritation. Just before their next game at Nottingham Forest and a few days ahead of the trip to Rome, he said: 'We're facing a tricky and crucial part of the season and as far as the players are concerned we would ideally have liked to have had the managerial situation sorted out by this weekend. It is easy to say that as professionals we should forget about what is happening off the field and concentrate all our efforts on the pitch but it is difficult to put the manager situation out of your mind. The newspapers have daily stories about the club's bid to appoint a man to succeed George Graham and it's on television and the radio all the time as well. So it is almost impossible to escape from it.'

With nothing settled before the Forest match, O'Leary took a gamble and set out his stall for the job. In his controversial book *Leeds United on Trial*, he wrote: 'I told the players I felt I had let myself down against Leicester and that I was going to pick a team I really had faith in, even if it proved to be my last game in charge.' He made a number of changes. 'The players began to see the real David O'Leary,' he added. 'If I was going to do the job, I was going to do it my way and there was no question of simply going through the motions. If I was surplus to requirements, I'd walk out with my head held high.'

Given that Leeds had to play part of the game with ten men after Granville was sent off, a 1-1 draw was not a bad result at the City Ground and the fans seemed to react positively to the changes O'Leary had made. His chances of getting the job improved as Ridsdale became more impatient at the lack of movement at Leicester but the Irishman would have less opportunity to influence things in Rome because he was banned from the dressing room and the dug-out as punishment for an outburst in Maritimo. However, he'd prepared the squad and picked the team, so a good result would surely make him hot favourite.

Packed with top-class players, Roma were in good form and currently sitting second in Serie A. They started smoothly and eased into the lead when Marco Delvecchio shook off Lucas and ran on to a pass from Francesco Totti before firing past Nigel Martyn. Leeds gradually worked their way back into the match, a goalpost twice coming between them and the equaliser while at the other end they stood firm. Don Warters, reporting in the *YEP*, wrote: 'Radebe recovered from his slip and hardly put a foot wrong again as he fought bravely alongside Robert Molenaar to keep the talented Roma forwards out.' Despite their efforts, all looked lost when Bruno Ribeiro was sent off ten minutes into the second half for a second yellow card. Surely now Roma would brush the ten men aside? Leeds dug deep and showing bloody-minded resolve as well as considerable ability, they restricted the home side to that single goal. As Warters said it was 'an Herculean effort which has set up the prospect of a humdinger of a second leg clash at Elland Road in a couple of weeks' time.'

High in the seats of the Stadio Olimpico as the Leeds fans saluted their heroes, Ridsdale and his fellow directors had made up their mind. That gutsy performance showed the players were responding to O'Leary. He would get the job. That night, after they flew back to Leeds, Ridsdale and Jeremy Fenn went to the Irishman's house in Harrogate and asked him to be the new manager. To their amazement, O'Leary asked for time to think about it. The chairman was in shock: 'I couldn't believe it,' he admitted later. 'There we were, offering a coach with zero managerial experience the post at Leeds United, a job many would kill for, a break we knew he wanted and yet, instead of snatching our hands off, he played at procrastination.'

Over the next few months, O'Leary was often to repeat his 'aw shucks' routine, reminding people that he was just a 'naïve young manager', but his true character was clear to see that night. He'd learned well from his mentor Graham and knew better than to appear too keen, especially when the other side were now desperate to get matters settled. This was not the moment to be grateful and 'snatch their hand off', this was the chance to establish the balance of the relationship for the next few years. It took the nerve of a poker player, but O'Leary pulled it off. 'I was very flattered to have been offered a job of this magnitude for my first managerial job, but I was not given any details at that stage of what the package contained,' he told the *YEP*. 'I was not told anything about how much money would be available for spending on transfers and while personally I am not dependent on money, I was not told what my salary would be either. So I was not prepared to say yes until the details were given to me.'

In a further act of brinkmanship, O'Leary waited until after the next league game against Chelsea before announcing his decision. With Martyn injured, he played teenager Paul Robinson against one of the best attacks in England on a day when heavy rain made the pitch especially difficult for keepers. The youngster was outstanding, Leeds picked up a 0-0 draw and a new era started at Elland Road.

As far as Lucas was concerned it was the ideal solution. He liked O'Leary and had enjoyed working with him. It was the Irishman who had first dubbed him 'The Chief', a name that had instantly been taken up by his team-mates, the fans and the media. Most importantly, O'Leary's appointment meant continuity. 'David was a player here when I first came to Leeds so I've known him for quite a while. He told me what the English game was about and has helped me to develop as a centre back. I am sure he will be a great manager. He has worked well under George Graham and he obviously has a good understanding with the players,' Lucas said.

A few days later, O'Leary returned the compliment. Urging the board to give the South African a new contract, O'Leary said: 'He should never be allowed to leave. He should be put in concrete here, never mind nailed down. Lucas has no bigger supporter than me and there won't be any lack of effort on my part to keep him here.'

The manager and his captain were as one and they were to form the backbone of a period of exceptional success at Elland Road.

Chapter 21

Value for money

David O'Leary's brinkmanship with the Leeds directors paid off. He cracked open a bottle of champagne with his solicitor Michael Kennedy after they thrashed out a two and a half year deal with Peter Ridsdale that would make the Irishman one of the best-paid managers in the Premiership. He had also won a commitment that there would be money to spend on strengthening the squad.

'I got the guarantees I was looking for about transfer money,' he said. 'I don't expect to have the funds of Chelsea, Manchester United, Arsenal and Liverpool - at this stage they are in a different league. But this club is going in the right direction. I started it with George two years ago. It's got a long way to go still but we've come a long way with what we've spent.' Ridsdale, who had found George Graham hard to get close to and a bit negative when it came to how fast Leeds could progress, liked the sound of 'at this stage' with all its implications that soon United would be on a par with the top clubs in the country. The new manager shared his vision of competing at the very top quickly. 'There are no differences at all between us and I'm hoping we'll be exercising the cheque book this week,' Ridsdale enthused.

The sensation of drive and ambition around Elland Road was tangible. It was exciting for players like Lucas who already knew they were part of the future though for others it spelled the end of the line. O'Leary's sights were set high and several players like Lee Sharpe and Scottish striker Derek Lilley were soon put on the transfer list. O'Leary had long been urging Graham to unleash some of the exceptionally talented teenagers coming through United's academy but the Scot was reluctant to blood too many too quickly. O'Leary had no such inhibitions and he planned to build his own team around those kids, a few key, experienced heads like Lucas, and some high profile signings that would make the football world sit up and take notice.

The first match of the new era was a pulsating derby with Bradford City in the Worthington Cup as the League Cup was now re-branded. City were enjoying a rare spell out of football's basement leagues and the often acrimonious rivalry increased as the Bradford fans saw a chance to put one over on the arrogant lot down the road. Telling people in South Africa about the clash, Lucas compared it to a Soweto derby, reporting that in both places 'the fans are fanatical about their teams and the games seem to bring out the deepest emotional ties.' He was named man of the match as Leeds edged through 1-0.

The next game wasn't nearly as enjoyable. Leeds drew 2-2 at Derby and five minutes into the second half Lucas got caught up in a melee in the United penalty area. As he went down, Dean Sturridge accidentally fell on top of him and he felt a sharp pain in his knee. There was no way he could continue and the fear was that he had seriously damaged the ligaments. The return match with Roma was only three days away and O'Leary told the post-Derby press conference 'It would be a major blow if we had to go into Tuesday's match without Lucas because he has been fantastic for us this season. I am always concerned when we are without him, especially for such an important match.'

By the following day it was clear he would not be fit to play. The physios were able to set his mind at rest that he didn't face another eight-month lay-off but calculated he would probably be out for two or three weeks. It was still frustrating because he was playing the best football of his life and he champed at the bit as he missed the next six matches, including some that stood out as key games of the season. They included a goalless draw with Roma in which Nigel Martyn performed heroically despite carrying an injury, another defeat by Leicester this time in the Worthington Cup, and a 3-2 loss at Manchester United. Along with most other footballers, Lucas didn't like watching matches in which he should have been playing but he confessed he'd enjoyed his view from the stand at Anfield as Leeds beat Liverpool 3-1. He particularly relished seeing another youngster sensationally grab the chance he'd been given by O'Leary, Alan Smith coming off the bench and scoring with his first touch in senior football.

It was while Lucas was recovering from injury that the South African Broadcasting Corporation made special arrangements for a live satellite link to Leeds so that O'Leary could present him with the SABC Sports Personality of the Year award. He had pipped Springbok Gary Teichmann and cricketer Jonty Rhodes and proudly told the audience back home that he was dedicating the award to his parents, whose guidance had been so important in his success.

Meanwhile, South African journalists were also following a story that had even more impact back home. According to the papers, Rhoo, who many still remembered as a tall skinny kid at the Chiefs, was in demand by some of the wealthiest clubs in Europe: 'Bafana Bafana captain Lucas Radebe is about to achieve multi-millionaire status as top clubs vie for his services in the mega-rich English Premier League. The deal that is finally clinched could make Radebe one of South Africa's richest sportsmen.'

The English press were equally interested and noted that many of the biggest clubs were tracking the Leeds defender. Lucas was believed to be top of Gerard Houllier's wish list at Liverpool, ahead of his eventual signing Sami Hypia, and reports linking Lucas with a move to Spurs wouldn't go away. Graham was said to be lining up a £4 million bid. 'George can line up what he likes, Lucas is going nowhere,' O'Leary said, clearly peeved in case his star defender should be unsettled before Leeds had managed to negotiate a new deal. Stories out of Italy revealed that several Serie A sides, including Lazio, were so impressed by Lucas's display against Roma that they wanted to sign him. Then there was Manchester United. Alex Ferguson had a track record of stirring things up by letting it be known he was interested in signing one of Leeds' top players just before the sides met. He'd done it in the past with Gary McAllister and sure enough, in the week United were due to go to Old Trafford, a story appeared saying he was thinking of signing Lucas. 'To be honest, I think everyone should be interested in Lucas because he is such a good player,' O'Leary said. 'But I can assure everybody that the club will be making Lucas a fantastic offer to sign a new, long contract with us. Whatever happens, Lucas will be here for the 18 months which still remain on his present contract.'

In fact, Lucas had made up his mind: providing the new contract was as good as Leeds were hinting, he wanted to stay. He and his family were settled in the area; he was at the peak of his form and enjoying his football; he was respected and liked by the club officials, the new manager and the rest of the coaching staff, his fellow players and the fans; he was captain of a club that was clearly going places. Why would he want to move? Nevertheless, he recognised that this was probably the most important contract of his career, so it had to be right. There was nothing to be gained by rushing.

Lucas's adviser Gary Blumberg was in his strongest negotiating position yet and determined his client would finally get the rewards his talent deserved. As the talks dragged on a few fans started to get anxious that their skipper might be wavering, perhaps considering a better offer. Blumberg sensed Ridsdale and Fenn were so confident Lucas wouldn't leave that they were not taking his demands seriously enough so he quickly let it be known that while Lucas felt great loyalty to Leeds, loyalty went both ways. The United captain deserved to be paid the going rate for a player of his quality and if Leeds wouldn't match that, then other clubs were keen to step in. That was enough to make the club move. They told the local media that the gap between what they had offered and what Blumberg had asked for was not great and the deal was duly completed early in December. It was reported that Lucas had doubled his salary to £20,000 a week and become one of the best-paid players in the club's history. The increased money brought security and, of course, a lifestyle he couldn't even have imagined as a kid in Diepkloof. In addition, it allowed him to help all his family back home and pay for them to come over and visit him regularly.

These were the early stages of the exponential rise in footballers' salaries that was about to threaten the balance sheets of several clubs, including Leeds, and created a gap between player and fan that was unbreachable, and to many, unfathomable. With the game awash with money, no one expected a return to the days when superstars like John Charles travelled to matches on the same bus as the fans but many feared things had gone too far. Only a month after Lucas put pen to paper there was a howl of protest from football followers when it was announced that Robbie Fowler was to be paid £35,000 a week at Liverpool. Yet, despite the fact that he was now earning more in a week than many of the Leeds fans were paid in a year, Lucas never suffered any form of backlash. United supporters knew the journey he had made to get where he was, the effort and the sacrifices involved. They also knew that he always gave everything to the cause, and put his body through pain in order to play for the team. Furthermore, he was a 'top man', he always had a moment for the supporters, spent time after matches signing autographs, and it was becoming increasingly apparent that he was one of the United players who was heavily involved in the club's community activities. The Chief, they believed, earned every penny he made.

Back in the treatment room, Lucas's injury was taking a frustratingly long time to heal. He had a setback when the knee didn't stand up to a reserve match against Birmingham City and he had to come off after an hour. O'Leary was getting desperate at a growing injury list in his already small squad and the problem was especially acute in defence. Martin Hiden had picked up knee ligament damage against Manchester United that put him out of action for a year so Lucas was hurried back for a 4-0 win over West Ham. He battled through that game but damaged his knee once more in the following match against Coventry. Twice he went down in agony and each time gingerly got to his feet and finished the game but he paid a price and had to sit out another five Leeds matches and miss South Africa's Nelson Mandela challenge against Egypt.

By the time Lucas was close to a comeback, Leeds had slipped from third to fifth in the table and been held to a goalless draw in the FA Cup at Football Conference side Rushden & Diamonds. The Leeds squad, as O'Leary regularly pointed out, was down to the 'bare bones.' Robert Molenaar had been stretchered off at Arsenal and was out for the season; David Batty's enthusiastically welcomed return to the club where he had started his career stalled when he picked up a rib injury, Stephen McPhail and Bruno Ribeiro were struggling with knocks and Jonathan Woodgate suffered a thigh strain. Lucas played for an hour in a reserve game and felt he could go on but the physios didn't want to risk it. The following day, the knee still felt good so it was decided he could return in the FA Cup replay against Rushden. The non-league outfit took an early lead but United's class eventually showed and they went through 3-1. Lucas felt rusty at first and a bit tentative about aggravating his injury. But gradually he got into the rhythm and pace of the match and by the end was feeling comfortable. The knee stood up to the test without any problems, which was just as well because he was in for a hectic second half to the season with matches coming thick and fast for Leeds and South Africa.

Chapter 22
Jet setter

On 18 January 1999, Leeds produced what Lucas described as 'one of our best performances since I joined the club' in beating Middlesbrough 2-0 with the rapidly emerging Lee Bowyer outstanding. But Lucas hardly had time to savour the win before dashing to Manchester Airport where he met up with Mark Fish to fly to Johannesburg. The following day, he was a guest at Fish's wedding and within 24 hours the pair of them joined up with the Bafana squad to fly to Mauritius for an African Cup of Nations qualifier.

Like David O'Leary at Leeds, Trott Moloto was giving young players their head and even though they only managed a 1-1 draw in a game they were expected to win, Lucas was impressed by some of his new international team-mates. He enjoyed the excitement and energy generated by talented youngsters and he got a kick out of guiding them and helping them improve. 'The likes of Bradley Carnell, Sibusiso Zuma, Benni McCarthy and Quinton Fortune are developing into fine players with potentially bright futures in international football,' he said.

From the heat of Mauritius, Lucas returned to Yorkshire where another bunch of youngsters was exceeding expectations but struggling for consistency. After a couple of defeats in the league, they faced a mouth-watering FA Cup tie against Spurs that would bring George Graham back to Elland Road for the first time. While Leeds's main priority was a high Premiership finish to qualify for Europe again, the FA Cup presented an alternative route and a realistic opportunity for silverware so it was always going to be a big match, whoever they faced. The Graham factor added extra spice to the mix.

On the evening before the match Feziwe went into labour and Lucas drove her at top speed to the hospital. He needn't have rushed. At 3.30am she persuaded him that the birth wasn't imminent and he should go home and get some rest. He hardly seemed to have got to sleep when he was awakened at ten the next morning by a phone call from the maternity ward saying that if he wanted to see his child born, he had better hurry back. He raced to Fezi's side and marvelled as a fine son, Lucas Hugo, was born at around half past 11. It was hard for Lucas to drag himself away and he arrived at Elland Road just in time to lead the side out. It was a cagey game against a team predictably well organised by Graham.

Switched to right-back, Lucas kept Spurs' dangerman David Ginola quiet but neither side could get on top and the 1-1 draw added a replay to Lucas's exhausting schedule.

O'Leary's 'babies' were hitting form at just the right time. They played with little fear, relishing their success, safe in the knowledge that down the spine of the team they had the experience of Nigel Martyn, Lucas and, hopefully soon, David Batty to bail them out when they got in trouble. Two good wins improved their league position before the replay at White Hart Lane but this time Leeds were always second best.

There was no chance for Lucas to dwell on the 2-0 defeat. He had a plane to catch. South Africa had given special permission for him to miss their Castle Cup game against Botswana and play against Spurs on the Wednesday night even though they faced an African Cup of Nations qualifier against Gabon the following Saturday. The only available plane meant a stop over in Milan, cutting down any chance of resting on the flight. It was Lucas's 50th cap and he led Bafana Bafana to a 4-1 win. But there was scarcely time to show the family photos of the new baby before he was heading for the airport again because, with Woodgate suspended, Leeds needed him to play against Leicester on the Monday night.

Faced with the prospect of three games in six days on two continents, with many hours in the air in between, Lucas joked: 'I'm looking forward to it. The plane trips will let me catch up on some much needed sleep I have lost since the baby was born!' More seriously he explained: 'It will be very hard and tiring but I owe it to both my country and to Leeds United to play in every game if possible. It is the price I pay but I am willing to pay it.' In years to come, the true cost to his body would become clear.

Lucas only had two hours from the final whistle in Pretoria to travel the 30-odd miles to his flight at Johannesburg and not surprisingly, he arrived too late. Once again he had put himself under stress by accepting a crazy schedule but also by his inability to turn his back on anyone. Even though he was up against the clock, he admitted, he'd felt forced to stay and sign some autographs for adoring South African fans. 'It was a great honour for me to win my 50th cap. I was delighted with the way we played, and the fans after the game were unbelievable. They were really happy that we'd won and were so supportive it made it hard for us to leave the ground,' he said. Lucas's life would have been a lot easier and probably his body would have suffered a lot less pain if he had occasionally followed the example of less considerate sports stars and ignored the fans. But in his view, this was what came with the territory of being a highly-paid international footballer and you just got on with it.

Instead of arriving back on Sunday as planned, it was Monday morning before Lucas touched down in England. He was immediately whisked off to join his team-mates at their hotel in Leicester. A brief sleep didn't really help much but he shrugged off his weariness and led United to a 2-1 win at Filbert Street. Even he wasn't quite sure how he'd coped with the last six days. 'It was quite an experience. One I hope I never have to repeat,' Lucas reflected later. 'By the time the match at Leicester finished, even though we won, the only thing I could think of was getting to bed – and as quickly as possible. When we got back home I went straight to bed and slept through the night and all through Tuesday and the following morning as well.'

The victory over Leicester was followed by a revenge win over Spurs in the league and three more impressive displays saw Leeds in fourth place in the table and on course for a UEFA Cup place. Indeed, they were only two points behind Chelsea who were a further point behind Arsenal. Manchester United were clear of all three and hot favourites to be champions but a top three spot and Champions League place next season was a realistic and heady possibility. Even though Graham was picking up his first silverware at Tottenham in the form of the Worthington Cup, it still looked as though Lucas's decision to stay at Leeds had been a good one. The team had won their last seven matches in a row, equalling a club record that stretched back to the 1973-74 season. Their chance to break it would come when Liverpool arrived at Elland Road, a match that SkySports TV had insisted be switched to Monday 12 April, Lucas's 30th birthday. There would be little chance to celebrate – he was facing another madcap journey to and from Africa for an African Cup of Nations qualifier in Gabon on the tenth. It was not lost on Lucas that he had been able to go home to South Africa for a few days just two weeks before because there was an international break in England. If FIFA officials only got their act together and co-ordinated the international calendar, that could have been the weekend South Africa took on Gabon. But as usual, the problems of the players didn't come into the bureaucrats' calculations.

Bafana Bafana lost 1-0 to a last-minute penalty. It was a sickening result that even neutrals agreed was in large part due to some woeful refereeing. South Africa were on top throughout and had two solid penalty appeals turned down only to be hit by an injury-time sucker punch when the official awarded the home side a very dubious spot kick. Lucas was seething as he raced to the airport to catch a plane to Paris where United had a private jet waiting to whisk him back to Yorkshire. He touched down at Leeds-Bradford airport at 8am on the Sunday and spent most of the day in bed trying to give his body the maximum rest before the match. O'Leary was sympathetic but resolute. Agreeing it was no way to prepare for such a big match, he said: 'Bearing in mind the way Liverpool play with Michael Owen and Robbie Fowler up front, we really need Lucas in the team.'

It was a mark of the new respect Leeds were being given in the Premiership that Liverpool came to shut up shop, hoping to grab a goal on the break. O'Leary's men weren't experienced enough to break the deadlock and the game ended 0-0 with Lucas getting the SkySports pundits' vote as man of the match. Two more draws in a row as good as killed off United's hopes of a Champions League place but the UEFA cup was still a strong possibility and there was optimism in the camp, particularly after the second of those matches saw them hold Manchester United despite being forced to play teenage midfielder Matthew Jones in the unaccustomed right-back role, up against Ryan Giggs. The star of the show was another teenager, Jonathan Woodgate, and the youngster gave an insight into how United's young players viewed Lucas when he told the press: 'He's a great player to play alongside because he makes it so easy for you. I learn from him every single day, not only about football, but in other ways. He is not only a dedicated trainer and player, he always has a smile on his face. He helps pick you up when you're down – though he can hand out a rollicking too if he thinks it's necessary.'

Lucas climbed aboard yet another plane, this time heading for a friendly in Denmark where Bafana Bafana were keen to see if they had improved from when the sides met in the World Cup. In fact the result was an identical 1-1 draw and when Lucas got back to Leeds, O'Leary wasn't best pleased to find that he'd played the full 90 minutes when he was only supposed to play one half. With two weeks left of the season, United faced four more games including West Ham, who were still pushing for a European place, Arsenal and Chelsea, the sides immediately above them, before rounding things off at Coventry.

They thrashed West Ham 5-1 but went down 1-0 at Chelsea, which finally confirmed they couldn't overhaul the Londoners in the table. The final home game was against Arsenal and despite all the denials from Lucas and O'Leary, conspiracy theorists were convinced Leeds would go easy on the Gunners rather than do Manchester United a favour in the title race. There was only one way to kill the story off and Leeds did it brilliantly, beating Arsenal 1-0 with Lucas and Woodgate again the outstanding players as the Gunners threw forward Kanu and Diawara to join Anelka and Bergkamp in a bid to salvage something from the game. In the *YEP*, Don Warters paid the pair the compliment of comparing them to the best Arsenal defences, highlighting the moments when 'the United captain cleared off the line from Bergkamp while Woodgate headed a bullet shot from substitute Diawara off the line.'

A lifelong Arsenal supporter, Lucas's adviser Gary Blumberg sat and admired the outstanding performance from his client and his young sidekick but wished they had saved it for another occasion! But the Leeds fans were ecstatic and gave the team a standing ovation as they made their annual lap of honour. At last they felt they had a team that could perhaps deliver the kind of success they craved. Lucas's smile had seldom been wider. 'We took on the reigning champions, a side that still has the chance of winning the title, who were desperate to win and we gave them their first defeat in five months,' he exclaimed. 'We have proved that we are capable of competing with the best but we have to show we can do it on a regular basis if we are to challenge the top three for the major honours.'

With the UEFA Cup place safe, O'Leary made seven changes for the final game at Coventry and what Lucas described as 'the best season since I joined the club' came to an end with a 2-2 draw. Of course it was not yet finished for Lucas, who still had two more matches to play for South Africa. He'd been excused a tour of the West Indies, when Trott Moloto tried out some new, home-based players, but the captain was required for an African Cup of Nations qualifier against Mauritius in Durban.

Once again he boarded a plane and headed south. Bafana Bafana beat Mauritius 2-0 and so made sure they qualified for the finals. Moloto excused Lucas from playing in the final qualifier in Angola two weeks later but he did turn out in a friendly against Zimbabwe and squeezed in a trip to Australia to team up with George Weah, Zinedine Zidane and Marcelle Desailly for an exhibition match against the Socceroos to mark the opening of the Sydney Olympic stadium. Since returning from injury against Rushden & Diamonds on 13 January, Lucas had played 27 games and flown something like 85,000 miles. He was ready for a holiday.

Chapter 23

One for the archives

Lucas may have felt like enjoying a long, lazy rest while the sun recharged his batteries and aching limbs restored themselves, but even though David O'Leary gave him a few days' longer break than the rest of the Leeds players, he still only had three weeks before he joined the squad at their pre-season camp in Sweden. There were plenty of new people to get to know. O'Leary had set out his stall to buy talented, young, mainly English players who he could mould into the team of his vision; 'I don't want a ready-made team, I want a young side that will grow together and make Leeds proud,' he said. Since taking over from George Graham, he had only made one significant signing, paying £4.4 million for David Batty, but by the time Lucas arrived in Sweden a further £20 million had been splashed out and central defender Michael Duberry, full-back Danny Mills, midfielder Eirik Bakke and striker Michael Bridges had arrived. They were soon followed by pacy winger Darren Huckerby and yet another central defender, Danny Hay from New Zealand.

Lucas was excited at the potential of a squad bristling with energy, skill and ambition and he noted the terrific spirit that was already apparent in the camp. The squad had its fair share of practical jokers, which was great for generating camaraderie. The only jarring note to the harmony came from Jimmy Hasselbaink, who felt he was undervalued. The previous season, he had been the joint winner of the golden boot, awarded to the top league goalscorer, and felt he deserved not only to be the highest paid player in the club, but the highest by some margin. What's more, he insisted he should remain the top earner all the time he remained at the club. Hasselbaink was digging in his heels over a new contract, demanding £40,000 a week. When the fans got wind of it, they turned against the Dutchman, and some wrote letters of protest to the *YEP* with more than one declaring it would be an insult to Lucas if another player were to be paid more than him. Jimmy was in danger of creating disharmony in the camp and O'Leary finally decided to lance the boil and sell his top scorer. The Dutchman signed an extremely lucrative contract with Atletico Madrid while Leeds banked a £12 million transfer fee, giving them a £10 million profit over what they had paid for him.

Hasselbaink's departure put a massive onus on the young shoulders of Harry

Kewell, Alan Smith and Michael Bridges, who would be expected to come up with the goals. But that wouldn't be easy as the opening game of the season showed. Leeds' new status as a genuine title contender had changed the way opponents approached them. Derby County came to Elland Road with the aim of not getting beaten rather than trying to win the match and United battered against a mass defence in vain.

It was harder for teams to follow Derby's example when they were at home and the extra space Southampton gave Leeds at the Dell allowed United to carve open chance after chance. Bridges made his £5 million price tag look like money well spent when he grabbed all three goals that beat the Saints. So far Lucas had hardly had to break sweat but that changed when they visited Old Trafford. Despite going down 2-0, Leeds did enough to suggest they had reduced the gap between the two sides and Lucas felt optimistic as he flew home to play in a special match to mark Nelson Mandela's retirement as President of South Africa.

As it was a friendly, Leeds did not have to release Lucas, but they knew that nothing would stop him appearing in this match. Players travelled from around the world for the honour of taking part. Significantly played at Ellis Park, the home of Springbok Rugby Union where at one stage you would have been hard-pressed to see a black face in the crowd, the football was secondary. This was a celebration and thank you to the man who made the long walk to freedom without bitterness and then united a country torn apart by racial bigotry and inequality. The monumental task was far from over but Madiba had decided to hand over the day-to-day running of his country and Lucas was proud to be one of those chosen to mark the occasion.

As one of his country's most high-profile citizens, Lucas now found himself in the public eye for more than just his football prowess. No matter how often he and 1996 Miss South Africa, Peggy-Sue Kumalo, denied that their relationship was anything more than just a friendship, the gossip columnists pointed to photographs of the pair leaving a restaurant in London together and hinted at romance.

The other perennial fascination of society journalists round the world is, of course, money and a breathless column in the *Sowetan* spelled out what they thought Lucas must be earning in wages, bonuses and endorsements. It concluded: 'Radebe's total earnings are around R11.8 million a year, more than the entire South African cricket team and more than the combined salary of the first, second and third highest-paid rugby players on the planet.' But just as in England, there was no sense that this was undeserved: 'The perfectly timed tackle, the soaring header, the cleverly planned interception, the brave block:

these are the tools of Radebe's trade and the millions he has started to earn clearly represent his value.'

Back in England, a vibrant 2-1 win over Sunderland had Leeds fans wondering just how far this team could go. A story leaked out afterwards that demonstrated why Lucas was such a favourite among fans and perhaps suggests why they never felt he was overpaid. Before flying to the Mandela match, he'd spent some time at Thorp Arch with a group of young South African footballers who were visiting England. Although still weary from the return flight and the match against Sunderland, he spent another hour with the lads, signing autographs and having his picture taken. That was more than many players would have done but Lucas went even further and invited the whole group to a braai at his home the next day. It was all done without fuss and without telling anyone, and only came to light when the group got home and sent the club a letter thanking them for their hospitality.

O'Leary was concerned that expectations should be kept to a reasonable level – he rated his goal of a top three Champions League spot as very ambitious – and he pointed to the next performance against Liverpool as a prime example of what he meant. Leeds were dreadful and completely outplayed by Gerard Houllier's men. The 2-1 scoreline came nowhere near reflecting how one-sided the game was, with Titi Camara giving Danny Mills a torrid time, and United players losing their personal battles across the piece. To his dismay, Lucas gifted Liverpool their winner when he sliced a Patrick Berger centre into his own net.

In public O'Leary claimed it was no more than he had expected – 'maybe this will bring a few people within the club and outside who think we are going to win the title down to earth. We have a lot of very young players and they still have a lot to learn,' he said. But privately the Leeds boss was furious and let his side know it at the end of the game. 'David had a right go at us in the dressing room,' Lucas revealed. 'I've never seen him that angry. But he had every right to be like that. I don't blame him for such a rollicking because we couldn't get anything right.' O'Leary cancelled days off for the next week, bringing the team in for extra training. They might be 'naïve babies' but he was determined they wouldn't stay that way for long. It was time for them to move up to the next level.

And move on they did. At times playing almost carefree football, Leeds won seven of the next eight matches – the other a memorable 4-4 draw, played in pouring rain at Everton, which had the two managers tearing their hair out but sent the crowd home buzzing with excitement. The run included a win over Spurs and a victory against Newcastle where Lucas faced the inevitable physical battle with Alan Shearer, which included being caught in the face by a flying elbow, resulting in a verbal volley for the England striker. Then they beat Watford 2-1 and took over top spot in the Premiership. No matter how often O'Leary warned them it was still early days, United fans were dreaming of silverware. Lucas too was wondering if this might be the season when he picked up his first winners medal in England.

In addition to the their league form, Leeds knocked Blackburn out of the League Cup and were enjoying success in their UEFA Cup campaign, which got off to a memorable start for Lucas in Holland. United were drawn against Partizan Belgrade and after some dithering, UEFA finally decided it was too dangerous for the first leg to be staged in the Serbian capital after the recent Balkan conflict so they switched the match to the Abe Lenstra stadium in Heerenveen in the north of Holland. Leeds knew little about their opponents; their scouts had been unable to take a look at Partizan and they'd received no videos. So, O'Leary decided to pack the midfield and take a careful look, before being too adventurous. United started well with Kelly hitting the bar and Bridges shooting just wide but they went a goal down when Martyn parried a shot into the path of an onrushing forward. Leeds hit back with an equaliser from Bowyer but then Lucas got caught out and brought down Kezman and the referee pointed to the penalty shot. To the South African's great relief, Martyn again saved his blushes with a superb save.

The next telling action has entered the archives as one of Leeds United's most memorable moments. They were awarded a free-kick and for once, instead of being the defender to stay back at set-pieces, Lucas went up into the Partizan penalty area – 'He had to ask one of us the way!' Hopkin joked. Harte swung in a measured cross towards Woodgate, who climbed above his marker and flicked on. In his eagerness to get into the danger area, Lucas tripped. He landed on his backside, just as the ball dipped towards him. Instinctively he raised a leg and managed to hook the ball into the net. For a moment he was stunned. Then, as his laughing team-mates raced towards him, a massive smile creased his face.

Bowyer added a third for Leeds towards the end but all the talk was of that goal. The next time Lucas drove into Leeds' Thorp Arch training ground, last to arrive as usual, he was greeted by the sight of his team-mates sitting on the floor waving their legs in the air like demented crabs. Feigning hurt feelings, Lucas told laughing journalists: 'No one will listen when I tell them the move which led to that goal is practised in training every day – a Hartey free-kick, Woody flick-on and me finishing like a demon. The fact that I was on my back and put it in with an overhead kick only serves to demonstrate my striking prowess. The strikers better watch out now, I'm out to steal their thunder. I'm going to be one of the glory boys.'

Leeds finished the job with a 1-0 win at Elland Road and were drawn against Lokomotiv Moscow in the second round. Despite picking up a knee injury and being stretchered off with a thigh strain at Watford, Lucas was determined to keep battling on especially as Martin Hiden was still some way from being fit and Michael Duberry was also injured. The Russians arrived at Elland Road with a big reputation but the next day the *YEP's* new United reporter Phil Rostron declared: 'Leeds United passed their European examination with distinction last night, and in the process, lowered a 68-year-old club record of consecutive victories. Their 4-1 defeat of Lokomotiv Moscow surpassed the wildest dreams and set Elland Road alight as United waltzed to a breathtaking tenth successive victory in all competitions.'

Lucas was teased by his team-mates at the prospect of a trip to Moscow for the second leg. Knowing how much he hated the cold, they 'volunteered' him to be photographed in the fur Cossack hat when the press asked for the inevitable picture. The freezing temperatures on match night – kick-off wasn't until 9pm to accommodate British TV – made Lucas's early experiences at the Shay seem like balmy holidays. But Leeds cruised to a 3-0 win and a large section of the 1,000 or so travelling supporters convinced the Muscovites that the British really are crazy by stripping to the waist at half-time and waving their shirts in the air.

It was early November – far too early to start making claims - but it was already clear this was no ordinary team. With people like Lucas, Martyn and Batty to provide the steadiness, the rest were free to express themselves. Their enthusiasm rubbed off on the older players and the whole unit performed like a side who really enjoyed playing football, who had never heard the word pressure, or considered the possibility of failure. Incredibly they had achieved an unbeaten run that not even the great Revie side, so full of talent, guile and experience, had managed. Lucas was far too canny to make any extravagant claims but he was proud to captain this vibrant group and admitted: 'This young team of ours amazes me. Just when you think that an obstacle is put in their way, all they do is knock it over.'

The late departure from Moscow, the time difference and probably the heady feeling of invincibility took their toll and Leeds' record breaking run came to an end in the least glamorous of fixtures, away to Wimbledon. O'Leary used the defeat to make the point that as exciting as his team was, his squad wasn't nearly big enough to cope with the number of games they would face. He needed more players and he had every reason to believe that he would be getting them because it was not only football supporters who were sitting up and taking notice of what was happening at Leeds. Investors were homing in on them as an exciting prospect and Rupert Murdoch's BskyB company negotiated a deal to be the club's media partner which boosted United's coffers by £9.2 million. Leeds also had companies queuing up to put their name on the team shirts and Bulmers Cider finally paid £6 million to have Strongbow on players' chests for the next three years.

Lucas was captain of a club that was on the brink of joining the elite of Europe. He was proud of what they had achieved in such a short time and he was also proud of the difference they were making off the pitch.

Chapter 24

Mentioned in Parliament

Three stories appeared in the *YEP* in the early months of 2001 that go a long way to showing how much more than just a star footballer Lucas had become in both Leeds and South Africa. In the first, feature writer Anne Pickles berated critics of David Beckham, pointing out that for all his faults, the England captain was a much better influence on kids than the likes of pop stars Eminem, Robbie Williams and Liam Gallagher. She then reminded readers that Leeds United had their own outstanding role model in Lucas: 'a good egg with the welfare and future of children firmly set on his personal agenda…He is a man determined to lead by example and therefore one who fully appreciates the inspirational value of what he does,' she wrote.

At an apparently more trivial, yet in reality deeply significant level, a story about a United supporter told of his five-month-old son, named Lucas. That white youngster is one of several in the Leeds area who when asked how he got his unusual name will shrug and say: 'My mum and dad were United fans. They loved Lucas Radebe.'

Finally there was a report of a tour of South Africa by two members of Leeds United's staff to talk about an educational initiative that had proved successful in England and which was now being considered in other countries. It was sponsored by the British Council and in choosing Emma Stanford and Steve Smith, they were not only getting two of the most influential people in the scheme's success but the added bonus that fans, clubs, educationalists and potential sponsors in South Africa would all be keen to talk to people from Rhoo's club.

The trip to South Africa was the latest acknowledgement of how far Leeds United had turned round their community involvement in recent years and just as he had been at the heart of Leeds' growing success on the pitch, Lucas was again an important figure in Community United. According to Emma Joussemet, then Stanford, who created the department and was its driving force, Lucas was one of the major factors in making it such a groundbreaking success.

Like most football clubs in the early 1990s Leeds United took very little notice of the local community beyond selling them tickets to matches and sending a few, often ill-prepared and under-equipped ex-professionals into schools to do some coaching. United fans were considered among the worst in Britain, both for violence and racism. But apart from issuing a few half-hearted statements of disapproval, the club felt there was little they could do. It was mainly 'society's' problem.

Caspian's takeover of Leeds United saw that attitude start to change. Partly it was a straightforward business decision – Leeds wanted planning permission for their ambitious arena scheme, which was vehemently opposed by many of the residents near the stadium. People living close to Elland Road felt the club did little for them. The directors lived in affluent north Leeds and didn't give a thought to the poorer south side of the city. The local council saw an opportunity and hinted that approval for the arena was much more likely to be forthcoming if the club were to take a little more care of their own back yard. But the change in approach was not entirely cynical. People like Jeremy Fenn and Peter Ridsdale were from a corporate background where it was considered normal and cost-effective for companies to invest time and effort in their local area and they, along with fellow director David Spencer, could see the advantages of putting some resources into a proper community department.

The takeover coincided with a government initiative to use youngsters' passion for sport to persuade them to do better at school by linking education to their favourite football club. Three Premiership clubs were approached to run a trial and when one dropped out, United enthusiastically took up the challenge. The first thing they did was to hire Emma, who had been involved in community work with Northern Dance. They then spent £2 million creating a welcoming, well-equipped 'school' running the width of the pitch under Elland Road's South Stand. No blackboards and no rows and rows of desks here; instead, state of the art computers, big pictures of United stars on the wall, even football magazines among the books on the shelves. Steve Smith, one of the most innovative teachers in the area, came on board as head of the study services.

'It was one of those rare occasions when a big idea and the right people with energy, understanding of what was possible and the funds to make it work all came together at the same time. And Lucas was an important factor in that,' Emma said. 'Community United would not have been nearly as successful if the Leeds players had not been involved and I was lucky because soon after I arrived George Graham made Lucas captain. I went up to talk to him and he immediately understood what we were attempting to do and was always ready to help out. There were a lot of young players at the club at the time and if Lucas had been indifferent, they would have probably followed his lead. But because he set the example, many of them came on board too.'

While the Learning Centre and Playing for Success were the flagship projects, with children from 23 primary schools producing spectacular improvements in their literacy, numeracy and IT skills, Community United quickly expanded its sphere of influence and at the height of its power employed 30 full-time and 25 part-time staff – more than the club's commercial department - and recruited 100 volunteer mentors. They gave supporters a voice through fans' forums, improved the facilities for the disabled, helped channel the work of charities and went a long way to tackle the scourge of racism both through their own activities and support for the national Kick It Out campaign.

All this meant extra work for Lucas, visiting schools, talking to children at the Learning Centre, handing out awards, raising the profile of charities, and spending time after the match with groups like Leeds United's Disability Organisation. 'He was always the first to volunteer and the great thing was that he didn't have to be briefed – he found it easy to mix with people and always said the right thing,' Emma said.

It seems obvious that Lucas would be at the forefront of United's anti-racism campaign and he was, but it wasn't always in the way that might be expected from someone who grew up under the apartheid regime. Lucas would talk about his childhood and the injustices that he and his comrades felt but when it came to racism in English football he hadn't personally experienced very much – two of his later team-mates, Frenchman Olivier Dacourt and Croatian-born Australian Mark Viduka, had much more harrowing stories to tell. And yet he remained a potent symbol. It was as though by becoming so admired as a player and loved as a person, he was a living cxample of the futility of racism.

Leeds United used this to help get over their message time and time again, not least when they faced a major problem with some of their supporters whose latest bout of racism involved a visit to Elland Road by Leicester City. The Midlands city has a high proportion of Asian residents and a small group of Leeds followers chanted inflammatory, anti-Asian songs. There was widespread condemnation across the country and once again United's reputation was dragged through the mud. With a visit to Filbert Street coming up, Leeds' management were desperate to avoid a repetition and Emma recalled: 'We hit on the idea of a personal message from Peter Ridsdale and Lucas as chairman and captain. They were probably the two most respected people in the club and of course, as a black South African, Lucas's words carried extra power. We produced a leaflet with a plea from both of them to cut out racist chants and handed them out at the turnstiles as people went into the ground. Our press officer, Liz Dimitrievicz, and I sat among the fans to monitor the reaction and it was one of the most satisfying moments I can remember at the club. They behaved so well that at the end of the match, the Leicester City stadium manager went on the tannoy and thanked them.'

Working closely with Lucas, Emma had plenty of chance to get to know him and to witness the impact he was able to have on people's lives. Like most people who met him, she was instantly charmed, enjoyed his sense of humour and admired his selfless dedication. She also recalled that he helped her settle into a job that could be intimidating to a newcomer. 'As I was to learn, footballers in a group love to try to tease people, especially women, and at times they seemed to enjoy making you feel uncomfortable. Lucas always had a twinkle in his eye yet somehow the fact that he was there meant it was not as threatening as it might have been. There was something reassuring about his presence that made you feel safe.'

While Emma often saw the effect of Lucas's personality on people around Leeds, she only really appreciated how much of an icon he was in South Africa when she and Steve Smith made two visits to the country to talk about the Learning Centre and Playing for Success. Everyone was keen to talk to these people who worked with Rhoo. His name opened many doors and got things done. Perhaps the most bizarre occasion was when they were invited to watch a soccer tournament in Johannesburg. Their host for the day turned up late, arriving in a squeal of brakes and driving right up to the main entrance where he parked his car on the pavement. When a policeman approached him to move it, he protested that Steve and Emma were personal friends of Lucas Radebe and if there was any trouble it was important that they could get to the car quickly. 'Rhoo will be very angry if you make me move the car and something happens to his friends,' he said. And the policeman allowed the car to stay where it was.

But the influence Lucas had at home went far beyond helping latecomers use an illegal parking spot. He was probably an even greater role model there than in Leeds. The fact that he was able to captain a Premiership side was proof that with the right attitude and hard work, everything was possible. And just as in England he used his influence to good effect. Nowhere was this more apparent than when, following the 1998 World Cup, FIFA invited him to be their ambassador in South Africa to SOS Children's Villages. He immediately jumped at the idea. Having benefited from his own home upbringing, he was impressed by the fact that rather than keep orphaned and abandoned children in large institutions, the charity provides communities in which the children live in smaller, family-style units. He became a powerful voice on behalf of the SOS. He visited most of their villages in South Africa whenever he went home, was an enthusiastic fundraiser and spread the word back in England. Thanks to Lucas, Community United arranged a book collection and sent more than 3,000 children's books to villages in South Africa. And Leeds fan Kathy Darley was so impressed by what she read in the club's matchday programme about his SOS work, that she threw herself into raising money and took a three-month sabbatical from work to go to South Africa and work in the villages.

Lucas is, of course, not alone among footballers in spending time working for the good of the community and promoting charities but it is doubtful if many have been as wholehearted or successful at it as he. Certainly not many have had their efforts acknowledged in the House of Commons. In his fulsome praise the work of Community United in a debate in February 2002, Colin Burgon the MP for Elmet, near Leeds, quoted something Nelson Mandela had said to Lucas: 'We can reach far more people through sport than we can through political or educational programmes. In this way, sport is more powerful than politics.' And later the MP added: 'Lucas Radebe has been centrally involved with the Leeds United campaign against racism. Along with fellow players such as Olivier Dacourt, Mark Viduka and Rio Ferdinand, he has visited schools to talk about the need to combat racism.'

Lucas has never made a big deal about his community work. It is his way of showing how grateful he is for the chances he has been given and even if there are moments when the demands cut across things he would like to do for himself, he always remembers why he became involved in the first place. 'I want to excel in everything I do. I want to be somebody who makes a difference in life. There is nothing better than giving back. Sometimes you can have everything but you have to be aware of your responsibilities.'

Chapter 25

Three for a tenner

Lucas had picked up a third European yellow card in the victory over Lokomotiv Moscow so while his team-mates headed back to the Russian capital to face Spartak Moscow and temperatures of minus 20 degrees, he caught a plane to Pretoria and a friendly against Sweden played in warm sunshine. The difference did not go unnoticed among his colleagues and even though he pointed out that he had received the booking before he knew they would be returning to Moscow, there were still a few who laughed and shook their head knowingly.

The Nelson Mandela challenge was one of those international matches that Lucas might normally have considered missing and certainly David O'Leary was keen that his star defender should politely tell his country he wasn't available. But there was much more riding on this than another entry in the record books – South Africa's ruling body was using every match to push their bid to host the World Cup in 2006. The voting was now only a few months away and South Africa was among the front-runners. Their infrastructure, match-staging ability and the enthusiasm of the fans would all be on show, and it was just as important that the team demonstrated it was good enough to be the host nation. SAFA wanted the best team possible to turn out and certainly wanted their highly respected captain on hand to meet and greet all the high profile FIFA guests.

Lucas felt it was his duty to be there, supporting the bid. The idea of South Africa hosting the 2006 World Cup had appealed to him when it was first put forward in 1996, although in those days he was thinking mainly in terms of what a great experience it would be as a player. But as his reputation grew, especially in Europe, he became something of an unofficial spokesman for the bid, never missing the chance to push the fairness of Africa at last staging the event and particularly the reasons South Africa was the logical country on the continent to receive the honour.

One of the main opponents was England, who felt it would be just perfect to take the World Cup back to the birthplace of football 40 years after it had last staged and won the competition. As well as boasting of their own preparedness, part of England's campaign involved pointing out the high crime levels and violence in South Africa, conveniently playing down the dismal record of some England fans who had taken drunken loutishness and violent chaos to a new level wherever they went.

Some of the adverse publicity drummed up against South Africa at the very least hinted at paternalism and could be interpreted as colonial. Even Tony Blair's bid envoy, left-wing MP Tony Banks, sounded condescending when he claimed the rivalry between England and South Africa was friendly but added: 'If they are successful then we will offer whatever assistance and professional advice necessary.' The 'dark continent' surely couldn't stage something this big without the help of England!

Lucas was one of the few people in a position to regularly push South Africa's cause in England and often pointed out that while his homeland had its problems like everywhere else, it was certainly not a third-world country and would stage a brilliant World Cup. Playing against Sweden would give him another chance to mention the bid in the English press.

The match looked as though it was heading for a goalless draw until Trott Moloto sent on Siyabonga Nomvethe in the 83rd minute. Five minutes later he grabbed his first goal for his country and Bafana Bafana had beaten European opposition for the first time since returning to international football. The players had done their part in the charm offensive.

It had optimistically been arranged for Lucas to be subbed ten minutes from the end so he could catch a flight back to England and play against Southampton the following day. In fact he played the full 90 minutes and despite being upgraded to first class so he could sleep, it was expecting too much even for someone with his renowned stamina. O'Leary took one look at his jet-lagged skipper and decided he needed more rest.

The remainder of the Leeds team were also feeling the effects of too much travel. Their trip to Moscow had been in vain because the pitch was too dangerous for the game to go ahead. After a weary-looking 1-0 win over the Saints, they set off again to face Spartak, this time in Belgrade where the temperature was only just below freezing. Even though he was still suspended Lucas was keen to go and support his team-mates but was ordered to stay behind and rest ready for a heavy programme that was coming up over Christmas. Leeds struggled without him and returned to England 2-1 down.

Lucas came back into the side with a man of the match display as United beat Derby 1-0 and was ready for the challenge of the UEFA Cup second leg. Few gave Leeds much chance against the Russian title-holders who had started the campaign in the Champions League, but United did have an away goal, which might prove crucial. The match was a classic. Fast, entertaining and full of incident as both sides went on the attack, chasing the opening goal that would swing the advantage their way. It was one of those nights that have fans on the edge of their seats – and often on their feet – but with goalkeepers Nigel Martyn and Andrei Smetanin athletically withstanding everything thrown at them, it looked destined to end goalless. There were just six minutes to go when Michael Bridges' persistence won Leeds a corner. Stephen McPhail clipped an in-swinger towards the far post and for once Smetanin misjudged the flight, his attempted punch nowhere near the ball. Lucas came in behind him and headed firmly into the net. The shock on his face was clearly visible in the TV replays before he was engulfed by whooping team-mates. Later Lucas laughed and said: 'I didn't know what to do, how to celebrate. I just stood there until everybody else came to me. I can go up for set plays a hundred times and the ball never comes to me. But this one did. What a goal!' Leeds went through on the away-goal rule and Lucas quickly reminded Dave Swift of a bet they had struck at the start of the season that would mean the physio paying Lucas ten pounds for every goal he scored after three. 'He tried to persuade me that the two European goals and his own-goal against Liverpool already made it three but I wasn't having that,' Swift laughed.

One of the first of football's often-repeated truisms that Lucas learned when he came to England was that 'whenever things are going well, football will kick you up the backside.' After enjoying a comfortable FA Cup win over Port Vale, Lucas received his kick up the rear courtesy of referee Graham Barber. It came towards the end of yet another tight Worthington Cup clash with Leicester. The sides had played several crunch games in recent years and a bit of feeling had developed between the two sets of players. Seldom critical of fellow professionals, Lucas did admit to finding the Foxes' long-haired blond midfielder Robbie Savage 'too flash and mouthy.' Lucas's friend David Share was so surprised to hear such a condemnation that it stuck in his mind and years later when Lucas arrived back at Leeds-Bradford airport after a trip to South Africa, he found that Share had plastered his car with pictures of Savage as a joke.

But it wasn't Savage who upset Lucas at Filbert Street, it was Leicester's powerful striker Emile Heskey. The pair had a physical battle all evening and Lucas was a bit surprised when the referee booked him for what he considered was a 50-50 tackle. He shrugged it off. These things happen and the call could have gone either way. But with the game locked at 0-0 and extra-time only a couple of minutes away, Barber made a decision that had Lucas uncharacteristically furious with both the official and his opponent. Lucas and Heskey went for a ball just outside the Leeds area and as they turned, the striker collapsed in a heap on the ground. Out came the second yellow card, followed by the red. Leeds had to play extra-time with ten men and even though they held out, Leicester won the shoot-out to go into the next round. The game ended in a mass confrontation in the centre circle as incensed United players confronted Heskey and the referee. They felt cheated.

For once Lucas didn't measure his words when talking to the Press. Barely concealing his anger and frustration, he said: 'Heskey took a dive and coerced the referee into sending me off. His behaviour was scandalous. I never touched the guy and I couldn't believe it when he threw himself to the ground. Life for defenders is becoming almost impossible. You go into a tackle, time it to perfection and because the opponent goes over you get a yellow card. If it happens twice, you're off. What about the fans? They pay good money to watch a game of football not people throwing themselves about as though they have been pole-axed. What really annoys me is that a rule has been brought in this season introducing yellow cards for players who take a dive. I have yet to play in a match in which that has happened, but I have played in enough where it should have. If ever there was a case for a yellow card for diving then Heskey's was it.'

Leeds regrouped and won a fierce encounter at Chelsea that saw Dennis Wise and Lee Bowyer go head to head like two diminutive fighting cocks, and gained some satisfaction by beating Leicester in the league on Boxing Day. The final game of 1999 took United to Arsenal but they couldn't live up to their billing as the brightest young team on the block, crashing to a 3-0 defeat that could have been worse. Nevertheless, the name at the top of the Premiership as the world entered a new millennium was Leeds United. You would have got long odds on that the day Lucas first walked into Elland Road.

He could only sit in the stand while he served his 'Heskey' suspension and watch Leeds go down to another defeat against Aston Villa but returned to lead the side for the first time in the new century and enjoy a surprisingly easy 5-2 FA Cup win over Manchester City. That was all he could contribute to Leeds for a while. His duty now was to join up with the national squad who were preparing to head for the African Cup of Nations, about to be staged jointly in Ghana and Nigeria.

The two host nations – sharing the tournament after it was taken away from strife-torn Zimbabwe – were the joint favourites to lift the trophy but as they assembled at their initial training camp in Mafeking, Lucas felt Bafana Bafana might cause an upset. He was aware their recent dismal away record – only one win in nine since losing the final to Egypt two years before – but that had been a period in which new players had been blooded and he was confident they would raise their game for the tournament. One concern was the absence of their two most prolific goal scorers – Phil Masinga was injured and Benni McCarthy had announced his retirement from international football after falling out with SAFA and his change of heart had come too late to be included – but they should still be too good for most of the teams involved. 'We know where the cup belongs and we will bring it back,' Lucas told reporters as South Africa arrived in Kumasi ready for the group stages. 'I think we've got a good chance. We've got great players who are hungry for success ... We want to be there again. We want to keep that momentum going.'

The players were pleasantly surprised by Kumasi. The training pitch might not have been up to the standards they were used to back home but the players couldn't fault the way their hosts were putting themselves out to make their stay as comfortable as possible. Local fans turned up in large numbers to watch training sessions and hundreds of small boys hovered around the perimeter fence of the Flossid Hotel, hoping to catch a glimpse of 'Feesh' or 'Rhoo'.

Goalkeeper Andre Arendse, now playing his club football at Oxford United, was impressed with the preparations: 'The spirit of the team that won the tournament in 1996 was unbelievable but I must say we've got a very good mood in this camp, too. It could be even better because we are away from home and know we have to pull together to be successful.'

Bafana were in Group B with Algeria, Congo and their first opponents, Gabon, and were expected to go through very comfortably. Perhaps the players took it a little too easily in the opening game because they found themselves behind after only 21 minutes to a goal from 16-year-old Chiva Star Nzigou, the youngest player in the tournament's history. That was the kick in the backside they needed to shake them out of their complacency and they stepped up a gear. Dumisa Ngobe equalised with a glancing header just before the interval and two second-half goals from Shaun Bartlett sealed the victory.

Bartlett was on target again with the only goal of the game as South Africa beat Congo to ensure their place in the quarter-finals. Lucas thought he'd earned that tenner off Dave Swift when his shot looked bound for the net but Congo's Michel Dinzey got back and headed off the line. South Africa only needed a draw in the final match to ensure they would remain in Kumasi and avoid the upheaval of moving to Nigeria. There was little interest among the Ghanaian public, only 2,000 turning up to watch and with qualification already assured, Moloto used the game to give some of his fringe players a run out. Lucas was still playing, as was Bartlett who was on fire in front of goal. His second-minute strike took his international tally to 16 and level with Masinga as South Africa's all-time leading scorer. Algeria equalised just before the end to go through as group runners-up.

Ghanaian indifference turned to a desperate scramble for quarter-final tickets. It seemed the whole of the country wanted to be at the Asokwa Stadium, hoping to see their team gain revenge for that 1996 semi-final defeat. But while the fans turned up in noisy, colourful support, the Ghana team was muted and South Africa should have been out of sight long before Syabonga Nomvethe put them ahead five minutes before half-time.

There was a quiet confidence in the Bafana dressing room at the break but that was dented five minutes after the restart when combative midfielder Eric Tinkler picked up a second yellow card and was sent off. Warning bells started to sound within a minute as Ghana surged forward and crashed a shot against the crossbar. Their tails were up. From then on, Bafana were battling to hold on to what they had. The back three of Lucas, Mark Fish and Pierre Issa played out of their skins, thwarting everything thrown at them and a last-minute header off the line by Fish made sure South Africa were in the semi-finals again.

Having knocked out one of the host nations, Bafana now had to move to Lagos ready to tackle the other one. There were only three days between matches but the media managed to cram in enough words to portray the significance of this mighty confrontation, so often promised and now finally here. This would decide whether the 'Boys' of South Africa or the 'Super Eagles' of Nigeria were the kings of African football. Such was the anticipation that army troops were put on standby in case fans' enthusiasm got out of hand. People across the continent wanted to see the clash of the Titans and the television coverage attracted record viewer numbers in Africa.

Inside the stadium, the noise levels were incredible as the teams took to the pitch but they soared even higher 40 seconds after the referee blew his whistle to start the game. Tijani Babangida picked up the ball from midfield, ran at the back-peddling Bafana defence and smashed a shot past Andre Arendse from 20 yards. Bafana were rocked and without the suspended Tinkler to steady things in midfield and with legs still weary from playing with ten men in the steamy heat of Ghana, they were unable to respond. Just before half-time, Babangida found space to the left of South Africa's penalty area and curled a shot into the top corner of the net. There was no way back and it took a last-ditch tackle from Lucas to prevent Raphael Chukwu putting the Super Eagles even further ahead.

There was massive disappointment in the camp and back home where there were the inevitable calls for Moloto to be sacked. But before the tournament could be analysed and future paths decided on, the team had to play the third-placed play-off match against Tunisia, which meant a trip back to Ghana. While players, freed from the tension of a tournament, often produce entertaining football in these matches, there is always an element of 'after the Lord Mayor's show'. The game attracted only 3,000 people who looked lost in the 40,000-seater Accra Sports Stadium. Those who stayed away probably made the right decision: it wasn't particularly thrilling to watch, notable mainly for Bartlett scoring his fifth goal of the tournament to become South Africa's leading scorer, and a penalty save by Arendse. Tunisia scored in the 91st minute to set up a penalty shoot-out, which South Africa won 4-3 after some tired-looking spot kicks.

By this time, Lucas was back in the dressing room having been carried off just before half-time with a leg injury. The rumour went round that he had broken his leg but it turned out to be a very sore shin. There was only a week before Leeds were due to play Manchester United so he hoped the flight home wasn't going to make the situation worse. He was already feeling apprehensive because while he had been away, Leeds had hit a sticky patch. It wasn't totally surprising because soon after Lucas arrived in South Africa, two of his team-mates had been arrested in the back streets of Leeds.

Chapter 26

Arrested development

As Lucas went straight from the FA Cup win over Manchester City to catch his plane to the African Cup of Nations, the rest of the United squad were wondering how to enjoy a few days off. With an international weekend coming up and their next opponents, Manchester United, in Brazil taking part in the World Club Challenge, Leeds didn't have a game for two weeks. David O'Leary wondered about taking the players away to the sun for a while but decided against it, reckoning their families would welcome the chance to spend some time with them. How different Leeds United's history might have been if he'd whisked them away to Ibiza.

Instead, events in the streets of Leeds in the early hours of the following Thursday morning cast a shadow over a group of players and a pall over the whole squad. And 18 months later, O'Leary's take on events and his observations on some of the players, revealed in a book, would be a major factor in him losing the trust of the dressing room and eventually to him getting the sack.

Some time after midnight on 12 January 2000, a dispute outside the Majestyk nightclub in Leeds city centre resulted in two brothers, Sarfraz and Shazad Najeib, and three of their friends being chased across the road by a gang of young men. The report in the *YEP* read: 'As they turned into Mill Hill, Sarfraz was grabbed and viciously assaulted. He suffered a broken nose, broken leg and head injuries, which kept him in hospital for a week. His brother was also assaulted but suffered relatively minor injuries.' As the paper followed up the story, they found an eye witness, who had been working in a nearby kebab shop. He told the reporter: 'We ran outside and saw a group of three or four Asian lads. One was on the floor and he was getting kicked by three white lads. Eventually they stopped and ran off. It was very, very bad. It was barbaric.'

The following Monday, the police made two arrests and next day's front page headlines shouted: 'UNITED STARS IN ASSAULT QUIZ.' Lee Bowyer and Jonathan Woodgate had been arrested on suspicion of being involved in the attack. A few weeks later, reserve striker Tony Hackworth was also arrested. The three of them, along with Woodgate's friends, Neale Caveney and Paul Clifford, were later charged with causing grievous bodily harm and affray, while Woodgate, Clifford, Caveney and United defender Michael Duberry were also accused of trying to pervert the course of justice.

Leeds United was rocked to its core.

The club was under scrutiny as never before. It took only a few days before anonymous calls started to be received, threatening retribution. The national media were in hot pursuit of a massive story, wanting to know how the club was going to respond. Leeds' management held meetings with the players involved, who protested their innocence even though later they admitted to having consumed vast quantities of alcohol and being involved in the chase. At this stage the club's biggest dilemma was whether or not O'Leary should continue to include the players in matches. They decided that on the basis everyone is innocent until proven guilty, they would continue to pick them, a decision that horrified some sections of the public and led to anti-Nazi league protesters turning up outside United matches, handing out leaflets calling for Bowyer and Woodgate to be suspended.

Leeds beat Sunderland the weekend after the story broke but were then bundled out of the FA Cup by Aston Villa and went down 3-1 at Liverpool. It is impossible to say how much off-the-field events affected results – O'Leary pointed out that a major factor was the absence of Lucas and David Batty – but it is hard to believe that there was no effect.

Lucas arrived back to a very subdued camp but one with a lot of emotion not far below the surface. Leeds were regularly fielding sides in which eight members of the team were under 25 years old, several barely out of their teens. From a happy, slightly cocky bunch, used to having praise heaped on them and being idolised by fans, they were suddenly confronted by the other side of fame. Out of the blue, there was a downside to 'all for one and one for all' and some of the players were shocked that accusations against a couple of them appeared, in some people's minds, to cast doubt on them all. It hurt and it was confusing and it was starting to affect their play. The burden on Lucas as captain and one of the few senior players was heavier than ever. He would need all that fabled charisma to try and calm things down and get minds back on some important games that were just around the corner.

The team performed well against Manchester United, creating a string of chances and hitting the woodwork three times, but they still went down 1-0 after Andy Cole flicked the ball over Lucas and raced past him to score. The result gave their rivals a six-point advantage over them with only 13 games to go. It would be a tall order but Lucas was determined his young team-mates should not give up the chase. 'We are all disappointed but we will try to win every game now,' he said. 'The title race is not over. We still have a chance but we have to get our heads up and look forward to the next game. We cannot think we have lost everything. We are hungry for success and have to keep working hard.' With the UEFA Cup about to resume, it was a timely reminder.

Leeds flew out to Italy to face AS Roma, the side who had knocked them out of the competition the previous season. They were followed by seven planes filled with Leeds fans and in all, United expected more than 6,000 supporters to be shouting them on in the Olympic Stadium. Roma had been too good for Leeds last year and since then they had been strengthened under new manager Fabio Capello. O'Leary watched them twice and could find few weaknesses. He warned his players that the Roma strike force of Marco Delvecchio and Francesco Totti was as lethal as ever and to counter their threat, the Irishman selected a three-man central defence, playing Alfie Haaland alongside Lucas and Jonathan Woodgate. The trio were in impressive form and even when the Italians managed to get past them, they found Nigel Martyn unbeatable. The Cornishman pulled off a string of world-class saves that had Capello kicking his dug-out in frustration and earned Leeds a goalless draw.

Leeds kept their title hopes alive with a 3-0 win over Coventry before Roma turned up at Elland Road determined to dispatch the English upstarts. Once again the United defence was brilliant. This time they didn't have to rely on the keeper because very little reached him – 'We felt we owed him after the match in Rome so we made sure he didn't have too much to do,' said Lucas with a grin. Harry Kewell won the match with a goal worthy of such a high-profile encounter and Roma disintegrated, finishing with only nine men after Vincent Candela and Antonio Carlos Zago were sent off.

United came through a high-tempo, passionate derby with Bradford City days before Slavia Prague arrived at Elland Road for the next stage of the European adventure. Woodgate was out with an injury but the rest of the build-up was dominated by discussion about whether Bowyer should play with his first court appearance coming up the following day. In the event the midfielder produced one of his finest performances in weeks, scoring a superb goal in an impressive 3-0 victory. It was to prove a foretaste of how the trial was to affect Bowyer, who turned to football, the thing in life he most understood, as a release from an alien process that threatened to engulf him.

Leeds thumped Wimbledon 4-1 then travelled to Prague, scored an early away goal and although they lost 2-1 on the night they had booked their place in the semi-finals of the UEFA Cup, with the mouth-watering prospect of facing Arsenal in the final. And they were still second in the Premiership, only four points behind Manchester United. The jauntiness had returned to Leeds players' step; confidence was high once more: 'Our style of play is no secret,' Lucas said in his weekly *YEP* column. 'It is based entirely on stamina, speed, quick passing and an attitude that no matter who the opposition is, we are capable of going out and beating them…The feeling among the players is that we have not come this far in a European competition, to fall at this particular hurdle.'

But it was not to be. Four weeks later, they were out of Europe, fourth in the league and 18 points behind Alex Ferguson's side. They had also been through a traumatic night that saw two men killed just because they were following Leeds United.

Chapter 27

Welcome to Hell!

For years, Leeds have boasted of 'Fortress Elland Road', where the passion of the crowd spurs on United while reducing all but the strongest opponents into a shadow of their normal selves. Many other clubs try to turn their stadium into an intimidating place for visiting teams. The psychology ranges from the baying of a hostile crowd to more subtle touches like the sign Liverpool manager Bill Shankly hung above the tunnel to remind his own players and the opposition that 'This is Anfield', with everything that implied. But nothing in English football came close to the intimidation felt by teams visiting United's next European opponents, Turkish champions Galatasaray.

Former Liverpool hard man, Tommy Smith, who according to Shankly was not born but quarried from granite, looked back at a visit he and his team-mates made and warned the Leeds players they had not experienced anything like the atmosphere that awaited them in Istanbul. 'It was the worst place I had ever been to in my life. We think some of our supporters are noisy but they are nothing compared to the Turks. They are absolutely fanatical.' Chelsea had been to Galatasaray a year before Leeds and instead of 'Welcome to Anfield' they had been greeted by fans holding placards reading 'Welcome to Hell!'

Leeds' confidence had already taken a dent when they lost league matches to bogey side Leicester and Chelsea and the youngsters' ability to withstand a full campaign was being questioned. Several of Lucas's Bafana team-mates played their club football in Turkey so he had picked their brains about what to expect from Galatasaray. John Moshoeu was among those who said, 'Don't take them lightly, they have some very good players'. The team were staying in five-star luxury, with stunning views across the Bosphorus that links Europe to Asia, but when they went to train on the match pitch that night, the Ali Sami Yen stadium looked dilapidated and didn't compare to Elland Road or other top English grounds. After a good session, they went back to the hotel and eased into their pre-match routine.

Out in the streets of Istanbul, Leeds fans were wandering around looking for somewhere to eat and a bar where they could pass the evening. There was the usual banter with local supporters, as groups of United supporters sang 'Marching on Together!' and chanted 'We are Leeds!' But with the warnings they had received before setting out and still mindful that four United fans had been stabbed when leaving the stadium in Rome, they seemed less boisterous than usual. Yet, some time after 10pm, a disturbance started in a McDonald's restaurant. It spilled out into the street and turned into a fight. Knives were drawn and by the time the police arrived to break it up, several fans were bloodstained. Christopher Loftus and father of two, Kevin Speight were fatally injured.

Peter Ridsdale was dining with the directors of Galatasaray when he heard the news and he and fellow director David Spencer hurried to the Taksim hospital where the chairman had the harrowing task of accompanying Darren Loftus as he identified his brother's dead body. The situation at the hospital was chaotic. Spencer had to use his credit card to pay for blood and even then it had to be collected by Ridsdale's driver so a fan could receive a transfusion. And Leeds also had to pay before an ambulance would take another injured fan to the city's German hospital where suitable treatment was available.

Having dealt with the situation at the hospital as best he could, the exhausted and traumatised Ridsdale was then faced with a meeting with UEFA officials in the early hours of the morning. To his amazement, the governing body were insisting the game should go ahead and threatened that if Leeds refused to play, they would forfeit the tie. 'I had to think on my feet,' Ridsdale wrote in his book. 'I couldn't shift the sight of Christopher Loftus's body from my mind. I couldn't stop hearing his brother's screams. Football had lost all its importance. But in that split second I also pictured his murderers and the Galatasaray fans draped in red flags, dancing in celebration that we'd forfeited the match, dancing on the graves of our two fans. "We'll honour the fixture," I said in a snap decision.'

UEFA compounded their insensitivity at refusing to postpone the fixture by declaring that it would not be appropriate to hold a minute's silence before the match and that the teams should not wear black arm bands. For years, people had been saying that the atmosphere at matches in Turkey went far beyond what was acceptable and had urged UEFA to act. They had failed to do so and now seemed spineless in the face of a tragedy that earlier intervention might have avoided.

Back in the hotel, the players were unaware what had happened. In his room, Lucas's phone rang and when he picked up the receiver, a voice screamed: 'You! Lucas! I am going to kill you tomorrow.' Memories of his youth came back but he tried to put it to the back of his mind and dismiss it as one of the crank calls they had been warned to expect.

Far from subduing the Turkish fans, the deaths seemed to ramp up their hostility to new heights. The team bus needed a police escort front and rear as it made its way to the match. Anxious faces peered out of the windows as they arrived at the stadium. The area around the ground was filled with armed police with water cannons standing by. But no one seemed able to calm the baying mob who were yelling abuse at the players, several of them drawing a finger across their throat in an unmistakable warning. The stadium that had just seemed old and weary the previous night, was now filled with menace. The PA system was turned up to rock concert volume and yet above that it was still possible to hear the chanting and yelling crowd. The rhythmic stamping of their feet made the whole stadium shake as though a small earthquake was imminent. Vivid red flares lit up the terraces and were tossed down on to the pitch. Hell was not a bad description.

The noise could be heard deep in the dressing room under the stand, where the Leeds team ignored UEFA and pulled on black armbands. As Lucas led his side out of the tunnel at one end of the ground, it was like entering a war zone. They had to thread their way through a cordon of police holding riot shields high above their heads in an attempt to protect the players from missiles. A message of condolence read in English was drowned out by the screaming mob. The group of Leeds supporters behind one goal turned their backs to the pitch and held their fists in the air in defiance to the Turkish fans and UEFA.

Football, the game that was loved around the world, that had once marked a moment of sanity in the madness of the First World War, that Nelson Mandela had used to help unite a divided country, was suddenly completely irrelevant. Leeds lost the surrealistic match 2-0 but the only emotion the players felt was relief as the plane's wheels lifted off from Turkish soil.

They arrived home to find that Elland Road had been turned into a shrine to the dead fans. Supporters from far and near came to leave replica shirts, scarves, flowers and messages along the fence and especially around the Bremner statue that had been erected earlier that year. Lucas and Feziwe were among the people who came to read the messages of condolence and pay their respects.

Behind the scenes, Leeds were trying to get all Turkish fans banned from the second leg, fearful of how United supporters might react. Galatasaray objected and even suggested the game should be played in a neutral country. Once again UEFA dithered and it was some time before they finally ruled that the Turks would receive only 80 complementary tickets for officials and family members. Meanwhile, bizarrely, they fined Leeds for 'failing to control their players' in the first leg after United had picked up four yellow cards.

Leeds players were finding it hard to concentrate on football. They lost at Aston Villa and again at home to Arsenal. Lucas missed the emotional first match at Elland Road since the killings with a knee ligament injury but came back to lead his side in the second leg against Galatasaray. United took out a full page advertisement in newspapers in which Peter Ridsdale begged fans to behave themselves: 'During a week in which I, my colleagues on the board, David O'Leary and representatives of the players have attended the funerals of Christopher Loftus and Kevin Speight, it is important that all of us take the opportunity tonight to show the world's TV and Press that we will not allow the futility of violence and personal injury to cast a shadow over football in this country,' he wrote. Leeds had 350 police on duty, more than three times the number for a normal match. A West Yorkshire police spokesman reported 'Tensions were obviously running high but I'm pleased that the outcome was no worse than a normal high category game.'

The match was over as a contest after four minutes when Woodgate conceded a penalty and the Turks took a 3-0 aggregate lead. United managed to fight back to 2-2 on the night in an acrimonious game that saw Kewell and Galatasaray's Emre Belozoglu sent off. United's dream of a fairy-tale trip to the final had ended but somehow it didn't matter. The feelings of most Leeds fans were summed up by the front page of the *YEP* the following night. Over a picture of Bowyer on his knees at the end of the match, the headline read: 'THANK GOD IT'S OVER!'

While pundits were writing off United's season and O'Leary was reminding people that he'd warned that his squad didn't have the strength in depth to cope with such a hectic campaign, Lucas was determined to focus his young team-mates' eyes on what they had achieved and what they still needed to do. 'All the players have felt for a long time that we would win something this season and after losing sight of Manchester United at the top of the Premiership, going out of the FA Cup, Worthington Cup and now the UEFA Cup, what we are left with as a priority is finishing in the top three to get us into next season's Champions League,' he said. 'It has been tough – very tough – but we should rejoice at our performances in getting to within a single match of the UEFA Cup final in Copenhagen next month rather than dwell on our last-fence fall.'

Leeds hadn't won a match since 19 March and despite going 2-0 up at Newcastle, they had to settle for a point when Alan Shearer added two more to his impressive tally against United and Ian Harte missed a penalty. Leeds were in fourth place, two points behind Arsenal, who had a game in hand, and five behind Liverpool. They badly needed a change of fortune.

Arsenal were to prove the strongest of the trio, losing only one match in their run-in to second place before going down 4-1 in a penalty shoot-out after holding

Galatasaray to a goalless draw in the UEFA Cup final. Leeds' sights had to be set on Liverpool.

They went level on points with the Anfield outfit after beating Sheffield Wednesday 3-0 while their rivals lost to Chelsea. A 3-1 win over relegated Watford saw Lucas pick up an injury but the skipper's pain was eased when he heard that Leicester, the team who had been such a thorn in Leeds' side, had done them a favour by beating Liverpool. Two games to go and Leeds were in third place with a one-point advantage. Lucas's injury meant he missed the 1-1 draw against Everton and with Gerard Houllier's side also drawing, both teams went into the final match of the campaign with everything to play for, although Liverpool were slight favourites because they were against relegation-threatened Bradford while Leeds had to travel to West Ham.

Lucas led his side out at Upton Park for a difficult, tense encounter. The result may have meant nothing to the Hammers but you would never have guessed it by the way they scrapped for every ball. As so often that season, United's defence was at the top of its game, but the often-prolific strike-force couldn't get the all-important goal at the other end and after a 0-0 draw, everything depended on what had happened at Valley Parade.

There the game was settled by a solitary goal. Lucas's former central defensive partner David Wetherall bravely flung himself at a free-kick from another ex-Leeds player, Gunnar Halle, and headed past Sander Westerveld in the Liverpool goal. He had saved Bradford City from relegation and clinched Leeds' place in the Champions League. Little wonder that as they travelled back from London, the United players rang their former team mate and joyfully sang 'There's only one David Wetherall!'

Chapter 28
Seven o'clock - in the morning!

Lucas headed for South Africa on crutches after an operation to clean up his knee and shave down an overgrown bone in his ankle. He was looking forward to seeing his family and having a break from football. While he was the first to admit that the rewards for being a top player gave him a lifestyle most people could only dream of, there came a point where there didn't seem to be much time to enjoy it. He'd only had a few weeks between seasons for the last two years and at the age of 31 that wasn't enough. Those small knocks and strains that all players pick up were taking longer to heal and while he had shown time and time again his willingness to play through the pain barrier, he was starting to feel concerned that the wear and tear, especially on his knees, could cut short his career. He desperately wanted to carry on playing for as long as possible.

Having bent over backwards for years to accommodate club and country – often caught in the middle of rows where it seemed that his welfare was the last consideration – he decided it was time to make a stand. After the African Cup of Nations he'd told SAFA that he felt he had to concentrate all his efforts on Leeds's push for the title and UEFA Cup. In some parts of the media that was interpreted as him quitting international football and he hastily pointed out that wasn't the case. 'The South African management fully understand my desire to be exclusively involved with my club until the last ball of the season is kicked,' he said.

He had intended to return to the Bafana Bafana squad for at least the World Cup qualifier against Zimbabwe in July but the operations ruled out even that. For the first time since he was made captain, South Africa played ten games without Lucas. It was not a good period for the team: they lost all but one of the last six in that series including being thumped 4-0 by Zimbabwe.

The time freed by not playing was soon packed with other engagements including a visit to Bopaseantla, his former school in Diepkloof, to see a new computer learning centre, addressing the National Youth Alliance's Supercop Forum about tackling youth crime, and dropping into the SAFA school of excellence to encourage the next generation of young players.

There was also a series of fund-raising breakfasts for SOS Children's Villages which, for Lucas, required a special sacrifice. Unless Nelson Mandela was coming to visit the team hotel, 8am was not a time that Lucas bothered with very much and he was still incredulous when he related events to the Leeds United programme a few weeks later: 'I had to be there in a jacket and tie with a speech prepared at eight o'clock in the morning!' he said. 'In Cape Town it was SEVEN! I told the organisers, "Man, nobody's going to turn out at that time," but it was packed, just like all the others.' After each of the breakfasts, Lucas headed off to the nearest SOS village to see the children. 'That was the best time, coaching the kids. I hardly had time to put on my boots before I was surrounded by 60 or so kids – some of them very small – who just wanted to get started.' On the visit to the Cape Town village, his mind went back to his days as a small boy in Diepkloof. 'There was one little kid staring at me and when I said hello to him in Zulu he turned to his friend wide-eyed and said, "He speaks Zulu!" I was reminded of when I was about his age and used to watch teams like Liverpool on the TV. I used to think the players lived in their own world, somewhere near God. I said to this boy, "Sure I speak Zulu. I'm just like you. When I was your age I used to play in the streets and get into mischief." I just hope that if children like that see I'm just an ordinary person like them, they will have the motivation to do something with their lives.'

As well as the charitable work, there were also some commercial deals to be taken care of. Gary Blumberg had quickly realised that Lucas was becoming the biggest name in South African sport. That provided plenty of opportunities but also the danger that he could become swamped with requests for endorsements and personal appearances in the short time he had in his homeland each year. As well as footballers, Blumberg had worked with some of the world's top golfers like Nick Price and Ernie Els and used the model of how they were managed as a pattern for looking after Lucas's interests. There were differences, of course. Whereas a golfer's whole programme will be worked out with his or her advisers, a team player like Lucas only has a few weeks a year when his diary isn't controlled by the club. But in most other ways, Lucas's pre-eminent position required a full management team to oversee his affairs, looking after everything from contracts, to marketing opportunities, investments to personal appearances. Glyn Binkin, a marketing expert who knew Lucas and Gary from his days as a successful team manager of Bafana Bafana, came on board and the trio quickly established a solid working relationship that has guided Lucas's career since.

In many ways this was pioneering work. There had been successful sports-based marketing around rugby, cricket and golf, but compared with football they were niche markets in South Africa. Lucas was the first South African soccer superstar and as well as appealing to the football-mad black population, he was popular with white fans whose main soccer interest lay in the Premier League in England.

Binkin laughs as he explains that he quickly became Dr No. 'Lucas hates to turn anyone down and when asked to do something will often say, "I'd like to do it, but you had better see Glyn." If we had accepted every offer he received, Lucas would never have had time to play football, let alone time to himself, so I became the person that said no when necessary. From day one, our policy has been quality not quantity. We established relationships and long-term contracts with a small number of blue chip companies and many of those early partnerships have lasted beyond Lucas's playing days.'

Blumberg adds: 'In many ways we were ploughing an untrodden furrow in South Africa but we have always been guided by what is best for Lucas, professionally and personally. There were times during his playing days when we could possibly have made more money by moving to a different club and, similarly, there were times when it would hve been financially beneficial to switch his commercial contracts but one of Lucas's greatest personal qualities is his loyalty and we have reflected that both with Leeds United and with his sponsors and business partners. It's been a policy that Lucas feels most comfortable with and I think is to his credit.'

One of the first things the expanding management team arranged was to create Lucas's own logo – a green and red square with an easily recognisable silhouette of his head. It made one of its first appearances on a range of personal leisurewear, launched in the summer of 2000 in cojunction with Leeds United retail department. It was all manufactured in South Africa and he was lined up to promote it in a series of stores at home during his 'holiday'. Once again his enormous popularity was there for all to see. Arriving on an open-top bus at a store in Durban, there were so many people inside and outside the shop that it took him ages just to get through to where the clothing was on display.

The local press were intrigued when they caught wind of the fact that Lucas's representatives were looking at the possibility of taking over South Africa Premier Soccer League club, Wits University. Gary Blumberg had once been a goalkeeper on the club's books and his negotiations were in the very early stages when a journalist first approached Lucas with questions. He made light of it, saying he was just trying to keep up with his mum. Only a few months before, Emily had become a director of second division club Robertsham Callies, where three of Lucas's brothers played and which were managed by his uncle Johannes Tlhong. Lucas was interested in the idea of following in the footsteps of Jomo Sono and Kaizer Motaung by owning his own club. He knew that his Bafana team-mate Mark Fish, who was now playing at Bolton, was thinking about taking over first division club Arcadia Shepherds so why not him? He could see all kinds of possibilities opening up to give young players from South Africa and England the chance to gain experience through exchange visits between Wits and Leeds United. The discussions were congenial but, finally, no agreement was reached. Meanwhile Emily went from strength to strength and still has high hopes of seeing her team, now known as Diepkloof Leeds United, playing in the Premier Division.

While the leisurewear and thoughts of football club ownership were part of several long-term plans his management company were pursuing to secure Lucas's future after he finished playing, another opportunity offered the possibility of making him one of the wealthiest people in football. Fabio Capello was preparing a £7 million bid to take Lucas to Roma. After he took over as England manager, Capello recalled: 'In my first season with Roma we faced Leeds United in the UEFA Cup, and over two very close legs we were unfortunate to go out of the competition. We did not score a goal in either game, and certainly the presence of Lucas Radebe in defence was a big reason for this, particularly at the Stadio Olimpico in the first leg when he was calm and in control of his defence. He impressed me and we looked to bring him to Roma.'

Lucas was used to being linked with big clubs – Chelsea and Arsenal had recently shown interest in luring him away from Elland Road - but apart from a fleeting thought towards following George Graham to Tottenham, he had never seriously considered leaving Leeds. But a move to Roma needed proper consideration, especially at this stage of his career. This might be his last chance of a major move. 'It was a big club and I had to ask myself if it was a step up or would it be a sideways move?' Lucas said. 'I also had to take into account the effect on my family and ask if I really wanted to start again in a new country with a new language.' After wrestling with the pros and cons through a few sleepless nights, Lucas made up his mind. 'I decided not to go. I was settled at Leeds and enjoyed the way of life there. We were now in the Champions League. In a way my own progress and the club's were going in parallel. It was as though we'd started to crawl together, then learned to walk and all of a sudden we were running. I decided I would stay and try to get Leeds United to the highest level.'

The big disappointment of the summer came with FIFA's announcement of the venue for the 2006 World Cup. Lucas was one of many people who had campaigned long and hard for South Africa. It would mean so much to the whole continent but especially to the emerging Rainbow Nation. He could also imagine himself at the age of 36 leading Bafana Bafana out at Soccer City to provide a triumphant finale to his international career. The campaign had gone well and he was encouraged by the news that came out of a meeting a few days before the vote in Zurich. South Africa and Brazil had reached an agreement that the South Americans would withdraw their application to stage the tournament and vote for South Africa in return for the favour being returned for 2010. Their biggest rivals Germany sounded as if they had as good as thrown in the towel. With England's challenge failing fast, Morocco not really in the race and Nelson Mandela working the phones, urging delegates that 'It's Africa's time', all looked set for South Africa to win the big prize. The vote would still be close but SAFA calculated that, at the very worst, the final ballot might split 12-12 and they were confident that Sepp Blatter's casting vote would go their way.

Their maths appeared to be spot on. Morocco were eliminated after the first round of voting and England departed after round two, having picked up only two votes. South Africa and Germany were locked at 11-11. As expected one of England's votes, from Scotland, went to Germany. The other from Oceania, was due to go to South Africa. But acting against instructions from his board, their delegate, a 78-year-old Scottish-born official from New Zealand, Charlie Dempsey, decided to abstain. Explaining only that his decision was for 'personal' reasons, Dempsey resigned from FIFA a few hours later.

The crowds waiting in cities across South Africa to celebrate the expected good news were stunned and angry. As far as they were concerned, the snub to their country at the very least smacked of the old Euro-centricity but more likely corruption and probably racism. South Africa's bid committee immediately protested and sought legal advice to try to overturn the result or at least get a new vote. Not only had the country been denied the joy of having the world's best footballers perform in their cities, this vote had more significant implications. The BBC reported, 'It is ordinary South Africans, especially the soccer-mad black community, who have most to lose - jobs, investment, tourism and an injection of confidence into this new but still troubled country. Even South Africa's stock market fell on the news that the World Cup competition will not be coming here.'

Just as UEFA failed to right an obvious wrong in Istanbul, FIFA refused to consider addressing South Africa's claims that a second vote should be held. The most they could do was to give assurances that things would be different when it came to voting for 2010.

For once, it was club demands that cut short Lucas's hopes of a long summer break. The squad had to re-assemble earlier than usual because United's season was due to kick-off with a Champions League qualifier against TSV 1860

Munich ten days before the start of the Premiership. Only if they got through that successfully would they be in the lucrative group section with the guarantee of six big European nights. David O'Leary had already made two significant new signings. He paid a club record £7.2 million for classy French midfielder Olivier Dacourt and a further £6 million had gone on Celtic's Australian striker Mark Viduka, while Martin Hiden, David Hopkin and Alfie Haaland had departed. O'Leary claimed he wanted at least five new faces. The speculation that interested Lucas most had been in and out of the media for several months: Leeds were apparently after West Ham's highly-rated young central defender Rio Ferdinand. Hammers manager Harry Redknapp kept repeating that his young star was not for sale but before the season started, the player issued one of those 'I'm very happy where I am' statements that left enough room for doubt. 'As long as I'm happy at West Ham there isn't a problem,' he said. But how long would such an ambitious and talented player be happy at a club where the hope of European football seemed some way off?

United's tour of Sweden before the 2000-2001 season was something of a disaster. Although they won their games quite comfortably, they picked up a series of injuries and 11 days before the Munich match they only had ten players fit enough to train. New physio Dave Hancock, a man destined to play a major part in Lucas's life, was under enormous pressure before a ball had been kicked in anger.

To those who had come to know the way the Leeds boss worked, his early season playing down of United's chances came as no surprise. 'Liverpool have spent around £50 million and they are not in the Champions League and they have a wage bill of unbelievable proportions,' O'Leary reminded everyone. 'I don't think we'll have the problem of a lack of squad numbers in the Champions League come March because I'll be very surprised if we are still in it.'

Even the most sceptical of journalists had to agree he was up against it as his side went into their opening tie with a strong Munich side at Elland Road. David Batty, Harry Kewell, Jonathan Woodgate, Jason Wilcox, Stephen McPhail and Matthew Jones were definitely out and Lucas had to shake off the effects of a virus to play. The bench included teenagers Jamie McMaster, Gareth Evans and Tony Hackworth, none of whom had made his debut for the club.

Despite the doubts, things seemed to be going well for Leeds. Alan Smith and Ian Harte put them 2-0 up and Munich's Ned Zelic had been harshly sent off. It wasn't the only mistake referee Costas Kapitanis made that evening. He had what in football parlance could only be described as a 'mare', though to be fair, he was hopeless towards both sides. Dacourt was tripped but the official saw it as a dive and gave him a second yellow card, and Eirik Bakke was also dismissed in mysterious circumstances. Mr Kapitanis then found four minutes of added time from somewhere and, almost inevitably, at 90+3 Munich's Australian striker Paul Agostino headed a valuable away goal.

Having been forced to play three strikers because of the injury situation, O'Leary stuck with it in the opening league match against Everton and was rewarded with a 2-0 win, both goals coming from Smith, who was starting to fulfil the promise he'd shown in glimpses since coming into the side aged 17.

With Bakke and Dacourt suspended, Leeds again made use of Lucas's versatility by playing him in midfield, alongside Bowyer, Kelly and the half-fit Matthew Jones for the second leg of their Munich tie. The makeshift side withstood the early Munich pressure and finally won the game 1-0, Smith again on target. But Lucas's willingness to play out of position to help the team backfired. For the first time since taking over as manager, O'Leary dropped him.

Chapter 29
Pain in Spain

David O'Leary was unapologetic about dropping his captain. 'Lucas Radebe was on the bench because of the good form shown by Jonathan Woodgate and Michael Duberry as a central defensive pairing in Munich. Simple as that,' the Irishman declared. It wasn't quite that straight forward in Lucas's eyes. He was the first to agree that no player had an automatic right to a place and that if the guy who had the shirt played well, he should keep his place. But it seemed a bit harsh to lose out just because you had been willing to help your team in an emergency. He couldn't help wondering if the manager was having doubts about him, especially when Harry Redknapp revealed that West Ham had turned down a £15 million offer for Rio Ferdinand. O'Leary was clearly keen to add to his central defensive strength and at that kind of money, he wasn't looking to bring in back-up.

Lucas kept his thoughts to himself and when Woodgate picked up an injury 20 minutes into the match at Middlesbrough, he slotted in beside Duberry and helped his side to a 2-1 win. Despite all their injury woes, Leeds' 100 per cent pre-season record had been carried into the campaign but their winning run came to an end when Alfie Haaland returned with Manchester City and went home with all three points. That was followed by a goalless draw at Coventry and the pundits were apprehensive how Leeds would cope with their next challenge in Barcelona's famous Nou Camp stadium.

The draw for the Champions League groups gave Leeds a mouth-watering programme although most of the media agreed the fans should make the most of these matches because they weren't likely to get any more this season. As well as Barcelona, United would face another of Europe's richest and most successful clubs, AC Milan, and Turkish champions Besiktas, which would mean a too rapid return to Istanbul.

Barcelona is the capital of the Catalan people and fiercely proud of its heritage. In many ways their football team has become a symbol of the city's cultural, civic and, above all, Catalan pride. Over the years some of the world's greatest players have plied their trade at the Nou Camp including Johan Cruyff, Diego Maradona, Luis Figo and 1950s 'Mighty Magyar' Sandor Kocsis. The current bunch about to face Leeds weren't bad either, including World Player of the Year Rivaldo, Patrick Kluivert, Philip Cocu, Marc Overmars and Frank de Boer. Against them O'Leary could only field a patched-up side - Bakke, Kewell and Woodgate were left in Leeds receiving treatment while Viduka was with Australia at the Olympics.

The last time Leeds had played in the Nou Camp had been in 1992 when UEFA insisted they replayed a European Cup game on neutral territory after Stuttgart fielded an ineligible player in the tie at Elland Road. The 2,000 people who made it to the hastily arranged match looked lost in the steep-sided, three-tier stadium where Carl Shutt became a United hero by scoring the winning goal and righting what was seen as another UEFA injustice.

This time there were 85,000 looking down as Lucas led his side out. Those who came to support Leeds were about to have their worst fears fulfilled. It was men against boys. Barcelona were two-up after 20 minutes and the final 4-0 scoreline in no way flattered them. With a minute to go, Lucas went up for a ball with Duberry and Barcelona's Alfonso. There was a clash of heads, the South African fell awkwardly and lay absolutely still. Physio Dave Hancock sprinted to his side before the referee had chance to summon him and players from both sides clustered round anxiously. The stadium was silent as the treatment carried on for what seemed an eternity. It was almost seven minutes before Lucas was lifted gently on to the stretcher, his neck supported by a brace, and wheeled straight to a waiting ambulance, which sped him to hospital.

Hancock recalled: 'Lucas was out cold when I reached him. In a case like that you don't want to take any chances. I needed to secure his neck in a collar and put him on a spinal board in order to get him off the pitch. After he came round, I was checking his vital signs when the paramedics went to lift him on to an old canvas stretcher like something out of MASH. There's a photo of me shouting at them to stop but incredibly they didn't have any of the equipment I expected to be standard at a club as big as Barcelona. Fortunately I had a collar with me and Lucas was OK but it could have been dangerous and I think it was because of that incident that UEFA tightened up the regulations.'

Duberry remembered the event with horror: 'When the neck brace appeared I thought, "Oh God, this is really bad." He just didn't respond when the rest of the players and the physio spoke to him and it was clear he was out like a light. Thoughts of his family watching on TV at home in Leeds and South Africa raced through my mind.'

True enough, Emily was watching with other members of the family in Johannesburg. 'It was horrible,' she recalled. 'We didn't know what had happened to him and we couldn't get hold of anyone to tell us. Eventually we spoke to someone at the team hotel but while they said he was all right, they didn't seem to know any details of when he would be coming out of hospital or what he had done. It was very worrying.'

Leeds fans, too, were in shock. Not only had their team been trounced, it looked as though the Chief was seriously injured. Journalist Richard Sutcliffe had given up the chance to cover Leeds in Europe, preferring to follow them home and away as a fan. In his record of that season, *Marching on Together*, he recalled being told that Lucas had broken his neck and would never play again. 'I couldn't believe it. Our best defender forced to retire. The 4-0 defeat was nothing compared to this.'

After an anxious, sleepless night, Emily finally heard that Lucas wasn't as badly hurt as it had appeared. Scans had shown no breaks and even though he was still concussed and disorientated he was allowed to travel home with the rest of the squad. For the next few days, still suffering with severe headaches, Lucas was seen daily by a neurologist in Leeds. He was not allowed to drive and was told he had to take a complete rest. He could forget about playing football for a while. But AC Milan were due at Elland Road in a few days and he desperately wanted to be part of it. Each day he hoped the pain in his head would lift so he could declare himself fit but even he had to acknowledge he was in no state to face the Italians. Danny Mills slotted into central defence and Dominic Matteo, who had signed in the summer carrying a leg injury, was finally fit to make his debut as Mills' partner. On a rain-swept night, Leeds raised their game and Milan struggled to cope with the conditions. In the dying minutes, a speculative long-range effort from Lee Boywer squirmed past Brazilian keeper Dida and United had won. United's joy was even greater when they heard that Besiktas had beaten Barcelona. All four teams in the group had three points.

Lucas returned to the side the following Saturday as Leeds only managed a draw against ten-man Derby County. Having picked up just two points from the last five league matches, they had slipped to tenth in the table. Once again it looked as though they were unable to sustain both European matches and the bread and butter Premiership games and Lucas was concerned: 'Our mental approach is all wrong,' he said. 'If you look at Manchester United they are focused every time they go on the pitch. We aren't and it's dragging us down. We need to stay strong and maintain our standards in every match we play.'

Everyone at the club was focused on the next match, the arrival of Besiktas just five months after Christopher Loftus and Kevin Speight had been murdered on the streets of Istanbul. The two clubs went out of their way to create a harmonious atmosphere for the match and supporters' groups met to try and dispel any animosity. It was agreed that 500 Besiktas fans would be allowed to travel and Leeds United and West Yorkshire police mounted the biggest security operation ever seen at Elland Road. Duberry had picked up an Achilles tendon injury against Derby so Lucas lined up alongside full-back Mills in central defence. The makeshift partnership never looked like allowing their opponents a sight of goal. Whether or not the occasion got to Besiktas is unclear but certainly Leeds were at their irresistible best. They simply rolled over the Turks and their 6-0 triumph took them joint top of the group with AC Milan at the halfway stage.

It was time to get some league points in the bag but things didn't look too good when Sergei Rebrov fired Spurs in front early in their next match. Leeds had already lost Dacourt with a thigh injury when, just before half-time, Lucas and Les Ferdinand both threw themselves at a high ball. There was a sickening crack of heads that resounded round the stadium and both lay still. Ferdinand was carried off unconscious. Lucas received treatment on the sidelines and wanted to return to the action but Hancock, mindful that it was only just over two weeks since his concussion in Barcelona, took him off and sent him to hospital where doctors were concerned enough to keep an eye on him overnight. Meanwhile back at Elland Road, the game had turned into an extraordinary spectacle. Leeds scored four goals in 12 minutes but still came close to being pegged back when Spurs grabbed two in reply.

At the hospital, the specialist was adamant, there would be no quick return for Lucas this time. The concussed brain had to be given chance to heal completely. The news couldn't have come at a worse time for O'Leary. 'Lucas Radebe has not been up to the standard at which he can play until the Besiktas game, when he was back to his best and quite outstanding,' he said. O'Leary was able to welcome back fit-again Woodgate but pointed out that as Leeds went into their next game against Charlton, they would be fielding their fifth different central defensive partnership with only 12 fixtures fulfilled. 'Much of our training is built around the back four and we have not been able to work in anything like the way we should because of the injuries.'

Once footballers pass the age of 30, every match missed takes on a new importance. Lucas hated not playing and his latest injury was particularly annoying because it meant he missed out on Bafana Bafana's friendly against France, which was the first match under their new manager Carlos Queiroz, and he was also sidelined for United's return against Besiktas, the always massive clash at Manchester United, Barcelona's visit to Elland Road and the derby game against Bradford City. Who could tell how many more chances he would get to play in matches of this significance and intensity? Yet he was forced to accept the specialist was right. So determined was he to make the Barcelona match that he threw himself into training but had to leave the session because he was feeling ill. And even when he was allowed to come back, replacing Danny Hay in the 76th minute of a Worthington Cup tie at Tranmere, he had to admit he felt unwell afterwards. His mood wasn't helped by the fact that Leeds had again crashed out of a cup competition to lower division opposition, beaten 3-2 after being two goals up.

United's injury crisis continued to worsen. When they lined up against Liverpool on 4 November, O'Leary was only able to name four substitutes. He pointed out that he had a full Premier League quality team unavailable: Martyn, Mills, Duberry, Radebe, Harte, Bakke, Batty, Dacourt, Wilcox, Bridges and Kewell. Yet United still won a thrilling match 4-3 thanks to four goals from Viduka.

Next up was the final Group match against AC Milan at the San Siro and Leeds needed a point to be sure of going through to the next stage. Lucas wanted to play but the specialist wasn't sure he was ready. Physio Dave Hancock remembered. 'The club doctor and I took Lucas to see the neurologist and it wasn't good news. The date he set for Lucas to start playing was two days after the Milan match. The three of us were sitting in the car afterwards feeling gloomy and I asked the doctor what difference in terms of vital signs and scan results would those two days make. He didn't know so we went back to the specialist and asked him. He admitted they might make no difference at all. And when we explained what a massive game this was and how vital Lucas was to the team, he said if we brought him back the night before we left for Milan, he would take another look. So that's what we did, and he said Lucas could play.'

After only 14 minutes football in just over a month, Lucas's comeback couldn't have been tougher – countering the threat of two of Europe's top strikers, Andriy Shevchenko and Oliver Bierhoff. The odds were against Leeds. Milan had never been beaten by an English club at home, and on their six previous visits to Italy, United had never won and only scored one goal.

'I'm feeling fine,' Lucas told reporters who were surprised to see him at the airport. 'All the lads are hellbent on achieving something after what happened against Barcelona. That has acted as an extra incentive. It would be an unbelievable achievement for us to get through in what has been the toughest of the eight groups.'

If anyone gave credence to the conspiracy theory that Leeds and Milan had cooked up a deal to produce a meaningless draw so both would go through, the action at the San Siro will have convinced them they were wrong. Both sides were clearly determined to win. Leeds had a lucky escape after only 26 minutes when the home side were awarded a penalty. Schevchenko sent Paul Robinson the wrong way but his low shot cracked against the post and away to safety. Leeds went ahead just before half-time when Matteo got in front of his marker at the near post and headed home Bowyer's corner. The Italians were stung. They piled on the pressure after the break and it took all Lucas's skill and experience, well supported by Mills and young Robinson, to keep them out. In the end Milan managed an equaliser, Serginho skipping past Kelly and scoring. Lucas had made a triumphant return but his place in the team would soon be under threat once more.

Chapter 30
£18 million rival

Lucas had been sorry to see Jimmy Hasselbaink leave Leeds. The pair had become good friends and both enjoyed the tussles they'd had in training, neither afraid to give the other a 'dig' in order to come out on top. 'He's really strong and he knows how to upset defenders. Even in training he's always talking to you and pushing you around,' Lucas said, smiling at the memory. 'He didn't like tackling and being on the floor so he kept chatting and I kept trying to put him down. It was all in good spirits and it will be great to see him again.'

Only this time, with Leeds heading off to Chelsea where Jimmy had moved in a £15 million deal, it would be the real thing, no quarter asked or given. The Leeds squad was still on a high from their European progress and the news that they were now to compete in a group with Real Madrid, Lazio and Anderlecht. 'I think the other teams in Europe want us to keep knocking the big boys out of the way,' David O'Leary joked.

It is one of the extraordinary features of football that some rivalries between teams continue long after the original players have retired and most of the fans who witnessed the initial cause of the friction have been replaced by a new generation. Apart from the usual 'north-south divide' arguments, the tension between Chelsea and Leeds dated back to the 1970 FA Cup final when the Londoners beat United 2-1 at Old Trafford after a 2-2 draw at Wembley. The replay was one of the most ferocious finals for years, with Chelsea captain Ron 'Chopper' Harris making Eddie Gray virtually a passenger with an early scything tackle and Leeds' hard men, Jack Charlton, Billy Bremner, Norman Hunter and Johnny Giles, showing they were well able to hand out as good as they got. Years later, referee David Elleray watched a film of the match and declared that in the modern climate the sides would have been shown six red cards and 20 yellow cards between them.

It was now 30 years on but the rivalry was still as real and new animosities had grown up, the most recent involving Lee Bowyer and Dennis Wise, and Frank Le Boeuf and Harry Kewell. Almost every encounter between the two clubs was extremely physical and the last 16 meetings had produced 67 bookings.

This latest clash – a 1-1 draw - had its moments that were not for the squeamish but also produced some good football. Chelsea boss Claudio Ranieri didn't attempt to disguise his admiration for United's performance: 'They are certainly one of the best teams I have seen with a great will to win. They defended well and were very good on the counter-attack. Hasselbaink was isolated and that was through the merits of Leeds and not any defect of ours.' Writing in the *YEP*, Phil Rostron had no doubt where the credit lay for Jimmy's quietest game since joining the Blues. He started his match report: 'Satisfaction for United, maybe, with a hard-fought point from Stamford Bridge but an individual triumph, certainly, for their immaculate captain Lucas Radebe. Faced with one of the most difficult tasks in football, that of marking Jimmy Floyd Hasselbaink, the South African appeared to grow a foot taller, gain an extra yard of pace and acquire Swiss precision timing as he folded up the Dutchman and put him nicely in his pocket.'

Lucas felt justified pride in his performance and joked later, 'Jim told me afterwards he was a bit injured! We were good buddies when he was at Leeds. You have to be alert all the time because he will punish any mistakes. But I was feeling good before the game and thought "Yeah, I'll take him on." That game gave me confidence. I was making good, quick decisions and closing down early.' David O'Leary was equally impressed: 'There aren't many around better than Lucas at his best,' he said.

Although he didn't say so, there was one centre-half that O'Leary thought was already getting close to Lucas's standard and might in time prove even better. He was in action in United's next match at Elland Road and whereas Lucas struggled to contain Frederic Kanoute as West Ham won 1-0, at the other end of the pitch Rio Ferdinand was outstanding in marshalling the home attack. Rumours linking Ferdinand's move to Leeds were stoked up to boiling point. It seemed the player wanted to come to Leeds and West Ham were resigned to losing him. The only argument was over the price.

While Peter Ridsdale negotiated, United prepared for the next stage of the Champions League and the visit of the holders, Real Madrid. Leeds faced the threat of £37 million Luis Figo, Spanish star Raul, Brazilian dynamo Roberto Carlos and Lucas's oft-times opponent Steve McManaman. Meanwhile, because of injuries, their own midfield included full-back Gary Kelly and £250,000 Australian journeyman Jacob Burns. While it was nowhere near the humiliation of the Nou Camp, Leeds were second best throughout and comfortably beaten 2-0.

The high-priced signings in the summer had raised the bar on United's wage structure and Gary Blumberg was keen to negotiate a new deal to bring Lucas's pay in line. But it was hard to get Ridsdale's attention and it soon became apparent why. 'I remember driving to Leeds for a meeting I'd arranged with Peter Ridsdale, only to find that he had gone to London. It turned out later that he was doing the Ferdinand deal,' Blumberg said. The Leeds chairman had finally persuaded West Ham to sell their prized asset. That had been expected. The part that took the breath away was the size of the fee. It had cost Leeds £18 million, a British transfer record and the most ever paid anywhere for a defender. With the European Union threatening to outlaw the transfer market, many in football and even more in the City thought Ridsdale had lost his senses. But as far as he was concerned he was putting down a marker to show the rest of the Premiership, and indeed the rest of Europe, that Leeds were now a club to be reckoned with. 'Often in the past we have been criticised for not backing the desires of managers with money and no longer can that accusation be levelled,' he said.

In contrast, O'Leary suddenly sounded defensive as if concerned that this new signing would invalidate his mantra that any success Leeds enjoyed was a minor miracle because they couldn't compete financially with the top clubs. In an interview, he seemed to distance himself from the Ferdinand purchase. 'As my wife would say, I don't think anybody is worth that kind of money for kicking a silly white football around,' he said, adding: 'I'm the manager, we have a plc and in between there's the chairman to whom I say, "I recommend this player." Now I don't know the financial side of things. If they can go and get him, they get him. I don't make those decisions.'

Lucas realised he was facing the biggest threat to his place in the team since becoming captain but he welcomed the signing and even managed a joke: 'You have to be happy when top players like Rio join your club,' he said. 'It gives you a better chance of winning things – and that's the reason we are all here. I got a close up view of Rio when West Ham beat us 1-0 at Elland Road on Saturday. He looked an outstanding player. He was very impressive. Mind you, I think there were a few people at the game who he wanted to impress!'

The details couldn't be completed in time for Ferdinand to play against second-placed Arsenal that weekend but in another demonstration of United's status, Ridsdale arranged for the player and his family to be flown up by private jet so he could be presented to the fans before the game. Record signings didn't slog up the M1 in a car; even a scheduled flight was not sufficient. It was all a long way from Lucas's bucket-shop arrival.

If strengthening his defensive capability was in part to encourage the others, O'Leary must have been a happy man as he watched his side beat Arsenal 1-0. The two players most threatened by Ferdinand's arrival were immaculate. One report read: 'The existing central defensive pairing of Lucas Radebe and Jonathan Woodgate played with such authority that some pundits were moved to suggest that United could have saved themselves the expense of the new man watching from the stand.'

O'Leary had a dilemma ahead of the next game against Leicester. You don't leave £18 million players on the bench but, as Lucas had found out to his cost, one way in which the Leeds manager demonstrated he was fair to players was by saying the man with the shirt keeps it all the time he plays well. There was an added complication because Ferdinand had been signed after the Champions League window closed so would not be eligible for the trip to Lazio, which followed the Leicester match.

In a classic fudge, O'Leary picked all three and it backfired mightily. They'd had little time to work on a system they had not used before and no one seemed sure who was responsible for what. With the defence at sixes and sevens, Leicester went 3-0 up in the first 38 minutes. O'Leary took Woodgate off and reverted to a 4-4-2 formation but any slim hope of a recovery disappeared midway through the second half when Lucas was sent off for a second yellow card.

It was his second dismissal at Filbert Street and yet another defeat at the hands of Leicester. But those factors were not what disturbed Lucas most. He'd always claimed that he had been fortunate since arriving in England because he had faced little in the way of overt racism. However, as he led Leeds on to the pitch that afternoon, a voice from the crowd yelled: 'You South African kaffir.' This was someone who knew what he was doing and was deliberately targeting Lucas. Most racists in England use the epithet 'nigger' to insult a black person but this man knew that kaffir was the most insulting thing he could say to a South African. As he left the field following his red card, the same voice, soon joined by others, started to chant: 'Kaffir! Kaffir! Kaffir!' Lucas was shocked, hurt and angry.

The irony was not lost on Lucas that his name had been used to stop Leeds fans shouting racist abuse at Leicester a couple of years earlier. He had also recently been the figurehead launching a joint anti-racism initiative between Leeds United and the *YEP*. Only a few days before, he had explained to a group of children: 'We were called kaffir by the Afrikaaner, which means black, dumb and dirty. They thought because we were black we didn't have much skill and had poor backgrounds.' The kids had responded positively to him and Lucas clung to the thought that the actions of Community United at Leeds and the national efforts of the Kick It Out campaign had already improved the atmosphere at matches and that the next generation would be more tolerant than its predecessors.

The trip to Lazio was another surprise triumph for Leeds, who emerged as 1-0 winners. Having been given most of the blame by his manager for the disaster at Leicester, Woodgate responded with a brilliant display as he and Lucas snuffed out the threat of Hernan Crespo and Marcelo Salas, and later Fabrizio Ravenelli. Lucas was starting to enjoy his trips to Rome and the next one was to be one of the most pleasurable.

Just over a week later, he was back in the Eternal City, this time dressed immaculately in all black and accompanied by Feziwe as special guests at the glittering annual FIFA's Player of the Year Awards Dinner. Lucas was presented with the Fair Play Award, a prize that usually goes to associations, clubs or groups of supporters and only occasionally to individuals. He was being acknowledged both for his role as captain of Bafana Bafana and Leeds, and also his tireless efforts on behalf of SOS Children's Villages, his work for Community United and his contribution to football's anti-racism campaign. Dr Antonio Matarrese, the chairman of FIFA's Committee for Security and Fair Play, said: 'The choice of Lucas Radebe for this year's award serves a dual purpose. He is not only a fantastic and fair player on the field, but also a great personality off the pitch with a big heart for the children in the world. He is a real ambassador for Fair Play for our youth and all footballers.'

As he and Feziwe made their way back to their hotel that night, Lucas's mind swirled with mixed emotions. He was proud to have received such a prestigious award but increasingly concerned to know where he stood in O'Leary's plans. Did the arrival of Ferdinand spell the beginning of the end of his own love affair with Leeds United?

Chapter 31

Divided loyalties

Lucas had good reason to be alarmed. Two days before he collected his Fair Play award, David O'Leary had announced the team to face Southampton and the South African was on the bench. It was, the manager explained, because he was carrying a slight ankle injury and this would give him chance to rest it. In addition, his sending-off at Leicester meant he would be suspended for the following game against Sunderland, so it was as well to give the Ferdinand-Woodgate pairing a chance to play together. But O'Leary's comments after the 1-0 defeat by the Saints didn't do anything to settle Lucas's fears: 'I was delighted with Rio Ferdinand and Jonathan Woodgate,' the manager said. 'I thought they were excellent and to me that looks like a formation which I believe will get better and better in years to come, not just for Leeds but for England as well.'

Lucas was at the stage of his career where terms like 'stalwart' and 'long-serving' were starting to creep into reports alongside his name. In golf parlance he was on the back nine of his time as a player and he certainly didn't relish the idea of seeing out his last few years as an occasional player. He felt he still had a lot to offer. 'I don't want to spend too much time on the bench at this time of my career,' he told the *Mail & Guardian* in South Africa. 'I've only got a few years left. I'm not a young man and I want to be in the first team. I love playing for Leeds and things are moving in the right direction here but my life is built around being a professional footballer and I need to be in the first team. It isn't a case of me knocking on the manager's door but we'll have to wait and see what's going to happen. Obviously if nothing happens, there might be other doors open to me elsewhere.'

It came as no surprise when one or two reporters in England put together the arrival of Ferdinand at Leeds, Lucas's dropping to the bench, George Graham's known admiration for the South African and rumours that Sol Campbell would leave White Hart Lane at the end of the season and came up with a convincing re-hash of the Radebe for Tottenham story. Not wishing to miss out, other journalists linked him with different clubs who needed a top-rate central defender. Chelsea and Arsenal were mentioned and before long it became common currency that a move was imminent.

This was the last thing Leeds United wanted. While O'Leary might have seen the two younger players as the dream partnership, he also knew that Woodgate's trial was fast approaching so there was no telling how often he would be available and even if he were, how he would react to being in the dock. Leeds couldn't afford to lose Lucas and quickly asked his adviser Gary Blumberg to resume talks about a new contract. The proposed deal would not only give Lucas another increase in pay but also take him past ten years at Elland Road and so make him eligible for a testimonial season.

O'Leary and Peter Ridsdale made the right noises about how much they valued Lucas, telling him he shouldn't be concerned about the arrival of Ferdinand. They were just being realistic and recognising that with his injury history, Lucas's knees wouldn't stand up to the 50-plus games a season Leeds would face if they were to be successful. And they were also taking into account his desire to keep playing for his country. But make no mistake, they assured him, the club he had helped put on the map was going places and he was central to their plans.

There certainly seemed no end to the club's ambition. A recent report from accountants Deloitte & Touche had put Leeds 17th in a list of the world's 20 wealthiest football clubs. And the £18 million they had splashed on Ferdinand wasn't the end of their spending ambitions. Ridsdale was in the process of negotiating a deal to bring striker Robbie Keane from Inter Milan, at first on loan but then permanently, at a cost of £12 million. Another report showed Leeds were now the Premiership's top spenders on players. Not everyone was impressed by United's shopping spree and when one of the big institutional investors offloaded a chunk of shares, the price dropped dramatically to just over 12p. The project to catapult Leeds alongside clubs like Manchester United, who had taken years to get where they were, was proving to be a fine balancing act.

Lucas returned to the starting line-up for the match at Aston Villa, but in midfield in place of the suspended Olivier Dacourt, and he made way after 67 minutes for Keane's debut. Three days later, when United travelled to Newcastle for the Boxing Day fixture, Dacourt was back and Lucas sat out the match on the bench. Leeds lost 2-1, their fourth defeat in the last five league games. With a trip to Everton postponed, the Millennium year, which had been heralded in with United at the top of the Premier Division, ended with them wallowing in 12th place. They were in serious danger of missing out on next season's place in Europe and that would not only be humiliating for a club with such ambition, but financially disastrous.

For O'Leary, the situation was almost turning into a case of 'beware of what you wish for'. Having been allowed to sign a string of star players, he now had to keep a large, expensive and very talented squad happy. There were still only 11 slots on the teamsheet so he had to leave some big names on the sidelines. Even established managers had found this a hard trick to pull off, for the still comparatively inexperienced United boss it was a massive challenge.

Former Leeds player Peter Lorimer was the first to point out that while Ferdinand and Woodgate were highly talented players and could one day form a world-class partnership for club and country, right now they were both young and green. They were being caught in mistakes that a more experienced player wouldn't make. What was needed was an old head in there to guide them. What was needed was Lucas Radebe in the back four.

O'Leary may have taken that advice or he may have come to the same conclusion separately. Either way, Lucas was alongside Ferdinand for the New Year's Day draw with Middlesbrough and again for the FA Cup third round victory over Barnsley where 'he never put a foot wrong.' It seemed as though the Leeds boss had finally found his best defensive pairing but there was another snag looming. Increasingly concerned that it might be impossible to make up the points gap in the league, O'Leary saw the FA Cup as his best route into Europe next season and he was aware that the fourth round coincided with a Bafana World Cup qualifier against Burkina Faso. What's more, when Leeds returned to Champions League action, some of the matches clashed with international dates for Lucas and there was no way he could repeat the three games in six days on two continents feats of a few years back. The conflict had to be sorted out.

The next month was one of the most emotionally draining of Lucas's career and for once his off the field problems were reflected in below par displays on the pitch. As ever he wanted to try to please everyone, and as ever neither his club nor his country seemed willing to make any major compromise, leaving him subject to calls on his loyalty from both sides. In the past he had managed to calm the situation by pushing his body to the limits. He had paid a price for that. He had once spoken of his somewhat fanciful desire to stretch his career for another ten years but if he was to satisfy the demands of both club and country he would be lucky to last ten more months.

The debate simmered behind the scenes for some time. A couple of months before, Bafana coach Carlos Queiroz had visited Leeds to try and thrash out an agreement with O'Leary and agreed that Lucas would only be selected for World Cup qualifying games. That meant missing January's African Cup of Nations qualifier against Mauritius in which Bafana Bafana only managed an

Lucas and Feziwe on their never-to-be-forgotten wedding day. (© Yorkshire Post)

Madiba magic
(left) Lucas introduces Nelson Mandela in Leeds' Centenary Square.
(© Yorkshire Post)

(Top) Madiba welcomes Lucas, Feziwe and their children Lucas Hugo and Owami to his home.

(Below) Heroes - Lucas shakes hands with Nelson Mandela at Ellis Park watched by former South Africa rugby captain Francois Pienaar. The torch carried by Pienaar, was lit at one minute past midnight on Mandela's 87th birthday in the president's former cell on Robben Island, then carried in relay to Johannesburg. 46664 was Mandela's prison number. (© Press Association)

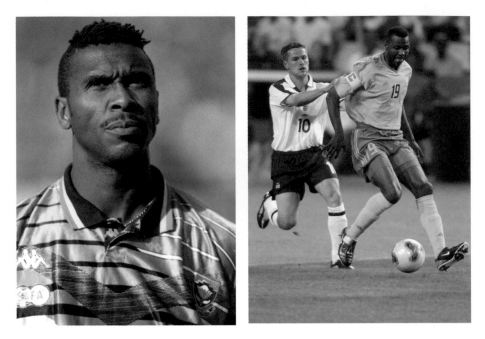

(Top left) Always proud to lead Bafana Bafana. (© Press Association)

(Top right) Lucas holds off Michael Owen as South Africa face England in Durban, his 70th and final cap for his country. (© Press Association)

(Below) Lucas heads the equaliser against Spain in the 1992 World Cup finals but a goal from Raul dashed their hopes of reaching the knock out stages.
(© Press Association)

A wistful moment. Lucas acknowledges the crowd as he takes off the South Africa captain's armband for the final time. (© Press Association)

An all too familiar sight – Leeds United physio Dave Hancock leads Lucas off the pitch with yet another injury. (© Yorkshire Post)

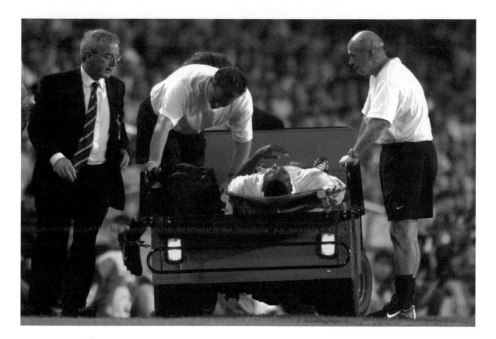

(top) Lucas is wheeled off the Nou Camp pitch in a neck brace while Leeds fans in the stadium and his family at home hold their breath in concern. (© Yorkshire Post)

(Below) Sowetan cartoonist Zapiro artfully sums up Lucas's constant club v country dilemma. (© Zapiro)

Lucas's testimonial at Elland Road

Top left: A colourful launch of his testimonial year.

Below left: Lucas had to fight back a tear when he saw how big the crowd was when he came out of the tunnel.

Right: Lucas Hugo gives dad a big hug as he thanks the crowd for making it such a special day.

(all pictures © Yorkshire Post)

(top) A wave to the crowd who packed Elland Road for his testimonial.
(© Yorkshire Post)

(Below) A word from Danny Pugh and Lucas takes to the pitch for his 200th
and final league match for Leeds United. (© Press Association)

(top) Lucas on the night he picked up his PFA Special Merit Award, flanked by Gary Blumberg (left) and Glyn Binkin, two of the key men in 'Team Lucas'.
(© Press Association)

(Below) Lucas with Inter Milan and Cameroon star Samuel Eto'o at the match to celebrate Nelson Mandela's birthday.

Proud dad – Lucas with Ofentse, Jessica, Owami and Lucas Hugo.

Lucas's wife Feziwe outside their Yorkshire home. (© Yorkshire Post)

The awards kept coming
Top left: Leeds United player of the year, presented by Supporters' Club chairman
Ray Fell. (© Yorkshire Post)
Below left: Leeds legend Peter Lorimer presents Lucas with a lifetime achievement
award. (© Yorkshire Post)
Right: Lucas and Feziwe with his FIFA Fair Play award, acknowledging his
contribution on and off the pitch. (© Press Association)

Lucas collects an honorary doctorate from Leeds Metropolitan University. 'My mum will be proud – she always wanted me to be a doctor.' (© Yorkshire Post)

embarrassing 1-1 draw. Queiroz was determined to have his captain for the Burkina Faso match and if Leeds wouldn't agree then South Africa would play hard-ball. They would invoke the FIFA regulation that allowed them to prevent the player turning out for his club if he refused to play for his country. The South Africa media were full of stories that Lucas's reign as South Africa's captain was about to end unless he agreed to commit himself to his country's matches. Queiroz was ratcheting up the pressure..

At Leeds, O'Leary made it clear that in his mind there was a simple solution – Lucas should retire from international football altogether or use his position as a superstar in South Africa to dictate terms to SAFA. He didn't appreciate how difficult that would be for Lucas. 'I don't think the club realised the situation in South Africa,' Gary Blumberg said. 'This wasn't like Alex Ferguson withdrawing a player from the England squad to save him for a Manchester United match. Even in post-apartheid South Africa it was still difficult for people to say no to authority, especially in football which was such an important symbol in the building of the Rainbow Nation.' Lucas had been part of the struggle to rid his country of an oppressive regime and he felt an obligation to do all he could to rebuild it. Showing little understanding of the turmoil being suffered by the player, the Irishman reminded Lucas that he had just signed a lucrative new four-year deal, accused him of being disloyal and he too threatened to give the armband to someone else.

In an article in the *Yorkshire Post*, football correspondent Jeremy Cross sprang to Lucas's defence, claiming: 'If players deserve to be chastised then so be it, but it is difficult to see what Radebe has done to justify such treatment from his manager and the circumstances are clearly having a detrimental effect on his game.' And it was noticeable that when Lucas spoke about his dilemma, following a meeting with O'Leary and Ridsdale held after the Newcastle game, he pointedly said: 'I had an opportunity to meet with the chairman and he understands my predicament. He has been very supportive of my position. I obviously realise the importance of my commitment to the club and he appreciates how hard a decision it is for me to withdraw from my international duties.' The manager's involvement in the meeting was ignored.

As much as it hurt, Lucas could see no alternative but to tell SAFA that unless they were willing to be more flexible about calling him up, the match against Burkina Faso would be his last for Bafana Bafana. He wanted to tell the officials personally and planned to make the formal announcement at a dinner in Johannesburg that was being attended by FIFA President Sepp Blatter. Lucas wasn't alone with this problem, most of the top African players were now signed for clubs in Europe so the situation was only going to get worse. Blatter and FIFA were the people in a position to resolve it by co-ordinating the two sets of fixtures so perhaps Lucas could use his own position as FIFA's Fair Play award winner and a man who had shown he was willing to make sacrifices to support his country, to demonstrate how impossible life was for African footballers. If he could put pressure on the governing body to make changes at least some good would come out of his retirement.

Inevitably news that Lucas was to quit leaked out into the press and fans in South Africa were shocked. Talking to an English journalist, Gary Blumberg said: 'I don't think Leeds United fans quite realise what a massive decision this has been. A South Africa team without Lucas in it will not seem like quite the same team for many South Africans.'

Shaun Bartlett, another player whose club had wanted him to stay behind and play in the FA Cup, scored the only goal as Bafana Bafana overcame Burkina Faso in Rustenburg. It was a highly-charged match for Lucas but he hardly had time to shower and change afterwards when he was whisked into the stadium's Presidential suite where South Africa cabinet minister Jeff Radebe urged him not to announce his retirement. 'Leave it for a while. Let's see if Danny Jordaan can sort something out with Leeds United,' he urged. Lucas was doubtful anything could be achieved but who was he to argue with a government minister? He agreed.

A meeting was called at United's Thorp Arch training ground early in February. South Africa showed how seriously they were taking it by sending over not just Jordaan, but also SAFA President Molefi Oliphant and vice President Irvin Khoza to argue their country's case. Leeds were represented by O'Leary and two directors. Lucas was on his own. It's not clear if SAFA insisted on Gary Blumberg being excluded from the meeting in the hope Lucas might be persuaded to change his mind, but if they did, they had misjudged Lucas again. Once again he showed that behind the ever-present smile and laid-back charm, there was a steel core. He showed it so seldom that it always came as a surprise, yet it shouldn't have because anyone who had watched him snuff out the challenge of world-class striker after world-class striker should have realised that was only possible by a strong-minded man.

Lucas told SAFA that as much as he loved his country, and as proud as he was to pull on the green and gold shirt and tug the armband high on his arm, unless they were willing to be completely flexible, they must look for a new centre-half and captain.

Both sides issued statements that sounded as though they had come away from the meeting with everything they wanted but back home in South Africa the press refused to be fooled. The *Sowetan* reported the story under the headline 'Leeds still hold all the aces' and columnist Bareng-Batho Kirtjaas wrote: 'By my interpretation the statement is a victory for the Elland Road team. They still have first call on Rhoo's services and they have SAFA conceding to their whims.' If only it had been that simple. The events of the last month had left Lucas hurt and angry. Some of his relationships would never be the same again.

To some observers from the outside it looked as though O'Leary was finding it hard to find the right balance between 'good cop' and 'bad cop' that is one of the secrets of successful football management. Having built such a strong 'family' atmosphere at the club in his early days in charge, he seemed to be changing his style, much more 'boss' than 'gaffer'. According to Ridsdale's book, Paul Robinson who had been playing out of his skin since Nigel Martyn had been injured, vowed, 'I'll never play for that bastard again.' It wasn't just that fit-again Martyn had been picked ahead of him for the Liverpool cup-tie that upset the young keeper, it was that he only learned about it when O'Leary uncovered the team on a flip chart in a team meeting. The least Robinson had expected was a quiet word of explanation in advance. He felt humiliated.

Leeds lost the match 2-0 and now faced an immense battle to claw their way up the table so they could qualify for Europe next season. They also needed to regain some form for the little matter of Champions League matches that were coming up.

The claim that a week is a long time in politics could equally be applied to football as Leeds demonstrated going into February 2001. In reality it was 11 days, but they crammed in four games, won two and drew two and with other results going their way, they found themselves back up to fifth in the table. Lucas and Ferdinand had been at the heart of a solid defence. The former West Ham star was making those who ridiculed his huge fee look foolish and Peter Lorimer claimed, 'Lucas Radebe all but matched him with an exemplary display. It is a formidable defensive pairing.'

At last, Leeds were showing something like their true form. The big question now was could they carry that on into the next two matches against Belgian champions Anderlecht?

Chapter 32

The other knee

There was a feeling at the Royals Sporting Club Anderlecht that although they were regularly champions of Belgium and had a good track record in European competitions, they were never quite given the respect they deserved. Maybe if they could put on a show against the upstarts from Leeds, who had made Real Madrid work hard and beaten Lazio, people might take notice.

The Champions League programme meant the sides met twice in the course of a week and Anderlecht were having the better of things at Elland Road. They took the lead in the 66th minute and Leeds' heads dropped a little. But then Ian Harte equalised with one of his trade-mark free-kicks and Lee Bowyer took a superb pass from Alan Smith to fire in the late winner.

Anderlecht coach Aime Anthuenis was not a happy man when he faced the Press: 'Leeds are not a good side. I was not at all impressed by them. Next week in Brussels is a different game. We will see what happens then,' he raged. Lucas could take some satisfaction from the fact that the coach also lambasted his prolific strike force of Jan Koller and Tomasz Radzinski for not doing better. He and Rio must have done their jobs.

Leeds fans, who in common with those of Anderlecht felt their side was too often slighted by the so-called bigger clubs, were insulted by Anthuenis's comments and they set off in large numbers for Brussels hoping the players would make him eat his words. They also knew that if Real Madrid could repeat their win over Lazio, victory would ensure Leeds a place in the quarter-finals. But Anderlecht had a 100 per cent record at home that season, including a Champions League win over Manchester United. Their coach had good reason to expect things to be very different at the Constant Vanden Stock stadium.

And they were. Olivier Dacourt translated Anthuenis's pre-match comments for the rest of his team-mates and David O'Leary's work was done. Asked what he thought of the remarks coming out of Brussels, Lucas gave one of his polite but to the point answers that his team-mates enjoyed reading. 'We know we didn't play particularly well in the first game, but who got the three points?' he said. 'The bad news for Anderlecht is that we are getting better. Anyway, it doesn't really matter what opposing coaches say. They are the ones sitting there on the touchline while we, the players, are the ones coming up with action instead of words.'

Lucas's judgement was spot on. Instead of a hesitant side fighting for form, Leeds were back to their fired-up best. Smith scored twice before half-time and Mark Viduka made it 3-0 before Anderlecht managed a consolation goal. Even then Leeds had the last word, Harte smashing in a penalty. The team that only a few weeks before had struggled to keep above the Premiership relegation zone, were now just two rounds away from the biggest final in club football. And they'd done it with two group games to spare.

After picking up five bookings, Lucas was suspended as Leeds ended Tottenham's nine-game unbeaten run. In theory he could have travelled home and played in South Africa's World Cup qualifier against Malawi, but with games against Manchester United and Real Madrid coming up, it was thought the travelling would be too tiring. That didn't stop South African journalist Sy Lerman accusing the Bafana captain of 'cocking a snook at the national side.' Lucas decided to ignore any criticism from home. If people questioned his loyalty after all his years of exemplary service to his country, then nothing he could say was likely to change their minds. He'd been forced to choose and in fact there had been no choice because if he wasn't playing regularly for Leeds, South Africa were unlikely to pick him anyway. It was time for him to do what was best for him and right now he was enjoying the fact that the old spirit was returning to the Leeds camp.

One of the most extraordinary features of United's revival was that it was achieved against a background of lurid headlines generated by the evidence being heard at Hull Crown Court. 'THE BLOOD ON BOWYER'S JACKET' yelled one. 'WOODGATE'S TEEN SHAME' screamed another. And, after Michael Duberry gave his evidence, yet another proclaimed: 'MY LIES TO POLICE TO SAVE A MATE.' Day after day, as details of the horrific attack on Sarfraz Najeib were revealed, the reputation of Leeds United was sullied and the club that had worked so hard to restore a tarnished image, was again considered a pariah by many. Yet somehow the players managed to perform with a style that in football terms at least showed Leeds United were among the best in the country.

With the team playing well again, O'Leary was more relaxed and he positively relished the chance to go up against Sir Alex Ferguson, who had recently hinted, prematurely as it turned out, that he would retire at the end of the season. The title was clearly on its way back to Old Trafford this time but O'Leary said: 'What I would really like is to win the championship next season and give him the perfect send-off to retirement. A sort of present from Leeds United.' Whereas a few weeks before this would have been a fixture to approach with trepidation, now there was anticipation among the players, the fans and even in the local newspapers where 'The Clash of the Titans' was counted down every day.

Leeds took the game to their opponents from the opening whistle and after having the better of the first half should have gone ahead just before the break. Harte challenged Fabien Barthez and for some reason the French international keeper aimed a kick at United's full-back. The referee awarded a penalty but decided to let the offender off with a yellow card rather than red and Manchester United were immediately rewarded when Barthez saved Harte's spot kick. As ever with this fixture, the controversy didn't end there. Ole Gunnar Solskjaer put the visitors ahead in the 64th minute but Leeds deservedly equalised seven minutes from time when Viduka headed home Smith's cross. In the dying minutes, Reds' defender Wes Brown turned the ball into his own net but to his relief the goal was disallowed because Viduka was judged to be offside. To Leeds' players and fans it looked like the same old story. 'Referees are afraid of Manchester United,' Lucas said.

Leeds felt hard done by again three days later when they came away from the Bernebeu stadium with nothing although they had more than matched Real Madrid. Smith gave United an early lead, finishing off a move started by a sweeping pass from Lucas, but Raul equalised, using his hand to guide the ball into the net. Figo put the home side ahead with a shot that Nigel Martyn had covered until it hit a divot and bounced over the stranded keeper. Viduka managed to square things again but a quality – and fair – goal from Raul clinched the victory.

Lucas was back to his best form, reading the game well, strong in the tackle and quick to nip in for an interception that thwarted some of the world's best strikers. It was in stretching to cut out yet another dangerous pass that his studs stuck in the turf and he felt the pain in his battle-scarred right knee. He immediately knew he couldn't carry on and as always, any fresh damage to the joint that had come close to ending his career in 1995 brought a cold sweat of fear. As he limped away from the stadium on crutches, he told waiting journalists, 'I'll live but I'm hurting too much to talk right now.' The reporters weren't used to Lucas declining an interview and feared it must signal a serious injury.

Lucas spent an anxious 48 hours waiting for the swelling to go down so that the specialist could scan the knee but when the result came back it showed no major damage. With rest, he should soon be able to play again. That was a relief, even though it meant he missed the visit of Lazio and the trip to Charlton. At least he could look forward to what promised to be an exciting league run-in and the possibility of making history in the Champions League.

United's next game was at the Stadium of Light against a Sunderland team that Peter Reid, later to manage Leeds, had guided to fourth in the table. The physios had suggested Lucas should not be recalled for at least four weeks but with Matteo picking up a knock and Duberry and Woodgate unavailable because of the on-going court case, O'Leary decided to bring his old warrior back early. And Lucas wasn't going to turn down the chance to play and prove his fitness with the quarter-final against Deportivo la Coruna just around the corner. In the event, his right knee stood up to the stresses very well – it was his left that gave up on him. He injured himself early on tackling Don Hutchison but knowing that his side had no specialist cover on the bench, he continued to play on to half-time. Physio Dave Hancock examined him during the interval and didn't like what he saw. 'There's no way you can go back out there,' he said. Leeds won the game 2-0 and jumped over Sunderland into fourth place but for Lucas the season was over. A scan showed he had damaged medial ligaments and instead of playing in the quarter-final of the Champions League, Lucas found himself back in the operating theatre and facing another long lay-off. He was devastated. The physical pain and inconvenience were bad enough but the prospect of being on the sidelines as the club he had helped to build tackled their greatest test to date was just torture. He badly needed something to lift his spirits. Thankfully Madiba was on hand to provide it.

Chapter 33

He is my hero

Over the years at Leeds, Lucas had grown to enjoy the fans' sense of humour so even in the gloom following his knee operation, he had to smile when he was told of their latest gem. In the lead-up to the Champions League quarter-final, Deportivo coach Javier Irureta had declared that Leeds were the weakest side left in the competition. Once again, David O'Leary didn't have to motivate his players and as Leeds blitzed the Spanish side 3-0, the United faithful sang 'Three-nil to the weakest link!'

A 2-0 win over Southampton put Leeds up to third place and back in the Champions League spots in the Premiership. At Hull Crown Court the jury was out considering its verdict so even that shadow looked as though it was about to clear, one way or another. Tony Hackworth had already been freed on the orders of the judge and Michael Duberry was found not guilty of conspiring to pervert the course of justice in one of the first verdicts returned by the jury.

Like everyone else, Lucas realised it would take some time and possibly some upheaval before the effects of the trial worked themselves out in the squad. It was reported that Bowyer and Woodgate were hardly speaking and there were questions about whether Duberry and Woodgate would ever be able to play in the same team. But the end of the case would at least bring initial closure and those problems could be addressed.

Incredibly, with the jury sent home for the weekend and their final verdicts expected on the Monday morning, the *Sunday Mirror* decided to publish an interview with Sarfraz Najeib's father in which he claimed that the attack on his son had been racially motivated. The judge had already ruled that whatever else it had been, the assault was not racist, and when the court sat again, Mr Justice Poole announced that he had no choice but to dismiss the jury and order a re-trial. The newspaper was hit with £175,000 fine for contempt of court but Leeds United paid a much higher price.

Knowing how the first trial had affected the dressing room, Lucas feared the re-trial could be even more disruptive, allowing unhealed sores to become more raw. Once he was fit again he would have his part to play. But right now his main priority was to be able to walk without crutches by the end of April because he had an important date and nothing was going to keep him away. Out of the hundreds of invitations he received every year, Nelson Mandela had agreed that his first visit to the north of England would be to Leeds. Lucas could hardly believe it when he was told – he had met Madiba many times, but this would be the first time in the city he called his second home.

The city of Leeds has a long tradition of supporting human rights struggles. It was at the centre of the abolition of slavery campaign in England, the fight to improve the inhuman conditions of factory children and the chartist movement, demanding an extension of the right to vote. The link between Mandela and the city went back to 1965 when Leeds University Students Union made him their honorary President at a time when much of the establishment in England considered him to be a terrorist. Eight years later people at the university again showed their support by naming a nuclear particle they had discovered after him and as the anti-apartheid movement grew round the world, many people in Leeds embraced and supported it. In 1983 the city opened the Nelson Mandela Gardens to show their backing for the world's most famous prisoner and a year later, the Nelson Mandela Centre was opened in Chapeltown, the area of Leeds where a large Afro-Caribbean community live.

Madiba had agreed to visit Leeds to receive the Freedom of the City, re-dedicate his garden and attend a lunch to raise funds for his children's foundation. Lucas was invited to help welcome him and join in the celebrations. He took his place on the temporary stage erected in Millennium Square together with Channel 4 journalist Jon Snow. The square was packed. People had travelled from all over the north of England just to catch a glimpse of the South African statesman. Lucas was a little nervous – it was easier to play football in front of a big crowd than pick up a microphone – but he needn't have worried. He was given a rapturous reception. It meant a lot to him. Even after all these years, he was still surprised by just how much the people of Leeds had taken him to their hearts.

He spoke about the importance of Mandela and his experience of him: 'To me Mr Mandela is the greatest man alive. He not only changed the face of South Africa, he changed the whole world. When I was at school, we used to chant his name, though we weren't exactly sure who he was. But everyone knows now!' Lucas helped introduce a programme of entertainment from one of South Africa's favourite singing groups, Ladysmith Black Mambazo, dance artists, Shikisha, and a choir made up of 100 local children while the joyous crowd waited for the guest of honour to appear.

Having visited the garden named after him, Madiba finally made it to the platform where he was greeted by the loudest cheer of the day. As ever he charmed everyone, dancing his way across the stage to the sound of Ladysmith Black Mambazo and typically insisting on shaking hands with every one of the children in the choir. When he spoke to the crowd – a speech full of humour, humility and grace – there was an awed silence, broken by laughter as he said: 'For some time now I have been haunted by three misfortunes: I am a pensioner, I am unemployed and I have a criminal record. If, therefore, I do not have the courage and self-confidence that you would expect, you know the reason.'

This was one of the greatest days of Lucas's life. He knew Madiba had a soft spot for him but only then did he realise just how deeply the former President cared. As Madiba entered the council chamber for lunch and started to make his way past the applauding guests towards the top table, suddenly he stopped, did a double-take and went back to embrace Lucas. 'Here is my hero,' Madiba said. Lucas could still hardly believe it when he spoke to *Yorkshire Post* journalist, Matt Reeder: 'I just could not stop smiling. That was the moment of my life. I was really embarrassed because I did not know what to say but it was a great moment for me. It made the hairs on the back of my neck stand up. It was something I will never forget.'

Inspired by Mandela's visit, Lucas shrugged off the despair he had been feeling and threw himself into his work. He might not be able to play football at the moment but he could still make a difference to people's lives. One of his favourite projects was the Leeds United Book Challenge, aimed at persuading some of the 70 per cent of children who never used their public library to go along and see what a treasure chest of information and entertainment could be found there. He and five other United stars chose their favourite book and the club produced a collectable card for each, featuring a description of the book and a photo of the player. Each time they visited the library and took out a book, the kids would be given a card and anyone with all six was entered in a prize draw. The picture of Lucas smiling and holding a book like a roof on his head became the defining image of the campaign and he spent hours visiting libraries and talking to children, urging them to discover the magic of reading. Launching the scheme, he told how important books had been to him as a youngster, helping him discover more about the world, and he explained why he had chosen *One Step Behind Mandela* by Rory Steyn and Debora Patta as his recommended read: 'It is a moving account of the struggle for equal rights in my country and the recognition of the vast strength of the black people. It is an important book for young people to read.'

As Howard Wilkinson was later to point out, Lucas had the instinctive ability to mix comfortably with people of all ages and backgrounds. With youngsters he was like a big friendly uncle; on visits to teenagers he was hip enough to be accepted as one of them; with older fans he was happy to listen to their stories of the days of Bremner, Gray and Hunter and had picked up enough knowledge of the club's history to be able to talk about it.

With some audiences he had to go back to his own past to reach them, as on the day he was invited to visit a young offenders' institution to talk to the inmates. Many of them were hardened teenagers who already had several convictions to their name. As they sat around informally chatting, Lucas was urging them to make the most of their lives, that their past didn't have to foretell their future. 'We can't all be footballers,' he said, 'but we all have a talent for something and if we work hard at it, we can be successful.' While several of the young men were nodding, slightly in awe at being in the presence of a Premiership footballer, one lad refused to be impressed.

'It's OK for you with your twenty grand a week and your big car, it ain't so easy where I come from,' he challenged.

Lucas smiled, lifted his shirt and displayed the scar left when the bullet had entered his body in Diepkloof. 'It's not been easy where I came from,' he said, 'but you have to try.' The young man was paler but now listening attentively.

As much as Lucas enjoyed the opportunity to use his celebrity to affect people's lives in a positive way, he still felt enormous frustration at missing out on playing. No matter how close you are to your team-mates and how much they try to include you in the day-to-day banter, players with long-term injuries always find themselves on the edge of things. When the team goes out to train, you are on the treatment table, when they travel to away matches, you are left behind, when they play at home, you are in the stand. Most frustrating is that you still care about every result but you cannot do anything to affect the outcome.

The three-goal advantage Leeds built up in the first leg against Deportivo was enough to send them through to the semi-finals despite going down 2-0 in Spain. That brought another tie against Spanish opposition and Valencia proved too strong. The match at Elland Road was goalless but Leeds were never in the tie at the Estadio Mestalla. They were clearly feeling the effects of a long season and they lost 3-0. To cap a miserable night, Alan Smith was sent off for a petulant two-footed tackle.

In the league, United had just lost to Arsenal, their first defeat after a run of 13 unbeaten league outings. That put them back to fourth in the table, three points behind Liverpool. Lucas was by now starting to ease back in training and while he wasn't ready for the 6-1 hammering of Bradford City, he was back on the bench as an unused substitute for the final match of the season, a 3-1 victory over Leicester City. Unfortunately those three points were not enough. As impressive as their comeback had been after the mid-season crash, Leeds were pipped for the last Champions League place by Liverpool. They would have to make do with the UEFA Cup next season. As ever the summer looked like being a hectic time for Lucas. First he had a wedding to attend, then there was the small matter of an engagement party. His own.

Chapter 34

Losing the armband

It wasn't the most flattering picture of Lucas ever published but at least the shot of him running with his cheeks puffed out and tie flying back over his shoulder suggested that his knee could stand up to pounding the pavement. It also amused his team-mates to see Lucas caught on camera, late again, this time at Ian Harte's wedding, where he arrived even later than the bride and had to sneak into the back of the church, trying not to disturb the service.

He was starting to feel good about his injury. He'd trained with the first team and apart from the usual aching, which by now he took as normal, things seemed to be going well. With important games coming up in June it was tempting to make himself available for at least some of the busy summer Bafana programme. But physio Dave Hancock had been hammering home for months that he had to be patient and not rush a comeback and Lucas was at last beginning to realise that some of the wear and tear on his knees was due to his own willingness in the past to play before he was fully recovered. He knew that another major injury could mean the end of his career and his desire to go on for a few more years persuaded him to take the summer off. So he took a back seat as South Africa drew with Liberia and Congo in the African Cup of Nations qualifiers and then picked up another draw in Burkina Faso and a win over Malawi to book their place in the 2002 World Cup finals. The thought of ending his international career by captaining his country in another World Cup was even more incentive for him to buckle down and work on his fitness ready for the new campaign.

Organization is not one of Lucas's strongest talents so when he turned his mind to his engagement to Feziwe, he left David Share to take care of the little matter of designing and producing the engagement ring. Feziwe invited the Leeds jeweller to come over to South Africa for the party but urged him not to tell Lucas. It would be a surprise. David recalled, 'Fezi's parents lived at the end of a cul de sac and they'd put a marquee right across the road. It was packed. When I went in the house, Lucas was standing next to a curtain. He did a double-take when he spotted me then hid behind the curtain before peeping out again with that broad smile everybody loves.'

June and July of 2001 provided one of the longest and most enjoyable breaks Lucas had experienced since he'd joined Leeds seven years before. He was able to spend time with his fiancée, family and friends in South Africa, do some charity work and still get to the gym often enough to strengthen his knee and prepare his body for the rigours of pre-season training.

He was optimistic that United were in a good position to build on the last two seasons, which had seen them confirm their place as a top-five club in England and reach two European semi-finals. It was some achievement. But now was the time to deliver more. Lucas told the press: 'Hopefully we can be challenging for the Premiership and for some silverware. We thought it was going to happen last season but obviously we had our injury problems. Had it not been for that I think it would have been a close run thing with Manchester United. We had some bad times but we still pulled together and we showed the character and potential which will take us further. We have achieved a great deal with a club that started low and has come up, gradually improving each season. For me to look back at where the club was on the day I signed to where it is today gives me great pride. Now it is time to step up to another level. Since I took over as captain we have been through some thick and thin times but it would be a great moment for me to lift a trophy, especially if it was the championship.'

It had been just over four months since Lucas had played a competitive game and since then Dominic Matteo had been transformed from a fine midfielder to a solid central defender. There was also competition from Jonathan Woodgate and Michael Duberry for the spot alongside Rio Ferdinand so Lucas knew he faced a fight for his place. With doubts about his position, he could understand to some extent why David O'Leary decided to strip him of the captaincy and hand it to Ferdinand. What he found hard to take was the way it was done. Instead of inviting him into the office for a one-to-one chat to explain his thinking, O'Leary announced the change almost casually in the corridor outside the physios' room. Even Ferdinand felt the manager could have handled it better, as he revealed in his autobiography, *Rio: My Story*. 'The Chief was a man we all loved. He was one of the best defenders in the Premiership and he was our leader whether he was on the pitch or not,' he wrote, adding that on hearing the news, 'I was delighted and happy, of course, but also embarrassed because the Chief was there, right in front of me. It must have been hurting Lucas and I didn't feel at all comfortable, but he made it easy for me, he was a diamond geezer.' Ferdinand admitted he felt so bad that he wouldn't park in the space reserved at Thorp Arch for the captain's car until Lucas insisted. The new skipper wasn't alone in feeling for Lucas, one of his long-time team-mates came up to him and said: 'Chief, you will always be my captain.'

Everyone expects a manager to be ruthless, to make difficult decisions that the players didn't like, but there is a way of doing it that they can accept. Some senior people in the club thought this was an example of O'Leary having lost that ability, or maybe he no longer saw Lucas as important to his ambitions and so less worthy of consideration. Nevertheless the Irishman went out of his way to praise the man he had once described as indispensable when he made the public announcement, saying, 'Lucas has done a brilliant job. He is a wonderful man to have around the place and it is no reflection on him that Rio has got the job.' But it still hurt.

Lucas hid the pain in public and concentrated on trying to win a place in the team. He told Carlos Queiroz that if he were needed he would be willing to play in Bafana Bafana's friendly in Sweden. If he wasn't to be a regular in the Leeds side, then the problem of playing for his country was eased. But the right knee continued to be troublesome and he had to ask to be taken off during a United pre-season match. He missed the final warm-up game against Sparta Rotterdam, ending his hopes of playing for South Africa, and he took no part as United picked up seven points from their first three games.

Lucas was encouraged when he managed to get through a full reserve game in midfield against Liverpool. 'It was a good work-out and the knees are standing up OK but I know it will be a huge challenge to get back into the side,' he said afterwards. 'This is what you expect at a club like this. They are going to bring in quality players but I am working hard and I am determined to win my place back.'

Progress felt agonisingly slow and at times it seemed that for every step forward he took, there were two back. He was often in pain and spent his time either training or on the treatment table. There were only a few lighter moments to distract him. He launched his own CD, *Out of Africa – The Captain's Choice*, a compilation of South African songs by some of his favourite artists that allowed him to share his passion for music with his fans. And there was an enjoyable evening when he returned to Leeds city centre, where he'd introduced Nelson Mandela, and linked up with former United favourite Vinnie Jones to switch on the Christmas lights.

He was anxious to get back to playing but could only watch from the sidelines as Leeds made an impressive start to the season. By early December they had knocked Maritimo, Troyes and Grasshoppers of Zurich out of the UEFA Cup and a 2-1 win at Blackburn saw them third in the Premiership, only three points behind leaders Liverpool. Meanwhile, although Lucas had only managed one more reserve game against Manchester United, he bizarrely found himself in the middle of another club v country row after O'Leary said publicly that the Chief's career was in the balance and blamed South Africa for over-playing him. Danny Jordaan was incensed and hit back: 'Why should we be blamed when all the injuries sustained by Lucas came in Leeds United matches? The records show Lucas played just once in 12 qualifiers for the 2002 World Cup and African Nations Cup.' It was as though neither side felt their year was complete without a blast at each other, no matter what the situation was with Lucas.

He just wished the two sides would stop bickering over him. 'Both Leeds and South Africa mean a great deal to me and when I think about sacrificing one of them I become heartbroken,' he said, adding that he was aware he might well be forced to choose between them sooner rather than later. 'It really does tear me apart. As a player I always wanted to play for whoever asked me, but I believe that I may have pushed myself too far sometimes. At some stage you have to stop. I'm not getting any younger and I have to make sure that I have a career here at Leeds, which is a long-term option. I want to go out on top.' But even as his head was telling him to be sensible, his heart wouldn't quite listen. 'I have not ruled myself out of playing in the World Cup,' he said but realising how unlikely that sounded, added: 'It would be great for me to bow out by playing in the tournament again but I'm not going to push it. If it is not right, I'll have to sit it out.'

At that stage, the World Cup seemed a distant dream and he had a lot to do before he could realistically put himself forward for selection. However, he was making progress and with Christmas coming up and Leeds facing six matches in 16 days, he was hoping to get some more reserve games under his belt and put himself in contention for a recall. 'My career is a long way from over,' he assured reporters. 'I have another two years after this one and I aim to be playing at the end of my contract. I still feel I can play a big part in this season. The boys have done tremendously well and I think we have a good chance of winning something. To be honest that has given me a big boost in my recovery. To be back playing for this club without any problem with the knee would be fantastic. For the next two years I just want to end on a high note.'

Lucas's fight back to fitness earned him fulsome praise from one of Leeds United's most distinguished 'old boys' and long-time Lucas admirer, Peter Lorimer. In his *YEP* column, 'Lorro' echoed the thoughts of most United fans when he wrote: 'It is wonderful to see Lucas Radebe back in full training and I really hope that we see him come back and play again. He played a lot of games when he should not have done a few years ago and I don't think that has helped him. He has had a knee problem for quite some time but he kept on playing because there was nobody else in the side to take his place. In the end it caught up with him and he paid the price with a bad injury. He put the club's needs before his own and that shows what kind of lad he is.' In something of a sideswipe at O'Leary, Lorimer added: 'Some people have suggested that it was playing for his country which caused the problems, but you cannot blame him for wanting to represent his nation. He always wanted to do his best for both club and country.'

Lucas was more nervous than usual before the reserve match against Sheffield Wednesday, played in front of a few hundred people. It felt a bit strange and reports of the match said he looked 'ring rusty at first. But as the game went on, he started to look sharper and made a couple of good solid tackles and two or three very smart interceptions.' His feeling at the end of the 90 minutes was mainly relief and he admitted: 'I need to get back to reading the game and being in the right position. I need to be stronger and sharper. I hope after next week's game in the reserves I will get better and that I will then be available for selection in the first team..'

The knees creaked and ached after the game but he was used to that by now and he maintained the programme Dave Hancock had designed for him that put the minimum of strain on the joints while keeping him in condition to play. 'He lived in the swimming pool,' Hancock remembered. Lucas willed his body to respond, challenged himself to be ready for the reserve match at Sunderland where he could show more improvement and just maybe get a place on the bench for the first team match against Leicester that Sunday.

The match went better than even he expected. His old instinctive positioning started to kick in and he was able to tackle hard without any pain. He was feeling good. Then, after 70 minutes, he went up for a high ball and landed awkwardly. He felt a stab of pain in his ankle and heard an ominous crack. 'I tried to move my ankle and couldn't. That's when I knew it was bad,' he said later. Those around him feared he had broken a bone. By the time the stretcher reached the dressing room the ankle was swollen massively. Lucas stared at it and couldn't believe that he'd been struck down again. He was taken straight to hospital in Leeds where an X-ray showed there was no break but the specialist warned him there was extensive ligament damage. 'We will only know how bad when the swelling goes down and we can scan it properly but I should warn you, I don't think you will play football again this season,' he said. Lucas was shattered.

Chapter 35

Trials and tribulations

Lucas had built his philosophy of life on being positive, on believing that with hard work most things are possible, that each person is given talents they should cultivate, not giving up until they can achieve no more. But right now it was hard to be positive. How many times could he go through the endless rounds of medical check ups, surgery, prolonged treatment and then the slow, painful, often boring and lonely process of rehabilitation? He accepted injuries were part and parcel of the game, part of the price for earning a living doing what he loved. But for almost a year his life had consisted of the tedium and the torture with none of the adrenaline rushes that made it worthwhile. And now, it was starting all over again.

He forced himself to find something to help him get out of bed in the morning to face the endless hours in the gym, or in the treatment room with his foot stuck in a bucket of iced water, or on a bike riding round the roads near Wetherby. He reminded himself of the journey he had taken, of how hard that had been from time to time. He had succeeded then and he could again. He remembered how fortunate he was compared to some of the lads he'd grown up with, lads who had been more talented than he was but who hadn't got the breaks at the right time. He recalled how long Madiba had to sustain himself on Robben Island before he was able to fulfil his destiny. Lucas told himself he couldn't give up now. He had to dig deep. There would be bad times, but he would come through this and play again.

When *Yorkshire Post* journalist Matt Reeder phoned him for an update, Lucas said: 'The one bright spot is that I have now played two reserve matches and not felt any reaction in the knee that has kept me out of action since the summer. I have to look forward. I know I will be back again. Yes this is a set-back but it just means I will have to work harder and wait that bit longer for my return to the first team. If I can get a few games under my belt I will be delighted.' Football supporters up and down the country and back home in South Africa wished him well but privately many thought that this might be one injury too many for Lucas to overcome.

The next three months were physically and mentally tough for Lucas and his rehabilitation wasn't helped by having to stand by and watch the club he loved start to fall apart. His ankle injury and its aftermath meant he was missing from the club when the jury delivered their verdict from the second trial of those accused of attacking Sarfraz Najeib. Lee Bowyer was acquitted. Jonathan Woodgate was declared not guilty of grievous bodily harm but guilty of affray and sentenced to 100 hours' community service, as was his friend Neale Caveney. Woodgate's other friend, Paul Clifford, was found guilty of GBH and sentenced to six years in prison.

Lucas knew it would take time for the club to recover from the trial. In an interview he said: 'It destabilised the club. It was difficult to get things going, mentally and physically. The problems off the field crept into what was happening on the field. Players felt vulnerable because of all the rumours. At some point it was going to give, and it undoubtedly affected team spirit.'

Slowly the team regained some of its old sparkle - a New Year's Day win over West Ham saw Leeds two points clear of Arsenal at the top of the table – but there were other concerns behind the scenes. At the start of the season, Peter Ridsdale had said there was still money to support the manager's ambitions. He also announced that the club was to consult with fans about moving away from Elland Road to a new super stadium on the outskirts of Leeds that would allow United to increase revenue from gate money, merchandising and by selling stadium naming rights. It now transpired that United needed every penny it could muster. The club's finances were a fine balancing act and the signing of Robbie Keane had taken O'Leary's transfer spending to £76 million with only £30 million recouped by sales. And in October, Ridsdale sanctioned the signing of Robbic Fowler for £11 million and Seth Johnson for £7 million. When the club announced the figures for the second half of 2001, the wage bill had soared from £19 million a year to £23.2 million. With no Champions League money, the overall loss for six months was £13.8 million pounds. Ridsdale made no bones about it, the size of the squad would have to be cut, although he promised, 'We won't sell the family silver,' which was taken to mean that the top players would be staying at the club.

Sustaining United's expenditure required success on the field and certainly European football every season, preferably Champions League, but from their lofty New Year pinnacle, Leeds went into sharp decline. They lost a bad-tempered third round FA Cup clash at Division One Cardiff City, were knocked out of the UEFA Cup by PSV Eindhoven and picked up only four points from their next seven league matches, which saw them slump to fifth in the table.

O'Leary had no doubt where the blame lay. He said: 'I think this was always going to be a very difficult season for everyone at this club. A lot of people forget about the trial that we all went through and so much has come at us off the back of that court case.' But there was another factor the Irishman didn't mention. There was speculation in the media that the manager had 'lost the dressing room,' that 'the players are not happy to play for him any more.' Even though Ridsdale denied it at the time, he was coming to the same conclusion.

Paul Robinson and Gary Kelly had each had run-ins with O'Leary but any disputes had been kept behind closed doors. But in January of 2002, just before the disastrous run of results, O'Leary published his book, *Leeds United on Trial*. Many people criticised it as cashing in on the notoriety of the court case, although to be fair to O'Leary he had agreed to write the diary of the season before the re-trial was ordered and to an extent it was sanctioned by the club because it was ghost written by director David Walker. However, there is no doubting it brought adverse publicity. Perhaps the biggest damage from the publication was the effect it had on the players and their relationship with the manager. O'Leary had broken the code – he had revealed dressing room secrets and made public his sometimes uncomplimentary thoughts about people in the squad. What, some wondered, would have been his reaction if they had published their thoughts on him?

Later Ridsdale claimed the book set in train the decline of Leeds United. 'Contrary to public opinion, this slide had nothing to do with the fall-out of the Woodgate-Bowyer court case,' he wrote in *United We Fall*. 'If anything the trials had somehow galvanised the team, and brought the lads closer together…For me, the tipping point was that first week of January – the week when David's book was published and promoted. It would be some weeks later before a spokesman from the dressing room would make clear the team's feelings about the manager's literary contribution at such a delicately-balanced stage of the season.' Ridsdale also claimed that ten players or their agents indicated to him that they wanted to leave if O'Leary remained the manager.

With the club seemingly in free-fall, Lucas was desperate to try and get back on the pitch and do what he could to steady things. He might not be captain any more but he was sure his experience would help if he could only be part of the team again. He started to do some tentative ball work at the end of January and was delighted by the way the ankle responded only to be knocked back again when he twisted his wretched, delicate right knee and had to go back to the treatment room. It was early April before he was confident enough to tell the local press that he was hoping to resume full training any day. 'I can do everything now and I just want to go and train in the open after all the indoor work I have been doing. Then the next big hurdle will be to get through a reserve game without any problem. At the moment I'm not looking any further than that.'

The slowly-slowly approach seemed to be working, but then came the need to try and speed things up a little because other injuries were starting to take their toll on the squad. Duberry was struggling, Ferdinand picked up a knock and Woodgate was ruled out for the rest of the season when his jaw was broken in a brawl in his home town of Middlesbrough. Leeds weren't the only team urging Lucas to come back. Having won their group in the African Cup of Nations, Bafana Bafana then crashed out in the quarter-finals to Mali. Queiroz resigned but it didn't halt the slide. Defeats to Saudi Arabia and Georgia followed and there were draws against Botswana and Ecuador with Jomo Sono and Trott Moloto in temporary charge. It was now decided that Sono would lead them into the 2002 World Cup and he was desperate to get Lucas in the squad.

Finally, on 18 April, Lucas ran out on to a football pitch. It was only for 45 minutes and in the reserves but it was a start and there were no ill-effects. He followed that up with an hour in the next reserve match and revealed that he had been having talks with Sono. 'He wants me to play,' Lucas said. 'He desperately needs experienced players, people who have played in big tournaments and in European football. This is the biggest stage and I think the hopes of our country lie with us. The knee and the ankle are now fixed and are getting better with every day.' But there weren't many days left. Time had virtually run out on his hopes of a first-team recall at Leeds but he played the whole of a third reserve game and there was still Gary Kelly's testimonial for him to show he was ready to represent his country again.

Sono could only wait and hope. It didn't look good. He would shortly have to name his squad and the reality was that it would be an enormous gamble to include a player in the biggest tournament on earth when he had not made a first team appearance for over a year. The coach sounded pessimistic when he said: 'Lucas has played only three games for Leeds United reserves and has had to rest for six hours after each one. We need medical advice from the club doctors.'

Chapter 36

Woodwork halts the dancing

The youngest of 13 children, Gary Kelly joined Leeds as a skinny, homesick, teenager from Drogheda, the coastal town north of Dublin, once the site of a massacre by Oliver Cromwell and his army. Kelly arrived as a striker but despite an obvious talent, it was felt he was too small to make the grade and he was about to be sent home when Howard Wilkinson had a flash of inspiration. He tried the youngster at full-back during the 1993-4 pre-season and so quickly did the Irishman adapt, he was in the Leeds team for the whole campaign, after which he flew to America as part of his country's World Cup squad. It was a meteoric rise and unlike many overnight sensations, Kelly managed to build and sustain a career at the top.

Kelly was the main practical joker in the United dressing-room. From early on, he and Lucas found they laughed at the same things and became friends. In many ways they grew up together as men and players, they had both spent long hours together in the treatment room when Kelly suffered from shin splints, and had become the senior figures as the exciting new generation emerged under David O'Leary. Once asked how English he felt after his years in Leeds, Lucas replied: 'With Kells and all the other lads from Ireland, I think I'm more Irish than English.' So he was delighted that he was fit enough to line up in the Leeds team that took on Celtic to mark Kelly's ten years at the club. The match attracted over 26,000 people with all the proceeds going to cancer charities in memory of the Irishman's sister Mandy, who had recently died from breast cancer. It was not an over-strenuous work-out but Lucas came through with no ill-effects and finally the medical team were able to give him the green-light to join the South Africa squad in Durban.

As he looked around the Bafana Bafana camp, Lucas realised why Jomo Sono had been so eager to have him along. Compared to the squad that went to France, this was a very inexperienced group. He had 63 caps, Andre Arendse, who had made 50 appearances, was back in goal, then came players like Quinton Fortune, Pierre Issa and Benni McCarthy, who had represented their country more than 40 times, But there were also several youngsters who had only played half a dozen games. Leading this squad would be a challenge but it was one Lucas desperately wanted to take on. The first game of the World Cup was less than a month away and he would only have a few matches to prove to Sono that he should be part of the final 22 to travel to South Korea and Japan.

He eased his way back into senior action with 45 minutes against Madagascar before the squad flew to their training camp in Hong Kong to take part in a tournament. 'It feels good to be back. It's great for my confidence to be part of the set-up again,' Lucas said, all his enthusiasm bubbling to the surface. 'This will be my last World Cup and if I am going, I owe it to myself to give it my best.'

A bigger test came in the first Hong Kong match against Scotland, a young side eager to impress their new coach, Berti Vogts. Lucas played the full 90 minutes as Bafana outplayed their opponents and comfortably won the match 2-0. Sono was delighted. 'I was very impressed with Lucas,' he said. 'I've put my head on the block for him but I knew if he played a few games he would come through. He is such a good player and very inspirational. If he is fully fit for all the games then Lucas will be my World Cup captain.'

The whole camp was delighted with the progress their talismanic captain was making. Team manager Stanley Tshabalala reported: 'He is really getting stuck in, unlike when he started when he was struggling. Now he is the Lucas that we know. He is a big-name player and the other players respect him because of his leadership qualities and the way he plays. He is a leader and has brought some confidence into the team as soon as we started training.'

After playing another full game as South Africa beat Turkey 2-0 to win the tournament, Lucas was feeling on top of the world. In a burst of sheer exuberance at the end of one training session he started to kick balls at his team-mates and the training staff who scattered amid gales of laughter. The spree came to an end when one shot accidentally hit a young press officer in the chest and left her on her knees breathless. But there was no mistaking the bounce in his step as Lucas made his way to the team bus after checking she was OK.

South Africa moved to a training facility specially built for them in Gangneung, ready for their opening World Cup game against Paraguay in South Korea's second city Busan. As ever under Sono, it was a very happy camp. It looked as though the coach's prediction that 'my team will dance through the competition' was to prove accurate.

On the eve of the first match, Lucas confessed: 'I'm always nervous, no matter what game I am playing. I was nervous against Celtic in Gary Kelly's testimonial so you can imagine how I will feel having to play on this huge World Cup stage. My knees will be rattling with nerves. I am hoping I can put my recent injuries behind me, put on a good show and represent my country with honour.'

In recent years Lucas had been criticised at home for not playing more games and he wanted to show the fans how much playing for his country meant to him. 'When you look back at the history of our nation, I would never have thought that we would be playing in the World Cup. As an older player I must go out there and set a good example. I have a great deal of experience and by being there I think I can give them a boost.'

Whether it was the nerves, the sense of responsibility or, most likely, sheer ring-rustiness at the lack of football at that level, Lucas struggled in the first half against Paraguay. He was up against Roque Santa Cruz, and three times the 6ft 2in striker got the better of him. The third time it resulted in a goal. But Lucas wasn't tagged a warrior for nothing. In the second half he upped his game and the striker struggled to make any impact on the match. Paraguay edged into a 2-0 lead when Francisco Arce curled a free-kick just inside Arendse's near post but with their captain growing in confidence so did Bafana Bafana. Seven minutes later Tobogo Mokoena unleashed a long-range shot that the keeper diverted into his own goal. Constant South African pressure finally earned them a penalty in time added on for injuries. Despite having missed his previous spot kick against Mali, and despite barracking from the South American players, Quinton Fortune kept his cool and smashed the ball into the net. It was his first goal for his country and had earned them a valuable point.

Coming back from 2-0 down and salvaging a point at the death made the draw feel more like a win and it was a confident team that went into their second game in Daegu against Slovenia. Their opponents, in contrast, were in disarray after their best player, striker Zlatko Zahovic, was sent home. Lucas noticed the difference as the two sides lined up in the tunnel waiting for the signal to take the pitch. His own young guns were singing and dancing and clearly relishing the occasion while Slovenia were heads down and looking nervous. Within four minutes South Africa were in front, Siyabonga Nomvethe bundling home Fortune's cross. From then on there was only going to be one winner but while Bafana Bafana set up a series of chances, none would go in. Fortune had shots saved, Benni McCarthy saw a header come back off the angle of post and bar. It was frustrating and it was scrappy and although it made history as South Africa's first World Cup finals victory, the joy was tinged with disappointment at having not built up a better goal difference against a side ripe for the taking.

South Africa were currently second in Group B, three points clear of Paraguay but they now faced a tough game against Spain while the South Americans could be expected to beat Slovenia. Bafana Bafana needed at least a draw to be sure of reaching the second stage. Wherever you looked in the Spanish team there was class. Skipper Miguel Angel Nadal, once a target for Leeds, was a rock at the back; Lucas knew the midfield skills of Gaizka Mendieta from his exploits for Valencia, and had faced the threat of Raul in the Champions League clash with Real Madrid. It was for exactly this kind of match that Jomo Sono had wanted his captain on board.

This time, it was Bafana who suffered the nightmare start. Arendse was under no pressure as he went down on the wet surface to gather a through pass by Mendieta but somehow he let it squirm away from his body. Raul was following up, nicked the ball away from the keeper's despairing second lunge and walked it into the net. The keeper redeemed himself with a superb save from a close-range header from Fernando Morientes. Had that gone in, it would have been all up for South Africa but instead they seemed to grow in belief and deserved their equaliser when McCarthy hooked in a volley after Nomvethe headed down a Fortune cross. Mendieta curled a free-kick round the wall and past Arendse to restore Spain's advantage just before the break but South Africa were not out of it by any means and the good news from Sewopigo was that Slovenia had gone ahead against Paraguay in first-half injury time.

Eight minutes after the restart, South Africa levelled for the second time. Defender Enrique Romero tried to head away a corner but only succeeded in flicking it to the far edge of the six-yard box where Lucas reacted quickly, guiding his header just inside the post. Instead of a 33 year old with dodgy knees, he looked like a kid again as he raced away in celebration. 'I didn't know what to do when the ball went in,' Lucas admitted. 'I just decided to run and run and run. It was just a magnificent feeling.'

But the joy was short-lived. Three minutes later, Spain snuffed out a Bafana Bafana attack and broke quickly. The South Africans raced back in numbers but still Sanchez Joaquin managed to clip an inch-perfect ball to the far post and Raul rose high to head home from three yards out. There was no coming back from that. Ten minutes from the end Lucas was carried off with yet another concussion. For him, the World Cup was over forever. Paraguay scored three goals in the last 25 minutes and even though South Africa were level with them on points and both had a zero goal difference, the South Americans had scored six goals to Bafana Bafana's five and went through as a result. For the second World Cup in a row, South Africa had been denied progress to the knock-out stages by the slenderest of margins and they couldn't help but reflect on all those squandered chances against Slovenia.

It was agonising to have again come so close to that elusive second stage only to miss out but Lucas later reflected: 'I loved playing in the World Cup. It was one of the greatest footballing experiences of my life. I think what made it really special was that deep down I never really thought I would be fit enough to play out there.' This was the reward for all those tedious hours in the pool, the gym and on the treatment table, of staying positive when things looked blackest. But he knew it wasn't only down to him and when he returned to England, he gave each member of the Leeds physio staff a personalised, signed copy of Nelson Mandela's *Long Walk to Freedom*. And to head physio Dave Hancock, he handed the No19 shirt in which he scored his World Cup goal, signed 'To Juju Man with thanks, Lucas.'

Bafana Bafana's exit was met with some critical media coverage but the fans welcomed them back like heroes. Once again the airport was packed and as soon as he appeared on the balcony, Lucas was greeted with a huge chant of, 'Rhoo! Rhoo!' A banner read: 'Bafana Bafana you are still No 1 in the heart of South Africans' while another proclaimed, 'Welcome Home. You Made Us Proud. We Love You!'

It was great to feel the affection coming from his countrymen and having recovered much of his fitness, Lucas could start to look forward to the new season. Little did he realise that he was about to be embroiled in a chaotic situation with both club and country.

Chapter 37
Shake-up all round

With Leeds United's finances in a bad way, and a second successive season looming with no Champions League football, the board were determined to make considerable savings and that meant offloading players. David O'Leary, in contrast, wanted to strengthen the squad. It was a circle that could not be squared and with the relationship between chairman and manager in tatters, there was a sense of inevitability when Peter Ridsdale summoned O'Leary to his office and sacked him.

Leeds again hoped to turn to Martin O'Neill, who was now at Celtic, but once more the Irishman decided he would stay where he was. Leeds needed an alternative and quickly. Ridsdale later admitted, 'I was left scrambling around for second-best options with people I didn't believe in as much as Martin. The truth is I didn't enjoy a single day at Leeds from the moment David O'Leary walked out of the ground. Looking back, I should have quit as soon as Martin O'Neill said no, because it never went right from that moment on.'

But he ploughed on, even though the board wouldn't even approve his second choice, Steve McClaren. Instead he ended up going along with the majority view and hiring former England manager Terry Venables, a man he felt was wrong for the job. The vital relationship at the top of the club was doomed before it started. The new manager was warned players would have to be sold and there would be little scope for buying. Venables hardly had chance to assess his squad before Rio Ferdinand, a player he had introduced to international football six years before, was sold to Manchester United. It must have seemed all too familiar to him – on taking his first managerial job at Crystal Palace his immediate task was to sell their best player, Peter Taylor, and similarly when he arrived at Barcelona, Diego Maradona was sold straight away to raise money.

As the Leeds players set out for a pre-season tour of Australia and the Far East, the papers were filled with speculation that Olivier Dacourt, Robbie Keane and Lee Bowyer would also soon be leaving as the club sought to recoup £60 million.

Lucas was concerned, wondering if United were destined to become another mid-table side, unable to compete any longer at the highest level. It was out of his hands; all he could do was to continue to ignore the constant pain in his knees and give his best on and off the field. 'It's going to be tough to step into the side and take on the role left by Rio, but I am ready to do it. I'm ready in both body and mind to play for Leeds again,' he declared. He only made cameo appearances in the early part of pre-season but did well when he came on in the 27th minute against Glasgow Rangers. His new 'gaffer' was impressed: 'I think Lucas is a champion,' Venables said. 'He is the type of player you want and need around the club and I thought he was excellent against Rangers. He has been doing very, very well for a player who has only been playing in parts of games.'

Lucas was in central defence alongside new captain Dominic Matteo for the opening match of the 2002-03 season, a 3-0 win over Manchester City, managed by another former England boss Kevin Keegan. It was Lucas's first league game in almost 18 months and as his name was announced the crowd rose to applaud him and broke into his personal chant. Lucas said later. 'I was a bit nervous before the game but it was great to get another chance. It's been such a long time it almost felt like my first game again. The reception from the fans was very emotional for me.' Keegan thought the Leeds defender had been the difference between the sides. He said: 'I thought Radebe was outstanding. Considering that he has been out of the game for so long with injury, he came back and showed what a quality player he is. He did the simple things throughout the match, nothing fancy, nothing clever and that's what you need.'

In his weekly *Yorkshire Post* column the following week, long-time Lucas admirer Matt Reeder claimed: 'Had former manager David O'Leary still been in charge at Elland Road for Saturday's Premiership opener, Lucas Radebe would not have been anywhere near the first team. In fact the South African international, who, quite rightly, is regarded as one of the true gentlemen of the sport, would never have played for Leeds United again had the Irishman not been dumped...Well, Mr O'Leary, I am afraid that last Saturday's display by the Chief would have had you eating those words, together with a pint of Guinness, as you continue to drown in your oh, so sour sorrows. Lucas is a legend, a true great. I know too many people are handed that label today, but there is simply no other word to describe the man.'

Lucas was substitute in Leeds' second match and played the whole of the third. After each game he packed ice around his knees to bring down the swelling and for most of the time in between was restricted to light training and rehabilitation exercises. Leeds were determined to wrap him in cotton wool so he could play as many games as possible but there was no disguising that the Chief had lost some of his pace and often walked with a limp.

Even the kid-gloves treatment didn't work when the swelling in the right knee wouldn't go down in time for him to play against Birmingham City. With the newly introduced transfer window about to slam shut, alarm bells sounded for Venables. He'd already signed Nicky Barmby for £2.75 million and little-known Australian Paul Okon on a free transfer from Watford but he needed cover at the back and, with minutes to spare, he brought in Swedish defender Teddy Lucic on loan. Meanwhile Keane went to Spurs for £7 million. That fee and the £30 million Leeds had received for Ferdinand was clearly not going on players. United were back in the bargain basement.

Lucas's renewed injury problem also sparked another row between Leeds and South Africa. Ephraim 'Shakes' Mashaba had made a winning start to his reign as Bafana Bafana coach, beating Swaziland 4-1, but he wanted his best players available for the African Cup of Nations qualifier against Ivory Coast, including Lucas. The defender wanted to go but Leeds were adamant – they insisted he rested, ready to face Newcastle United. Bafana general manager Stanley Tshabalala was outraged and wrote to FIFA to ask them to intervene. He told the press: 'Even when I explained to Terry Venables the importance of our game in Abidjan, he insisted Radebe's body could not take the pressure. Lucas called us and told us he wanted to play but the situation was in the hands of Leeds United. What really gets to me is that Leeds had written off Lucas. We gambled on him in the World Cup and now we are being snubbed.'

Lucas could scarcely believe that the old club v country tug of war was happening all over again. 'Whatever I do, someone is going to be disappointed,' he said. 'I want to play in every important fixture for my country, especially at this stage of my career. I don't want people to think that I am no longer interested in playing for South Africa now that the World Cup is out of the way. That is not the case. But what can I do? I want someone to make a decision so I know where I stand. This problem has gone on a long time and I don't like it.' FIFA were satisfied with the medical certificate supplied by Leeds and Lucas didn't travel. Neither was he fit to play against Newcastle.

Apart from the South Africa row, Lucas was happy with the way things were going at Leeds. The divisions of the latter part of the O'Leary era had disappeared and Venables' renowned man management skills seemed to have created a buoyant dressing room once again. 'Terry Venables has brought a breath of fresh air to the place and life here is exciting,' Lucas said. 'He has changed things around quite a bit and the way he communicates to the players one-on-one gives them confidence.' Laughing, he added: 'I feel like a 19 year old again. The younger lads keep asking how old I am and I won't answer. I just tell them I will be right behind them, waiting to take their place. I want to play first-team football and I will keep pushing for that.'

His next opportunity came when he was sent on to replace Matteo in the second half against Manchester United. It was Ferdinand's first time back at Elland Road and he received the predictable cries of 'Judas' from the home crowd. Kewell scored the only goal of the game, giving Leeds their first win over their old foes for five years, raising ecstatic chants of 'Rio, Rio what's the score?' Lucas knew how much it meant to the Leeds faithful and he shared their joy: 'I've lost too many times to Manchester United so to beat them is tremendous,' he said. 'In the last minute I kept looking at the referee and willing him to blow his whistle.'

If anything the next game was even more satisfying, closing the chapter on another, deeper hurt. With Matteo still struggling to shake off an ankle injury, Venables gave Lucas the armband for the first UEFA Cup match of the season against the Ukranian side Metalurg Zaporizhzhia and he proudly led United to a 1-0 win. Maybe Lucas was 19 again! But no, the knee problems returned and couldn't be shaken off.

The fresh injury coincided with another Bafana qualifier against Burundi and even though Lucas wasn't playing for his club, SAFA refused to take Leeds' word that he was too injured to travel. Under international regulations, an injured player is still supposed to join up with his squad so his country's medical staff can make an independent assessment. Venables protested that it was ludicrous to force Lucas to fly, probably making his injury worse. The row became personal when Mashaba publicly accused Lucas of cheating his country. 'I think that is outrageous,' Venables said. 'Anyone who knows Lucas knows he wouldn't let anyone down. They felt he should go back so they could check him, which is understandable. I asked if it was possible for someone to come over here and examine him. They said it would be too expensive so we even offered to pay.'

South Africa were in disarray with Delron Buckley also withdrawing and Benni McCarthy left out of the squad because he wouldn't apologise for critical comments he made about SAFA. Lucas felt he had to do something to ease the situation. He was hurt at being called unpatriotic and decided the only way he could convince the Bafana management was to see them face to face. So he paid his own fare to Johannesburg to try and clear the air, explaining that he had no intention of turning his back on his country but that the condition of his knees meant he couldn't tell from one day to the next if he was able to play.

Mashaba seemed unimpressed by the gesture and afterwards told the press he didn't want to talk about Lucas. 'I have 25 players here in camp who are looking forward to playing for their country. I don't know why there's so much concern about Lucas being captain,' he said. And as if to prove a point, the Bafana coach left Lucas out of the squad for the Nelson Mandela challenge against Sweden, even though he had indicated he was willing to play.

Lucas had been through bad spells with Bafana Bafana before but this was the first time he'd felt the national coach didn't value him. It was also a grim time back at Leeds United. After the heady atmosphere when the club beat Manchester United and moved to second in the table, they hit a bad patch and slumped to tenth. Rumours started to circulate that some players were unhappy with the way Venables switched tactics from game to game and even within games, and there was a sense of disillusion as a squad that still consisted largely of the players who had reached the semi-finals of the Champions League seemed unable to pick up points.

Lucas admitted his own frustration after 17-year-old wonder-kid Wayne Rooney skipped by him to score the only goal as Leeds lost to Everton. Leeds were now down to 13th and Lucas said: 'It hurts and it is embarrassing. I can't put my finger on what is wrong but it is up to us now, we have to look at ourselves.'

Morale grew worse as United crashed out of the League Cup at First Division Sheffield United in Lucas's absence but hopes were renewed when they managed a 4-3 win over West Ham and then booked their place in the third round of the UEFA Cup by beating Hapoel Tel Aviv thanks to four goals from Alan Smith. It was bitter-sweet for Lucas, whose match ended when he went down in a tackle after 67 minutes. Afterwards Venables revealed the South African had wanted to stay on the pitch, even though it was clear he was badly hurt. 'I don't think I have come across an amazing guy like him ever,' the Leeds boss said. 'I never use the word lightly but the Chief is a champion both as a sportsman and a person. It was amazing what he did. He was down on the floor injured and couldn't get up but I couldn't catch his eye because he knew I was going to take him off. He called over and asked us to leave it five minutes to see if the injury would go but he'd done his groin and couldn't even get up. The way he and Dominic Matteo have been playing this season when they probably shouldn't have been out there because of injuries has been brilliant. But it's come at a cost – Dom's had to have an operation and the Chief's broken down. I don't think we will see him back again for a while.'

In fact it was 13 matches before Lucas was able to return to first team football and he could only watch as Leeds looked more likely to be sucked into a relegation battle than compete for a place in Europe. They had a crippling injury list, which included Lucas, Matteo, Kelly, Harte, Dacourt, Woodgate, Batty,

Johnson, Lucic, Okon, Bakke, Milosevic and Fowler. As Lucas made a tentative comeback attempt, he found himself in a reserve side with a £27 million strike force.

In stark contrast to this picture of a club in terminal decline, Leeds unveiled their new £5 million building at the Thorp Arch training ground. It was a match for any club in Europe with everything a top team could need, including a half-sized indoor pitch, offices, changing rooms, canteen, state of the art gym and arguably the best medical facilities in the Premiership designed by physio Dave Hancock. As well as practically every mechanical device known to sports medicine, there was a large 'wet room' for hydrotherapy and a specially designed, Olympic sized, rehabilitation swimming pool that included powerful jets allowing players to swim against the resistance and so get the maximum fitness benefit with the minimum wear and tear on limbs. It was just what Lucas needed.

Leeds players were now training in a football palace but they were still performing like waifs and strays. They slumped to 16th in the table, just three points above the relegation zone, and went out of the UEFA Cup, beaten by Malaga. In *United We Fall*, Peter Ridsdale revealed that he had reached agreement with Martin O'Neill to take over as manager at the start of the following season. He now convinced his fellow board members to sack Venables and appoint a caretaker boss until O'Neill finally arrived. They decided the axe would fall after the next game against Bolton but just before that, £30 million of talent played another reserve match and some were ready to return to the first team. Leeds beat Bolton 3-0 and started a run with only one defeat in nine matches. Ridsdale had to hold fire. Lucas returned to action in a drab goalless draw against West Brom. As ever he was optimistic that things were looking up, but on the eve of the transfer deadline came the decision that shattered the harmony at the club.

Chapter 38

Like an elephant's hoof

Lucas was impressed by the way Jonathan Woodgate had come back from his trial and the later fracas in Middlesbrough. He sensed a new attitude and said: 'He's more mature mentally than ever before. I honestly think he's learned his lesson and I've seen a change in him. Sometimes in life you have to learn the hard way and I think that is what Woody has done – but he's come through it well.' Woodgate had been around so long it was hard to remember that he was still only 22 years old. He was starting to live up to his early promise on the pitch and Lucas was convinced 'Woody's got the potential to be a really great player, not just in the Premiership but worldwide.'

The fans were also impressed by Woodgate so there was alarm when the rumours started to circulate that Newcastle United had bid £10 million for the defender and the Leeds board were going to accept. There were plenty of players they would happily have seen sold but not Woody. That would be a betrayal too far. He was a key part of the 'family silver' Ridsdale had sworn to keep. Not knowing that the decision to sack him had already been taken, Venables felt the rug was being torn out from under him: 'I am beside myself with anger,' he said. 'I would be seriously unhappy if he goes and I'll do anything I can and more to keep him.'

But United were desperate for cash and everybody knew it, so negotiating became difficult. Fowler was sold to Manchester City for £7 million but Leeds had to continue paying part of his salary; Bowyer, who was almost out of contract, joined West Ham for a mere £100,000; and Dacourt went on loan to Roma. That hardly dented the problem. Woodgate had to go.

The press conference announcing his sale was one of the most bizarre in the club's history. Venables sat, arms folded, stony-faced, demonstrating as clearly as he could that he was adamantly opposed to the transfer. Ridsdale had told him that if he sold Fowler, Woodgate could stay. He felt let down. Pale and clearly shaken, Ridsdale tried to explain why he was forced to break his promise.

Angry Leeds fans protested, some tearing up their season tickets. The already fragile relationship between manager and chairman was fractured completely. And the players realised that Leeds United's time in the sun was over. Those with ambition to play at the highest level started to talk to their agents about getting away.

The only hope of salvaging something from the season was the FA Cup and briefly the players seemed to rally round Venables. They beat Crystal Palace 2-1 to reach the quarter-finals and Lucas said: 'I think we've got a real chance in the cup. It's been a while since we had a good run in the competition but this might be our year. We know we have been through a bad time but the players have stuck together and that has helped us get results like this one.' But two successive league defeats and an ignominious FA Cup exit at Sheffield United were the final straw. Ridsdale walked out of the next match against Middlesbrough at half-time, too upset to take any more abuse from the fans who had completely turned against him. Two days later, he sacked Venables and appointed former Manchester City and Sunderland boss Peter Reid to hold the fort until the end of the season.

Born on Merseyside and a former Everton player, Reid couldn't have asked for a tougher United baptism, away at Liverpool. It was a match that made him an instant Lucas fan, as physio Dave Hancock recalled. 'Peter Reid had a reputation for being ruthless and had been rumoured to sack physios if he wasn't happy with their news. Lucas had injured his ankle in the Middlesbrough match and it blew up like a balloon. It looked like I was going to have to tell the new manager that his most experienced defender was unlikely to be fit for his first game and I wasn't looking forward to it. But you never gave up on Lucas so we worked on the ankle all week and took him with us to the hotel, planning to give him a fitness test on the morning of the match. Keep in mind he was due to mark Michael Owen, one of the quickest and most skilful strikers in the game at the time.

'I strapped his ankle and we went out to test it. We spent about ten minutes warming up. He was hobbling badly and could hardly move the ankle. When I got him to move sideways you could tell he was in pain but he kept saying "let's do a bit more." After about 20 minutes I told the manager there was no way he could play. Reidy said, "Let me have a word with him," and walked over to Lucas. When he came back, he said, "He's playing." We strapped the ankle again before the game. He didn't have a painkilling injection but went out and he was man of the match. I sat in the dug-out and I couldn't believe what I was watching. He was incredible, never shirking a tackle, putting his body on the line. Afterwards his ankle was like an elephant's hoof but he was still smiling. That summed up Lucas for me. He was definitely old school – pain was secondary to playing.'

Years after leaving Leeds to go to Chelsea and then on as physio to the New

York Knicks basketball team, Hancock still talks of Lucas with something approaching awe. 'To me he was someone who made the most of his opportunity,' he said. 'He was always professional, an incredible athlete, an ambassador for his club and his country and one of the nicest guys I ever met. He's a true gentleman.' And as if to echo those sentiments, when the awards were handed out to mark the tenth anniversary of the founding of the Premiership, Lucas was given the Contribution to the Community Award, 'in recognition of his achievements of making a real difference to people's lives in communities on two different continents.' The impact Lucas had made was also expressed in another, more unusual way when a group of young rock musicians, who were avid Leeds fans, approached him and said they were changing their name and out of admiration for Lucas would from now on be known as Kaiser Chiefs (the s in Kaiser was just in case Kaizer Motaung objected!).

Despite Lucas's gutsy efforts on the pitch, Leeds lost 3-1 at Liverpool and were still only five points above the relegation zone. But they responded to Reid's blunt talking and thrashed Charlton 6-1 with Viduka, one of the players who hadn't enjoyed Venables' constant changes of tactics, scoring a hat-trick. Leeds took a valuable point off Spurs on Lucas's 34th birthday and he celebrated with two last-ditch interventions that prevented Sheringham and Keane from scoring. But in doing so, he aggravated his injuries and then picked up a virus so was forced to miss the next three games, which only produced one win.

The upheavals kept coming at Elland Road. With the club more than £70 million in debt, Ridsdale eventually accepted the inevitable and resigned. It was a sad end for a lifelong fan who had 'lived the dream' only to see it turn into a nightmare. He was replaced by a 65-year-old economics academic with little football experience. Professor John McKenzie made the right noises but was soon seen to be out of his depth.

Lucas came back into the team for the vital last two matches of the season. Leeds were only three points clear of relegation and faced a trip to title-chasing Arsenal and a home game against Aston Villa, who were only just above United in the league. By the time Leeds ran out at Highbury on the Sunday, the two sides below them, Bolton and West Ham, had drawn level on points. Few gave Reid's men any hope and thought Lucas and Duberry were in for a torrid time against Footballer of the Year Thierry Henry. The Frenchman did score but according to the *Yorkshire Post* report the two central defenders were, 'absolutely superb, winning virtually everything in the air and throwing themselves into countless blocks in and around the penalty area. Radebe's performance was particularly impressive given that he has been beset by knee problems all season, and with fellow invalid Dominic Matteo equally eye-catching at the heart of midfield, United's patched up duo finally dispelled any notions that the players had no stomach for a fight.' A reinvigorated Viduka scored the winning goal as Leeds picked up three points and for the second time in four years handed Manchester United the Premiership trophy.

No amount of pain was going to prevent Lucas playing in the final match, which Leeds won 3-1. The celebrations afterwards were as much relief as anything else and they were tinged with sadness because everyone in Elland Road expected that several of the players on show would not be there when the new campaign got underway in August.

It had been a long, painful, tiring and mentally taxing season. Common sense told Lucas it was time to take a rest but he had set his heart on just one more match. Bafana Bafana were to play England in Durban to announce the launch of South Africa's bid for the 2010 World Cup. He could think of no better way to end his international career than in his homeland against players he had come to know from playing against them week-in, week-out for his club. There was only one snag. Ephraim Mashaba was still angry with him for missing matches earlier in the season and refused to pick him. 'I am very disappointed that I won't be able to participate. It is a historic moment for South Africa to play against England, especially in Durban where there is great support. But these things happen in life and you just have to look forward to better times. I'll sit down and watch and cheer as one of the fans,' Lucas said.

There had been plenty of Bafana fans ready to criticise Lucas when he didn't make himself available but despite that they still held him in great esteem and acknowledged his contribution to his country's emergence from the dark days when they were excluded from international competition. Rhoo's success at Leeds had made them proud – he had forged the path for others to follow; he had captained a Premiership club with distinction; he had been recognised as a great player throughout the world. He deserved to be able to say his international farewell with dignity. Shakes was taking his dispute too far.

The South African coach dug his heels in and threatened to resign if Lucas was selected over his head. For him it was a matter of principle and not just over Lucas but all the overseas-based players who were too often not available when their country needed them. 'Let us not forget we are Africans and we are playing in Africa,' Mashaba said. 'England players are selected from their own Premier League, so why can't we select our players from our Premier League?' SAFA were not happy that the coach had chosen to make a stand at this prestigious match, which was designed to show off South Africa's international credentials.

They sacked him and once again the irrepressible and loyal Jomo Sono answered his country's call. When he announced his squad, Lucas, Benni McCarthy, Quinton Fortune and Shaun Bartlett were back. 'You can't discard legends and Lucas is a legend. He deserves to play,' Sono said.

The decision was greeted with enthusiasm back in England. Opposing captain David Beckham said: 'I have great respect for Lucas. He deserves the ovation he will get when he leads his side out.' Peter Reid retold the story of how Lucas had defied the pain to play for him at Liverpool and added: 'His attitude sets a great example to other players and he has a real will to win. His strength is quite amazing and he always walks around with a smile on his face. That's just the kind of man you want around a club. This match will be a fitting way to end his international career.'

In the build-up to the international, both sides were invited to meet Nelson Mandela and Lucas was photographed on one side of his former President with David Beckham on the other, two superstars reduced to small boys in the presence of a unique human being. Amazingly, some of the England players preferred to remain in their hotel 'to let their bodies rest for the game.' Lucas had long since come to terms with the fact that many footballers had little interest in anything outside their self-obsessed world but this he couldn't understand. This was a rare chance to shake hands with a man who had changed history. How often did an opportunity like that come, even to footballers?

Winning his 70th and final cap was an emotional night for Lucas and he was close to tears at the reception he received from the crowd and the acknowledgements from players, coaches and officials. Only afterwards as he confirmed his international career was over, did he reveal how close he had come to retiring during the previous season: 'There was a point a few games ago when I was very disappointed because I was limping and it was so painful I couldn't even get up the stairs at home. I said to Feziwe that I may have to call it quits because I didn't feel it was worth suffering all the pain.' But Lucas knows himself better than anyone and added: 'Then I said I would have to think about it, and once I said that I knew I was never going to make the decision, but it was really close.' Showing his scarred knees, the man United's physios called the Warrior added: 'They are my battle scars. I think they are good scars because I got them doing what I like most. I enjoy the pain after games because I know that I am willing to do the best I can. You only get one chance to do this and that time is now.'

Chapter 39
Dancing into married life

Over the years Lucas had grown into the English lifestyle. He even got used to the weather - but never the food. He loved listening to music – especially soul and R&B – and like most footballers, he enjoyed playing golf, a game he only took up after moving to Leeds. 'He was very enthusiastic about his golf,' David Share remembered, 'although some of his antics might not have gone down too well at some of the snootier clubs. I remember after he scored a gross birdie at one hole he threw himself into a full-length dive, as though he'd scored a goal, and on another occasion when a club slipped out of his hand and went into a lake, he waded in and retrieved it.'

But with a hectic playing schedule and the demands on his time of charity work, Lucas tried to spend as much time as possible at home with the family. Feziwe wasn't keen on going out and while she never stopped him having a night out with the lads, she was always happier when he turned his team-mates' invitations down and spent time with her. Throughout the last few years, when he had often struggled to get his aching legs out of bed and occasionally faced dark nights of doubt and despair, she had often been the only person to realise what he was going through. She had been his rock. It was time for them to marry.

Timekeeping has never been one of Lucas's strong points – jeweller David Share said: 'I've sold him at least five excellent watches but he still manages to be late,' – but on the day of his wedding he arrived on time. Around 400 guests, including more than 50 from England, gathered at Sun City Palace for the glittering occasion. Lucas reflected his life on two continents by his choice of best man or rather men – from Africa he chose his friend Monyane, with whom he'd had that scrape on the border with Bophuthatswana, and from England David Share.

As is the bride's right, Feziwe kept everyone waiting - for an hour! – and as it started to get chilly, blankets were brought out to keep the guests warm. Lucas wandered among them chatting, clearly not concerned that his bride might have changed her mind. 'He was very relaxed about the wait as you would expect,' Share said. 'He's so laid back he seemed to spend the day in a world of his own, walking around with a big smile on his face.' The smile grew broader when Feziwe finally arrived, looking stunning in a dress of Thai silk. After the couple exchanged vows, the guests made their way to the banqueting hall for the reception and a moment that has lived in the memory of all who witnessed it. Emma Joussemet recalled: 'The whole weekend was magical. We were all staying in the same hotel and Lucas made sure everyone was taken care of. But the moment I remember most was when they came into the reception. Feziwe was a quiet person who usually kept out of the limelight, but she and Lucas danced into the room. She was leading the women and he the men in a traditional African dance and she was really getting down. It was fantastic.' Leeds team-mate Nigel Martyn added: 'I've seen days when Lucas could hardly walk because his knees were giving him so much pain, but they certainly looked OK when he danced into his wedding.'

The happiness and exuberance of the wedding was in stark contrast to the mood Lucas found when he returned to Elland Road. Peter Reid's temporary appointment had been made permanent and he had brought Kevin Blackwell in from Sheffield United as his assistant. But the fans were more concerned about who was going. Harry Kewell left for Liverpool under a cloud of acrimony when it was discovered that Leeds had received only £5 million out of which they had to pay his agent £2 million. Newcomers included Jody Morris, Jermaine Pennant and a string of overseas loan players none of the fans had heard of.

Lucas had another minor operation to clean up his knee, which delayed his involvement in pre-season. He finally came into a struggling team for a tournament in Dublin that also featured Aston Villa, now managed by former United boss David O'Leary. Villa won the tournament, Leeds were last. Reid picked Lucas for the opening game of the season against Newcastle but he struggled. He gave away the penalty that put the Geordies in front and also made a mistake as Alan Shearer netted their second. But Leeds salvaged a point and he was in the starting line-up for the next match at Tottenham. Leeds lost 2-1 in a game that was notable only for the debut of 16-year-old Aaron Lennon, the youngest player yet in the Premiership. Lucas had battled through the pain to try and help his side but each time his knees had swollen up and been almost too painful to walk. For the next ten weeks he managed only two brief appearances from the bench and one reserve match while Leeds made their worst start to a season for more than 20 years. They were also in desperate straits off the pitch and called in Trevor Birch, the man who had conjured up Roman Abramovich to rescue Chelsea, to try and sort out a situation that seemed to be heading for administration.

Reid was sacked after a 6-1 humiliation at Portsmouth left United bottom of the table. The ever-faithful Eddie Gray, dismissed from his coaching role by Reid a few months before, returned to take up the challenge and immediately threw Lucas back into the fray at Bolton. Leeds lost the game but took eight points from the next four matches as Lucas continued at centre half. But then the *Yorkshire Post* reported that towards the end of a 1-1 draw at Manchester City, 'The night was soured by the sight of Leeds stalwart Lucas Radebe being stretchered off. The old warhorse seemed to take an awkward fall while winning a tackle and by the way he gripped the stretcher, it was clear he was in serious pain.' Lucas had torn his hamstring.

It was two months before Gray could tell the press, 'Lucas is back and involved. He's the same as ever – kicking people in training with a smile on his face. He's an infectious character and he's good to have around.' The United boss was still wary of playing the veteran and kept him on the bench as Leeds drew with Manchester United and Liverpool and went on a run that saw them win three of the next five games. They were still just in the drop zone but level on points with the two sides above them, with Manchester City only two points better off. They might yet salvage something from the campaign.

The game at Old Trafford had been an emotional day on several fronts for Lucas. That morning it was announced that John Charles, arguably the greatest player to ever wear the club's shirt, had passed away. John had been one of the first United 'old boys' Lucas had met. The 'Gentle Giant' was a modest and loveable man and Lucas was sad to hear he had lost his fight against cancer. United fans were also clearly moved yet they also took the time to pay tribute to another of their heroes. When it came time for Lucas to warm up, he'd hardly stepped out of the dug-out before the fans greeted him with his personal chant. 'It was a great reception,' Lucas said. 'I didn't know where to put myself. The fans are tremendous and it was a special feeling. People don't have to ask why I love this club.'

Off the pitch, United were in financial meltdown and in danger of going out of business. Birch approached the players to see if they would ease the situation by taking a deferment of their wages. Under FA rules, footballers automatically become preferential creditors if a club goes under but still some of the squad seemed reluctant to help. It took an intervention from Lucas to make them see sense. Physio Dave Hancock said: 'Lucas wasn't one of those captains who made stirring speeches or geed the lads up, he led by example. But I'm told that when the squad held a private meeting to discuss the deferral he stood up and made a passionate speech, telling them: "This is something you have to do. This club is in peril and we have to do whatever we can." Some surprising people, players you would expect to be backing the club to the hilt, were reluctant to forego their wages but Lucas won the day.'

Eventually the club was saved from administration by a consortium headed by Gerald Krasner. Although relieved, United fans were uneasy. Krasner was an insolvency expert which raised fears he was about to asset strip. Deals appeared to have been done to slash the debt, which supporters were anxious would eventually come back to haunt them. They were particularly concerned at the prospect of Elland Road falling into the hands of developers. One thing was certain: even if Leeds managed to stay in the Premiership, there would be a massive clear-out of players at the end of the season and with his contract up, Lucas was expected to be among them. The *Yorkshire Post* reported: 'A sum of £11 million will be slashed from the £40 million player wage bill when David Batty, Lucas Radebe, Jason Wilcox, Michael Bridges and four loan players are released at the end of the season but it is unlikely to be enough.'

So it came as something of a surprise when the new board offered Lucas a one-year extension to his contract at the start of April. He had been toying with the idea of returning to South Africa to finish his career where it had started at the Chiefs. But when Leeds told him they needed him to stay to help guide the young players through what would be a tough baptism, he couldn't say no. Even though it meant a reduction on his wages, he never hesitated to sign.

Peter Lorimer, now a club director, explained their thinking: 'Lucas has been unbelievable for this club. Loyalty isn't always the same nowadays because of the masses of money in the game – but Lucas is a loyal guy. I think he sets a great example to younger players. He's good to have around because he's a popular bloke and, at a time when the club may have to look at bringing younger players through, his experience will be important."

Lucas smiled as his friend Nigel Martyn returned to Elland Road with Everton on 13 April and received a standing ovation from the crowd. But he was less amused when his former team-mate produced a stunning display to restrict United to a single goal and earned the Merseysiders a draw. It was Lucas's first game since just before Christmas and Eddie Gray had asked him to add some security to midfield.

United were still in the third relegation spot, two points below three other clubs with the worst goal difference of the quartet. With only two more home games and trips to Arsenal, Bolton and Chelsea to come, it was going to be very tight. Gray felt Lucas's reading of the game from just in front of the back four would help protect a vulnerable defence but there was nothing the South African could do at Highbury where Thierry Henry ran amok, scoring four in a 5-0 drubbing.

Now they faced Portsmouth, one of the sides just above them, and victory at Elland Road would lift United out of the bottom three. They were without Viduka, who had needlessly picked up a second yellow card for wasting time against Blackburn two weeks before, and in the end slumped to a 2-1 defeat. Other results meant that Manchester City, three points above United, were now the only side within realistic catching distance.

Lucas had damaged his knee again in the Portsmouth match and could only sit frustrated on the sidelines as United faced Bolton. Viduka fired them in front but the Aussie was again sent off and the ten men of United collapsed to a 4-1 defeat that ensured they were relegated. Plenty of tears were shed by players and fans alike as a club who had so recently challenged for the Champions League now faced life in the second tier of English football.

Lucas came on for the final few minutes of United's emotional last Premiership match at Elland Road against Charlton, where the fans somehow found the resilience to acknowledge him and players like Dominic Matteo and Alan Smith who they knew had given their all in the fight. Before the final match at Chelsea, Paul Robinson was sold to Spurs and Eddie Gray again stood down, with Kevin Blackwell taking charge. Lucas played the whole match as 'living the dream' came to an end with a 1-0 defeat.

All season, Lucas had tried to remain positive, to encourage and to inspire his team-mates. Every game he had played had been in pain but he had been willing to battle on to try and save the club he loved from relegation. Now that it was over, he finally allowed his frustration to spill out and he told the *YEP*: 'This season, I have seen a change in the attitude of some of the players during training. The players did not enjoy it as much, and some of them were just coming in to pass the time. I feel that most of the players just gave up and accepted the situation and some of them knew that they would be going somewhere else at the end of the season. It is disappointing when people have that attitude. We have responsibilities, we are not just here to take the money and it is hard to respect those players who were not trying. You would try hard to get the spirit back during the week only to find that during the game it would go again. But Dominic, Smithy and a few others always worked hard for the club and it is sad to see them end up in this situation.'

Chapter 40

Disaster at Molineux

The Leeds squad going into the 2004-05 season contained only Eirik Bakke from the starting line-up of the team that had faced Valencia in the Champions League semi-final three years before. Gary Kelly, who had been on the bench that night, and Lucas, Seth Johnson and Michael Duberry, who had been injured, were also still at the club. The rest had gone. Among the new recruits to what was now a Championship club was central defender Clarke Carlisle, who quickly paid tribute to the way Lucas had helped him settle in at Elland Road. 'I can learn a lot by playing alongside Lucas,' the 24 year old said. 'He's a great man and still a very good defender.' When it was pointed out that because of all his injuries, Lucas had only played one more game in England than Carlisle, the newcomer said: 'It doesn't matter how many games you have played, you can always learn, especially from someone like Lucas who has played his football at the highest level. I was in the back three in the pre-season game against Darlington, which was fairly new for me, but it was good to listen to Lucas and pick up some pointers.'

Another recruit who was impressed by Lucas was Paul Butler, the former Wolverhampton central defender who had been made captain and who set about the job of creating a unity among a group of players who hardly knew each other. 'It's great to have Lucas here,' Butler said. 'He's been very supportive and helpful to me. He knows the club and the fans and is tremendously respected by everyone. It's good to have someone like him that I can talk to.'

Meanwhile, Lucas's mood had been lifted on 20 July when Feziwe gave birth to their second child, a beautiful daughter they named Owami. And a few days later, his off-field work, which continued as committed as ever, was acknowledged once again when the Variety Club of Great Britain used their Yorkshire awards night to honour him with a special award for his charity work in England and South Africa.

United's life in the second tier of English football started at home to Derby County with seven players making their Leeds debut. The changes weren't confined to on the pitch - the days of packed houses at Elland Road had gone and only just over 30,000 turned up for the game – still massive by the standards of the division but well below what United had been used to. Lucas came off the bench after 65 minutes, replacing the latest of Leeds' teenage sensations, Simon Walton, who had strutted into the game like a seasoned professional. A tackle by Lucas started the move that ended with Frazer Richardson firing home the winner.

Lucas sat out the following match, a 2-1 defeat at Gillingham, which reminded everyone that getting out of the Championship was no easy matter, but he was delighted when Blackwell asked him to fill a gap in midfield for a visit to Wolves on 14 August 2004. He might be 35 years old now, and have battered knees, but his enthusiasm was as great as ever. He said: 'I remember when we went out, Paul Ince was teasing me saying, "Are you still here? I thought you'd be too old to play by now!" and I replied, "I thought you'd retired long ago." We both laughed.'

But his main memory of the match is less happy. After only 15 minutes a ball was played over his head and he recalled: 'I turned and it felt as though someone had kicked me in the ankle. But there was no one near me. I knew I'd done my Achilles. I heard it go.' Dave Hancock raced on to the pitch and as soon as he touched the foot, Lucas screamed in pain. There was no way he could go on. Looking back, Lucas said: 'I couldn't believe what happened. I had just come back from a serious injury and now this. I kept asking why? Why now? I wanted someone to explain to me what I had done wrong to deserve this.'

Kevin Blackwell spoke of his admiration for Lucas and how he had managed to continue to try to influence the game despite the despair and the pain. 'The man was still cheering the boys as they came into the changing room because he knew how important the point was for Leeds,' Blackwell said, adding that no matter how serious the injury, he still wanted the South African around for the rest of the season. 'I can't afford to lose someone with his enthusiasm. I still want him around no matter what – if he has to come in on crutches, he will be just as good on crutches for me. He does not know the meaning of the word adversity. He always has a smile on his face.'

When he reached the hospital, Lucas's worst fears were confirmed – he had torn his Achilles tendon and was unlikely to play again that season. In fact, he might never play again. Dave Hancock explained: 'The injury was almost entirely due to wear and tear. His muscles and bones were giving up on him and they couldn't take the strain any more. As it was he probably already needed complete knee reconstruction.'

Fearing they would never see the Chief on a football pitch again, a few journalists rang round to get quotes for what was virtually a career obituary. One of the most moving came from Howard Wilkinson, the man who had brought him to Leeds. 'Lucas Radebe has been a fantastic servant for Leeds United and a great ambassador for South Africa. He was a low maintenance player, a manager's dream. He didn't require a lot of attention, his temperament was great and he was a good player to have around the dressing room.' Speaking of the £250,000 that he had paid for Lucas and the early days alongside Phil Masinga, the former United boss added: 'It was a steal. I think Lucas went the distance because he had more steel and determination than Philemon. He was focused and probably a better athlete. He could play anywhere and do a job, even in goal. If Lucas had not suffered so many injuries and been so versatile, I think he would have commanded an even higher reputation.'

Most players aged 35 and in the last year of their contract would have called it a day after picking up an injury that has wrecked the careers of many younger players. But Lucas didn't want to finish his football life in a heap at Molineux. He didn't want Leeds fans' last view of him to be disappearing down the tunnel on a stretcher. He was determined to go out with a bit more dignity and style. So once again he listened carefully to what the physios said, put in the long hours in the pool and the gym and seven weeks after surgery to repair the Achilles, he told the *Yorkshire Post*: 'Time flies and it's looking good. At least I'm off the crutches and now I have to step it up in the physio's room. They said I was looking at seven months but hopefully it will be sooner than that so I can come back and play again. It makes a nice change to wear a pair of shoes and it's nice that I can walk again. When injuries come, especially big ones like mine, you feel sad and down and it's hard to feel part of the team. But when you are able to walk around the place it becomes easier.'

The new-look Leeds team were finding life in the Championship hard. At the end of 2004 they were in 14th spot in the table, equal distance from the play-offs and the relegation zone. Off the field there were still massive financial problems. Gerald Krasner and his board had secured a deal to sell and lease back both Elland Road and the Thorp Arch training complex. They'd tried a number of fund-raising schemes and talked to several would-be buyers, but no one came up with hard cash. The debt was like a dead weight dragging the club down and on 17 January it was revealed they had only ten days before Leeds United would be wound up.

Kevin Blackwell recalled: 'One Friday in January, out of the blue, the stock exchange pulled the plug. It was a terrible day with staff crying all around me. We weren't going into administration – all the assets had been sold – it was straight into liquidation. The doors were going to be closed on the Monday.'

What Blackwell and the staff hadn't known at that stage was that in the early hours of the Friday morning, Monaco-based, tax-exile Ken Bates had agreed to invest £10 million through a company in Geneva to take a controlling interest in the club. He had always been a controversial and outspoken figure, right back to his early days at Oldham Athletic and Wigan, and Leeds fans remembered how critical he had been of the Yorkshire club when he was chairman of Chelsea. But they needed a saviour and he was the only one in town. Bates said: 'Whereas a couple of weeks ago Leeds had their head above water gasping for breath, now they are on the surface swimming against the tide. The next job is to get them swimming with the tide.'

Lucas could only watch from the sidelines, relieved that Leeds had survived but, like the fans, wondering what the hard-headed Bates would do. Meanwhile, he continued to work on his fitness, undertake his charity work and support United's community work. 'This season has been a nightmare for me,' Lucas confessed. 'I have watched a lot of good games and seen some bad ones. Sometimes I have found it hard to go to matches because I don't like watching and I know how hard it is going to be. Charity work has helped me throughout my career. I've been able to do a lot of work with kids. That has been very fulfilling and it gives you a perspective on life.'

In February he flew back to South Africa with the Lord Mayor of Leeds to present £10,000 worth of AIDS home-based care kits that had been purchased by fundraisers in Yorkshire. He said: 'I am touched that people in my adopted home of Leeds are prepared to help people in my true home of South Africa.'

A week later he was back in the Nou Camp stadium in Barcelona and tentatively pulling on football boots for the first time since his injury. He had been asked to join an all-star team to play in an exhibition match to raise funds for the people in Asia whose lives had been devastated when a tsunami killed around 250,000 people and destroyed the homes of millions more on Boxing Day. It was a gentle work-out as Lucas lined up alongside Ronaldhino, Kaka and other big names in the World XI against Gerrard, Beckham, Zidane and Raul in a European side. He was on the winning team and while the main purpose was to raise money for the victims, it also raised his hopes that he might yet still make it back in the Leeds team before the end of the season.

Back in Leeds, he was also busy planning his testimonial. He had an enthusiastic committee of David Share and his brother Richard, former United director David Spencer and PR man Jason Madeley, who handled the arrangements while Lucas went around drumming up interest and enthusiasm. Meanwhile, another group, under the guidance of Glyn Binkin representing Lucas's management company, were planning events in South Africa. This was a dual celebration, giving fans in both countries a chance to say thank you to Lucas but at the same time, and as important to Lucas, giving him a chance to say thank you to the fans.

He was determined to make it an enormous success and pledged that part of the money raised would be shared among charities in England and South Africa. His adopted city was eager to mark a career that had touched so many lives and he was invited to Hillcrest Primary School where the council presented him with a unique Power to Change award for the work he had done in the Playing for Success scheme. It was the first of many awards that were to come his way.

Leeds fans were disappointed that their side's expected instant return to the Premiership had failed to materialise but they were safe in mid-table, had avoided being wound up and who knows, maybe next season? First it was time to party and salute the Chief.

Chapter 41

Honours overshadowed

Bank Holiday Monday, 2005, was a day Lucas will never forget. He had known for a long time that he was highly regarded by Leeds United fans but the outpouring of love towards him at his testimonial match was far more than he expected. It was overwhelming and he was not alone in shedding a tear at the thought of how a tall skinny kid from Diepkloof 4 had become an icon in a city thousands of miles away.

It was a day where raw emotion and sentimentality were mingled with laughter. Not everything went smoothly behind the scenes. David Share recalled that with two players stuck in traffic on the motorway, Phil Brown and Sam Allardyce, who were managing the international XI, realised they were short of players. 'We had to go into the other dressing room and arrange an instant transfer until half-time,' he said.

One of the highlights for the watching fans, who made up Leeds' biggest crowd of the season, was the appearance of pony-tailed Lucy Ward, a star of Leeds United ladies team, who came on and scored a goal. When the crowd started to chant, 'Are you Robbie Savage in disguise?' Lucas wondered if news of his antipathy for the Leicester star had leaked out. Later, United had to apologise to the FA for allowing a woman to play in a men's match.

The scoreline was irrelevant as top players from all parts of the game came to pay tribute to someone they held in great respect both as a footballer and as a man. Fans from all round the world had emailed in their tributes and they filled six pages of the testimonial brochure. From Denmark, Jan Okholm wrote: 'You have one of the greatest football hearts in Leeds' history. Therefore you will always be in my football heart.' Rob from Dublin said: 'I'm truly grateful for the blood, sweat and tears you gave for the greatest club in the world.' From Australia, Paul Carter sent: 'Lucas, you are truly one of the greatest players to have graced our ground and your off-field representation of the club we love is unique. Thank you for making us proud to love Leeds.' And writing from Lucas's adopted homeland, Tracey said: 'You will forever be in the hearts of Leeds United fans. Thank you for the loyalty and commitment you have shown the club over the years. You're a true gentleman and a legend.'

Reporters covering the match discovered similar sentiments among fans at the match. A journalist from Johannesburg found three young people waving the South African flag and wearing Bafana Bafana shirts. Approaching them to see which part of his homeland they were from, he was taken aback to be greeted by Yorkshire accents: 'We bought the shirts and the flag on the internet. We did it for Lucas,' they told him.

Lucas's family were deeply moved to witness how profoundly he had touched so many lives. And their pride was shared back home in South Africa. Former Bafana coach Clive Barker summed it up when he said: 'If you were a South African in that crowd and saw the reception Lucas was given and it didn't make the hairs on the back of your neck stand up, then there's something wrong with you.'

A memorable day continued to have an impact long after the crowds had gone home with the funds of ten charities chosen by Lucas and the organising committee benefiting from his decision to share the proceeds.

Lucas still had one more act as a footballer. The following Sunday, United's final game of the season at home to Rotherham, he came off the bench in the 85th minute to make his 200th league appearance for the club. The name on the back of his shirt was spelled correctly. As the crowd and both benches stood to applaud, Gary Kelly, who had been at the club the day Lucas arrived, trotted across and handed the Chief the captain's armband. 'It was a great finish with typical Yorkshire weather,' Lucas said with a smile. 'When I came here it was freezing cold and when I finish it is freezing cold and wet – it was just perfect. While the match lasted it was brilliant. I got a touch – I was tempted to have a shot but I was too far out. At the end it was sad and emotional for me. I have enjoyed my time here and Leeds United has become an important part of my life.'

Looking back on his Leeds United career, Lucas reflected: 'I consider myself to have been very fortunate. I have worked under seven different managers and learned from all of them. Each manager has shown faith in me: Howard Wilkinson took a big gamble taking me to Elland Road and was patient while I struggled to adapt to England even though it was a difficult time for him; George Graham pushed me to a new level and made me captain; David O'Leary often fought my case and led us through an unforgettable period of success; and, even when I was struggling against injury and less able to contribute to the team, Terry Venables, Peter Reid, Eddie Gray and Kevin Blackwell always made me feel wanted, made me feel I was an important member of the squad. Everyone at the club made me feel at home – my team-mates, the backroom staff, the office staff, the fans – so it was always much more than just a place where I earned my living.

I've never gone in for kissing the badge or other gestures like that, but I can say with all sincerity, it was a privilege for me to pull on a Leeds United shirt and to be a part of such a great club.'

Following Lucas's retirement, the tributes came pouring in. Leeds Metropolitan University and the University of Cape Town awarded him honorary doctorates. 'My mum will be very happy,' Lucas joked. 'She always said I should be a doctor.' In separate polls in South Africa, he and Feziwe were voted among the ten nicest celebrities, while Lucas was named second only to Nelson Mandela in the ten most trusted people in the country. Asked to name his favourite player, Amakhosi owner Kaizer Motaung paused then said: 'It has to be Lucas Radebe and also Doctor Khumalo. Lucas adopted me as his father and I am proud of his achievements.'

On 27 September, South Africa awarded Lucas The Order of Ikhamanga in Silver, an award 'given to citizens who have excelled in the fields of arts, culture, literature, music, journalism and sport.' His citation read: 'In a career spanning 20 years, Lucas Radebe has risen to the heights of his chosen occupation, enhanced the image of his home continent's footballers, fought against racism in soccer, inspired hundreds of thousands of young fellow countrymen and ploughed back the fruits of his endeavours into helping ill and deprived children, not only in South Africa but elsewhere in the world. He has brought honour to himself, his family and his country.'

Lucas was humbled and thrilled by these awards. It should have been a time for him to bask in the warmth of the admiration and love that was coming his way but there was a shadow over his life that prevented him enjoying them completely.

At the reception on the night of his testimonial, Lucas realised he had not seen Feziwe for a while and asked David Share to find her. David discovered she had gone home feeling unwell and even though she struggled back to join the party, she was clearly in pain. Soon after she was diagnosed as having cancer of the bowel. Lucas was horrified. Not long before, Bruce Craven, one of the physios at Leeds United, had died of skin cancer and Lucas had been at the forefront of the awareness campaign organised by Dave Hancock in his colleague's memory. 'Two days before Bruce died, I had been running with him,' Lucas recalled. 'It all happened so quickly.'

The doctors suggested it would be better for Lucas to break the news to Feziwe but it took three visits before he could summon up the courage to say the word cancer. In an interview with the *Sunday Mirror*, he said: 'When I was told she had cancer I went numb. When you hear the word, you fear the worst. I have had some lows in my time, including being shot at, but this has been the worst time of my life. I could so easily have lost her. She needed emergency surgery otherwise it could have been fatal. She was in a lot of pain. When she came home I kept checking to see if she was still breathing. I have to stay strong for the children. They know mum is sick but they don't know how serious it is.'

Feziwe had always preferred the quiet life, choosing to stay out of the spotlight and look after the family. In many ways she preferred life in Leeds because while there were still endless calls on Lucas's time, she was able to grab a few more moments with him. Back home she hardly saw him. He had promised that once he finished playing football, there would be much more time together. He would continue his charity work but the rest of the time would be for her and the kids. It was what she had been longing for.

The couple's instinct was to keep the news of her illness within the family but after discussing it they decided to go public, hence the *Sunday Mirror* article with Anthony Clavane. 'We thought we should try to raise awareness of cancer,' Lucas explained. 'In South Africa people are dying because they think it's a sin and they keep it secret. It's like AIDS. We want people to know it can kill you. You've got to raise this issue when it happens.' The response from the public was staggering with messages of support coming in from all round the world.

Feziwe's illness meant Lucas was unable to return to South Africa to announce the second stage of his testimonial. He went back for three days to fulfil his obligations to attend a dinner and play in the specially-arranged match at King's Park, which was a Who's Who of South African football and shown live on national television, then raced back to be at his wife's side.

As Feziwe started to respond to treatment, Lucas went back to fulfilling his engagements on behalf of various charities in Leeds and South Africa. On one visit to Thorp Arch to raise awareness for a children's group, he admitted how much he was missing football. 'Now and again I just wonder if I can get my boots out again and get in another season. I'm keeping pretty fit just in case Dave Wetherall phones me and says he needs a central defensive partner at Bradford City.' But each morning when he got up, his knees reminded him it was a hopeless dream.

Anyway Feziwe needed him around the place as she went through bout after bout of chemotherapy and other treatment. Doctors broke the news that she had to have a hysterectomy, which rocked Lucas who had not given up the thought of having more children. He had loved this woman since first seeing her at the African Cup of Nations but his admiration for her grew at the way she handled this life-threatening illness; always strong, never allowing her fear to show to the children. Like his mother before, Feziwe was the rock on which the family was built.

Lucas and Feziwe went home to South Africa for the holidays and, impressed by the treatment she received there and the support and help from family and friends, they decided to stay.

Chapter 42

Back from the brink

Having hung up his boots, it was time for Lucas to consider where his career would go next. Over the years, Gary Blumberg had recruited various people to join Lucas's management team. David Becker left a career in the City to specialise in sports law with Blumberg's law offices and he continues to serve on Lucas's board today, while also acting as head counsel for the International Cricket Conference. Johannesburg-based accountant Jonathan Segel was the first of a number of advisers invited by Blumberg to advise on financial and tax matters. More recently, Allan Nossel, a local businessman with experience in acquisitions, joined them to advise on corporate investments. They, along with various other specialists and support staff, such as Olivia Schoeman, Lucas's PA; continue to work with Blumberg and Glyn Binkin for 'Team Lucas'. Thus, a skilled and dedicated management team with a guiding vision was established well before his retirement with the foundations of commercial partnerships already in place to allow Lucas to follow any post-playing career path he chose. Blumberg chairs the company board, which also includes a global advisory group.

Lucas's return to South Africa enabled the company to build on the elements already in place. In a move complementary to his essential sponsorship deals, they made an investment in Penquin, a dynamic marketing and media company in which Lucas became a corporate director. Recently they commenced negotiations to acquire equity in one of South Africa's first five-a-side football centres, a move which would further his dual aims of social responsibility and commercial development. A lot of their strategy is geared toward one of Lucas' ultimate dreams - the building of a sports, education and community centre in Soweto.

'We were approached by many companies wanting to be involved with Lucas,' Binkin said.'But we stayed with our policy of quality rather than quantity and we all agreed it was important that Lucas's first obligation was to the companies who had been loyal to him while he was in England. They had been mainly using his image but now they had the chance to use the man himself and a lot of people wanted to meet him and talk to him.'

Lucas was also keen to continue to use his fame to make a difference in people's lives and the same approach was used, concentrating on a few causes close to his heart. He continued to work as an ambassador for SOS Children's Villages and over the next few years got involved with a hospice and issues of family bereavement, Starfish, a charity helping AIDS orphans, and Beyond Sport Organisation, the Laureus Organisation and FIFA's Football for Hope programme, all three of which use sport as a catalyst for social change.

Having worked hard to help South Africa bring the World Cup to the country, Lucas was proud when the announcement was made that the bid had been successful. Despite doubters around the world, he was convinced his homeland would stage a memorable and safe tournament, and it would also be a great and much-needed boost to the economy. He also believed that officials at SAFA had made it clear they wanted Lucas to be team manager for the Bafana Bafana side for the World Cup, using his experience and enthusiasm to back up the work of the coaching team.

It had been a bad time for the national side, in many ways mirroring the decline of Leeds United. From the highs of winning the African Cup of Nations, playing in World Cup finals and being acknowledged around the world, they had slumped into the doldrums. The fans were shocked when Bafana Bafana failed to score a single goal in the 2006 Nations finals. They had also failed to qualify for the World Cup finals and despite several changes of coach, seemed to be in increasing free-fall.

Lucas felt he could help but SAFA didn't fulfil his understanding of the job they wanted him to do. He was shattered and turned against the governing body. 'It's all politics and business,' he said. 'But I am interested in the football side. I would have given it my best shot to make sure I could develop our football and our players. It kills me. This is what I was always looking for when I was playing abroad. I always wanted to give back to football in South Africa.'

The situation worsened when SAFA official Sturu Pasiya told the parliamentary sports committee that Lucas had 'been economical with the truth.' Normally calm in any adversity, Lucas was angry and hurt. For a while he considered quitting South Africa for good but he couldn't turn his back on the country he loved. He continued to argue his case that SAFA were in danger of getting things very wrong and that the decline of Bafana Bafana could be firmly laid at their door. 'It's not down to the coach. It's down to the administration,' he said. 'We can bring in any coach you want but if you haven't got the players to work with, it's going to be a problem. It's clear we haven't produced enough players who can compete at the highest level. It's a big disappointment for me and for a lot of ex-players who really played a role in bringing the World Cup to South Africa. Players like Doctor Khumalo and John Moshoeu have been icons and role models and to see them not involved pains me.' Lucas made it clear his argument was with SAFA and not his country and he continued to promote the World Cup, eventually taking up a post with the South Africa Tourism Board that saw him travel the globe to encourage people to visit his homeland in 2010.

If the public were well aware of his troubles with SAFA, only a few close friends and family knew of the anguish in his private life. In April 2007 Feziwe told the *YEP* of her relief that her cancer had responded to the doctors' efforts. 'I don't need any treatment because it is under control,' she said. But less than a year later, the newspaper reported that the tumours had returned and she was again battling to survive. Doctors tried every treatment they knew but on 11 October 2008 the moment Lucas had been dreading arrived. His wife, lover and soul-mate passed away, aged 34.

Amid his grief, Lucas was again surprised by the sheer volume of messages of condolence he received from people he had never met, yet who somehow felt that he and Feziwe had touched their lives.

Lucas found it hard to speak about Feziwe at her memorial service but, watched by the couple's children, Lucas jnr and Owami, he managed to pay a moving tribute, stopping from time to time to compose himself and wipe away the tears. 'Times like this are not easy and it is when you realise the value of life,' he said. 'The memories of our time together are vivid in my mind and she has left an unimaginable void in my heart.' And in a final farewell, he added: 'Go well my beautiful one, I will forever be proud of you.'

Lucas tried to be strong for his children and to start to rebuild their lives without the woman who had been at the family's centre but the pain was not yet over. Shortly afterwards, he collapsed while working out in a gym. Suffering from stress and exhaustion, he was rushed to hospital where he was fitted with a heart defibrillator. A month later he was rocked by another blow when his beloved father Johannes passed away. Even the Chief, the warrior who had amazed physios with his resilience and strength, was struggling to keep going. Leeds United, who had been taken in and out of administration by Ken Bates and now slipped into the third tier of English football, twice arranged dinners in his honour, but each time he was too unwell to travel.

It took more than a year before Lucas started to look and act anything like his old self but with the love of his family and friends, he gradually grew stronger. He was determined to do his best to make the World Cup a success and once again overcame his fear of flying to travel the world to promote the event. The familiar smile started to reappear as he watched his four children grow and become an integral part of the Radebe clan that gathers regularly at Emily's house, where the shelves hold some of Lucas's many trophies and the walls are covered with photographs and paintings of her famous son, including one with Nelson Mandela. Madiba had told him that sport had an important role in rebuilding South Africa and Lucas is determined to continue to play his part and honour the man who has so often inspired him.

He remains a popular figure at home in South Africa. It is impossible for him to appear at any function without a chorus of 'Rhooooo' filling the air and a stream of people approaching him just wanting to shake hands or have a photograph taken. None is turned away. All are greeted with the trademark smile. His popularity- and in the case of Aquafresh, the smile – continue to attract sponsors who want to be associated with Lucas and his long-term relationships remain with companies like Coca Cola, First National Bank and Woolworth (the Marks & Spencer of South Africa).

Looking into the future, Lucas seems set to do more television and media work. He has long spoken of his desire to give something back to South African football and has plans for a soccer academy that will cover life skills as well as football coaching. The passion and pride he feels for South Africa is expressed in a willingness to serve, to see his country continue to grow and prosper, and to make sure that future generations have the chance to fulfil their potential and ambitions. That might take him into the world of politics or, more likely, to using his natural talents as an ambassador around the world.

Lucas is also conscious of the debt he owes to his 'second home' and is committed to help promote England's bid for the 2018 World Cup. And back in Leeds where he still keeps a home, Lucas remains a hero and a legend. On 24 April 2010, the day before picking up his PFA Award, he was at Elland Road to watch Leeds beat MK Dons 4-1 and take another step towards promotion to the Championship and the long climb towards Premier League football once more. He was surrounded by fans before and after the match, taking an hour and a half to get away from the ground as he posed for pictures and signed autographs. And when he went on to the pitch at half time to greet the crowd, the chant again soared around Elland Road:

Radebe!

Radebe!

Radebe, Radebe, Radebe!

Radebe-e, Radebe-e, Radebe-ee-ee-ee-ee-ee!

LUCAS!

Glossary

Here are some terms that might be unfamiliar to English readers

ANC	African National Congress – the oldest and largest black political organisation in South Africa, and the ruling party since full elections
Apartheid	Afrikaans word meaning 'separateness', which became the name given to the oppressive policies inflicted on the black majority population of South Africa by the white minority rulers
Boerewors	uniquely South African sausage, usually cooked on a Braai
Braai	a barbecue
Inkatha	a Zulu political party which opposed the ANC in the 1980s and 90s
Kaffir	literally 'one who does not believe in God' but became a racist term of abuse used by whites to demean blacks in South Africa
MK	Umkhonyo we Sizwe (Spear of the People) – a militant wing of the ANC, set up after the Sharpville shootings
Pap	a kind of porridge made from mealie meal
Piccanin	an offensive term for a black child
Sjambok	a leather whip
Tsotsi	township gangsters

Acknowledgements

The research for this book put me back in touch with some old friends and introduced me to some new ones and I have to thank them all for the help they gave me. Firstly, of course, my heartfelt appreciation goes to Lucas, still not easy to pin down, but as always a pleasure to work with. I am grateful to his mother Emily, who invited me into her home where it is easy to see why she is the Radebe matriarch, and his sister Lydia, who shared some memories of her brother, especially during their childhood together. I was also greatly assisted on my South Africa trip and since by Lucas's friend, Thami Ngubeni, and Michelle Leon and the staff at the Johnnic Communications library in Johannesburg. The trip was made even more pleasureable by Tony Mangadi - a terrific guide and someone who gave me useful insights into soccer in South Africa.

I am grateful to Kaizer Motaung, who went the extra mile to sign Lucas for Kaizer Chiefs, and Eddie Gray, who was at Leeds United for almost all of Lucas's career there. To have two such highly respected football men contribute a foreword is a privilege.

I would like to express my gratitude to Lucas's management company, especially Gary Blumberg, who provided unique insights over several hours on the phone, Glyn Binkin, who was able to expand on Lucas's life in South Africa and David Becker, whose initial intervention transformed the project.

It was great to catch up again with some of the people at Leeds United who were as helpful and considerate as ever – Liz Dimitrievicz, Emma Joussemet and Dick Wright were part of a team who played an important part in the club's rise and deserved better than to see their work spoiled by poor management. Lucas's friend David Share pointed me in the right direction in a number of things while former United physio Dave Hancock guided me through the medical details as well as coming up with a couple of superb stories I'd not heard before. Thanks to George Graham for his insights into one of the pivotal times in Lucas's life.

Caryl Phillips provided a fascinating perspective as a long-time, black Leeds fan; I was delighted Fabio Capello spared a moment from England's World Cup build up to recall the impact Lucas had on Europe; and I'm also grateful to my business partner, John Wray, whose impeccable record-keeping bailed me out on several occasions, though I hasten to add any mistakes that have crept in are mine, not his.

The book would not have been possible without access to the newspapers and books listed below and I am especially grateful to the staff at Leeds Central Library for their help while I worked my way through the microfiche of several years' copies of the *Yorkshire Evening Post*. And to Keith Hampshire, David Clay and their colleagues at the *Yorkshire Post*, who were so helpful in allowing me to access their on-line archive. I hope I have given a name check to all the journalists and authors I've quoted, if not please accept my apologies – it was an oversight not a snub.

I am also grateful to Barry Cox and the team at Great Northern Books who made the job of author a pleasant one and whose encouragement and belief in the project helped during those long hours chained to the computer. Special thanks to Andrew Collomosse for his thorough and helpful sub-editing.

Throughout the book I have used the local currency symbols: £ for the British pound and R for the South African rand. In 1992 the exchange rate was roughly R1.70 per £ but the South African currency has devalued over the years and in 2010 a pound buys around R11.

I have quoted from a number of newspapers, most particularly the *Yorkshire Post* and *Yorkshire Evening Post (YEP)* in England, and the *Sowetan* and *Sunday Times* in South Africa.

I have referred to the following books and DVDs, which were invaluable, and I have quoted from several of them.

Books

Douglas Booth (1998) *The Race Game: Sport and Politics in South Africa.* London: Frank Cass

John Carlin (2008) *Invictus (Playing the Enemy): Nelson Mandela and the Game that made a Nation.* London: Atlantic Books

Peter Davies (1997) *Chasing the Game: Sporting Trails from Jo'burg to Jamaica.* Sandton: Zebra Press

Tom Easton & Luke Alfred (eds) (2005) *Touchlines and Deadlines: A Compendium of South African Sports Writing.* Cape Town: Double Storey Books

Rio Ferdinand (2006) *Rio: My Story.* London: Headline

Graeme Friedman (2001) *Madiba's Boys.* West Wickham: Comerford & Miller

Ian Hawkey (2009) *Feet of the Chameleon: The story of African Football.* London: Anova Books

Tracey Hawthorne (Editor) (2006) *My Dad by South African Sons.* Cape Town: Two Dogs

Monique Marks (2001) *Young Warriors: Youth Politics, Identity and Violence in South Africa.* Witwatersand University Press.

David O'Leary (2002) *Leeds United on Trial.* London: Little, Brown

Peter Raath (2002) *Soccer through the years 1862-2002.* Soccer through the Years.com

Peter Ridsdale (2008) *United We Fall: Boardroom Truths about the Beautiful Game.* London: Pan

Martin Roberts (2003) *South Africa 1948-1994: The Rise and Fall of Apartheid.* Harlow: Longman

Joyce Sikakane (1977) *A Window on Soweto.* London: International Defence & Aid Fund.

Richard Sutcliffe (2001) *Marching On Together: Leeds United in Europe 2000-2001* Lockerbie: Terrace Banter

Various (1996) *South African Sports Year 1996.* Johannesburg: Royston Lamond

Don Warters (2000) *Inside Leeds United: The Story of the Millennium Season.* Leeds: Leeds United Publishing.

Don Warters (2001) *2001 A European Odyssey: Leeds United's UEFA Champions League Season.* Leeds: Leeds United Publishing

DVDs

Hold Up the Sun, Episode 5: Not the Kings & Generals 1983-1990. Impact Video

Lucas Radebe: The Chief's Story Leeds United

Sarafina! Videovision Entertainment